Relative Effectiveness of Alternative Microfinance-Driven Poverty Alleviation Programs in Bangladesh

Relative Effectiveness of Alternative Microfinance-Driven Poverty Alleviation Programs in Bangladesh

By

Tamgid Ahmed Chowdhury

CAMBRIDGE
SCHOLARS
PUBLISHING

Relative Effectiveness of Alternative Microfinance-Driven Poverty Alleviation Programs in Bangladesh
By Tamgid Ahmed Chowdhury

This book first published 2013

Cambridge Scholars Publishing

12 Back Chapman Street, Newcastle upon Tyne, NE6 2XX, UK

British Library Cataloguing in Publication Data
A catalogue record for this book is available from the British Library

ISBN (10): 1-4438-5275-9, ISBN (13): 978-1-4438-5275-3

This book is dedicated to my wife Sonia Chowdhury and son Towsif Chowdhury – This book might not have been in this position without their dedication and sacrifice.

TABLE OF CONTENTS

LIST OF TABLES

LIST OF FIGURES

ACKNOWLEDGEMENTS

I would like to express my deepest gratitude to my PhD supervisor Dr. Pundarik Mukhopadhaya for his consistent support, kindness, continuous encouragement, guidance, and time spent with me in our regular discussion sessions. His expertise and guidelines were crucial to the successful completion of this book.

I would like to thank Associate Professor Tony Bryant, my co-supervisor, for his competent guidance and other technical advice.

This project has been funded by Macquarie University Research Excellence Scholarship (MQRES), Australia and I acknowledge further financial support provided by Faculty of Business and Economics, Macquarie University to conduct the survey in Bangladesh.

I have presented various parts of the book in the 82nd Annual Conference of Southern Economic Association held in Sheraton, Atlanta-USA on November 19-21, 2010, the 12th International Convention of East Asian Economic Association at EWHA Women's University, Seoul-South Korea on October 2-3, 2010 and the 4th Poverty and Social Protection Conference held in Bangkok, Thailand on March 1-3, 2011 organized by Tomorrow People Organization. Comments of the participants of the conferences were extremely helpful. I would like to thank the participants of the above mentioned conferences for their insightful suggestions.

I thank Associate Professor Cynthia Webster (Macquarie University, Australia), Associate Professor Sean Turnell (Macquarie University) and Dr. Sunil Venaik (University of Queensland, Australia) for their contribution in the early stage item identification and purification of the scale that I have developed in this book.

Special thanks to Ms. Laura Billington, Md. Shibli Shahriar and Professor Dr. Mizanur Rahman for their editorial support which has helped substantially improve the presentation of this work.

I am also grateful to Sohel, Shafiq, Munna, Ridu, Khairul, Mohsin, Razu, Sumon, Ranju and Forhad for helping me in collecting data from remote rural areas in Bangladesh.

I am thankful to my parents and my in-laws for their continuous support and moral encouragement.

DECLARATION BY THE AUTHOR

- A paper titled, 'Poverty Alleviation and Service Delivery: Government and Non-Government Organizations in Rural Bangladesh' based on a significant portion of Chapter-5 of this book has been published in *Oxford Development Studies*, Vol. 39, No. 4, December 2011, page. 427-452.
- Another paper titled, 'Assessment of Multidimensional Poverty and Effectiveness of Microfinance-driven Government and NGO Projects in the Rural Bangladesh' based on the subject matter of Chapter-7 of this book has been published in *The Journal of Socio-Economics*, Vol. 41, Issue-5, 2012, page. 500-512.
- A third paper titled, 'Limitations of the Theories of Non-profits and Benchmarking Service Delivery Dimensions of Poverty Reduction Programs in Rural Bangladesh' based on the scale developed in Chapter-5 of this book has been published in the *Journal of Non-profit and Public Sector Marketing*, Vol. 24, Issue-4, 2012, page. 325-350.
- A fourth paper titled, 'Are women less efficient in converting microcredit into functionings: Evidence from Bangladesh' based on the poverty model developed in Chapter-7 of the book has been accepted for publication in the *European Journal of Development Research* (Forthcoming).

INTRODUCTORY NOTE

In general, the effectiveness of microfinance-driven poverty-alleviation programs run by Government Organizations (GOs) and Non-Government Organizations (NGOs) in developing countries such, as Bangladesh, is assessed by repayment rates, the number of beneficiaries, the area coverage, the amount of loans disbursed, the cost of operations, profitability and the financial sustainability of the projects. This book argues that these methods are quite restrictive because none of them reflect the perceptions of poor people concerning the effectiveness of the projects. The development agencies (such as GOs and NGOs) have never been compared on the basis of service delivery effectiveness [a *processed based* comparison], nor have they ever been compared on the basis of their relative contribution to raising the living standards of the poor [an *outcome based* comparison]; both of which are crucial to poverty reduction. The main reason behind the absence of such comparisons is the unavailability of the appropriate parameters that could be used for such a comparison.

For the process-based comparison, this study develops and validates a two-dimensional multi-item scale through construct, convergent, discriminant and nomological validity. The scale captures different aspects of effectiveness in the delivery of services. These aspects are termed the 'credibility dimension' and the 'focus towards beneficiaries dimension' of the service delivery in poverty-alleviation programs. For the output-based comparison, this study also develops and validates a 'multidimensional poverty model' to compare the effectiveness of GOs and NGOs in contributing to the economic, social, political, and cultural elements in the lives of the poor. The methodology is based on 930 samples collected from 12 districts and 107 randomly chosen villages in Bangladesh during September–December 2009.

The results derived from utilizing the scale items for comparative study show that in many important dimensions of service delivery, the performance of GOs is more effective than that of NGOs. Gender discrimination also is evident in poverty-alleviation programs in Bangladesh. This study reveals that female beneficiaries are disadvantaged not only due to cultural or religious customs, but also because of the less attention they receive from the managers and field staff of both GOs and NGOs.

The poverty model shows that GO agencies are more effective in improving the welfare of poor beneficiaries than NGOs as a whole. While the comparative study shows that government agencies are more effective in improving the economic wellbeing of the poor, NGOs are better at improving the social aspects of their lives.

Tamgid A. Chowdhury

List of Abbreviations

ADB	Asian Development Bank
APRSP	Accelerated Poverty Reduction Strategy Paper
BBS	Bangladesh Bureau of Statistics
BRAC	Bangladesh Rural Advancement Committee
CBN	Cost of Basic Needs
DCI	Direct Calorie Intake
DFID	Department for International Development
EWB	Economic Wellbeing
FEI	Food Energy Intake
FFW	Food For Work
GoB	Government of Bangladesh
GO	Government
HCR	Head Count Ratio
HDI	Human Development Index
HDR	Human Development Report
HIES	Household Income and Expenditure Survey
HPI	Human Poverty Index
i-PRSP	Interim Poverty Reduction Strategy Paper
MDGs	Millennium Development Goals
MFI	Microfinance Institutions
MRA	Microcredit Regulatory Authority
NGO	Non-government Organizations
NGOAB	NGO Affair Bureau Bangladesh
OMS	Open Market Sale
PPA	Participatory Poverty Assessment
PRSP	Poverty Reduction Strategy Paper
SWB	Social Wellbeing
UNDP	United Nations Development Program
VGD	Vulnerable Group Development
VGF	Vulnerable Group Feeding
WB	World Bank
WHO	World Health Organization

CHAPTER ONE

INTRODUCTION

Bangladesh has long been exemplified as a nation of poverty. Even though the history of poverty in Bangladesh dates back to the British colonial period (Siddiqui, 1982), the major studies on poverty have been conducted since the formation of the country in 1971, and particularly after the devastating famine of 1974 (Azam and Katsushi, 2009). The poverty rate in Bangladesh and its severity was first surveyed in 1973-74 through the Household Income and Expenditure Survey (HIES) in which Food Energy Intake (FEI) and Direct Caloric Intake (DCI) methods were used[1]. The country made commendable progress in reducing poverty throughout the 1980s and 1990s (Osmani, 1990; Hossain and Sen, 1992), resulting in the proportion of people living below the poverty line[2] dropping drastically (from 82.9% in 1973-74) to 49.8% by the early 2000s[3]. The number of people living below the poverty line declined by almost one and a half percentage points per year particularly during the 1990s[4], and around one percent per year during the 2000s[5] (see SUPRO, 2007 and Table 1.1). In 2003, Bangladesh entered into the 'medium human development' league for the first time according to the UNDP's Human Development Report (UNDP, 2003). In 2010, Bangladesh received an award from the United Nations (UN) for reducing its child mortality rate by nearly two-thirds, achieving a current rate of only 2%[6]. According to recent statistics, life expectancy has increased from 45 years in 1972 to 66.8 years in 2008, the percentage of people using sanitary latrines is 87%, and 85% of the rural population have access to safe drinking water (MOF, 2010). The MDG Progress Report of 2011 (GoB, MOF, 2011) by the Government reports that the incidence of poverty has declined at an annual rate of 2.46 in Bangladesh during 1992-2010 periods against the MDG target of 2.12 percent. The report further suggests that Bangladesh has already met one of the indicators of Target-1 by bringing down the Poverty Gap Ratio to 6.5, against 2015 target of 8. Based on projections by the Asian Development Bank (ADB, 2005), poverty rates will decline to 22% by 2015 if the current trends continue. These achievements were reported to be due to the success of government organizations (GOs) and Non-government Organizations (NGOs) in reducing population growth, promoting women's empowerment, large scale micro-credit disbursement with wider coverage, effective disaster management capacity, and most notably, success in human development. Table 1.1 portrays trends in poverty rates in Bangladesh from 1983-84; the reduction of poverty in urban areas and changes in the poverty gap are notable. The rates in rural areas, however, remain alarming (column 4) even though these are the areas that receive the most resources from both the Government of Bangladesh (APRSP, 2005; i-PRSP, 2003) and NGOs.

Table 1.1: Trend of poverty in Bangladesh: 1983–2007

Year	National (%)	Urban (%)	Rural (%)	Poverty gap	Squared poverty gap
1983/84	52.3	40.9	53.8	15.0	5.9
1988/89	47.8	35.9	49.7	13.1	4.8
1991/92	49.7	33.6	52.9	14.6	5.6
1995/96	53.1	35.0	56.7	15.5	5.7
2000	49.8	36.6	53.1	13.8	4.8
2005	40	28.4	43.8	9.8	3.1
2007	47.3	-	-	16.5	7.8

Source: Sen (2003); figures for 2005 and 2007 are taken from BBS (2005) and Hossain (2009) respectively.

The Human Poverty Index (HPI)[7] for Bangladesh has dropped from 0.61 in 1982–83 to 0.47 in 1993–94 and further to 0.36 in 2000, at a time when the income poverty reduction rate was negligible, especially in the rural areas of Bangladesh (see Table 1.1) where most of the poor people live. Different studies have claimed that public action along with microfinance through Government policies and the active role of Non-government Organizations (NGOs) in the delivery of microfinance and social services have made this possible.[8]

Microfinance has been used as an effective tool for poverty alleviation around the world for decades. This approach not only created poor's access toward capital, but also allowed them to improve their business which in turn increased personal income and increased personal spending on children's education, family illness, and improved housing and nutrition (known as multiplier effect of microcredit, Morduch, 2000; Coleman, 2005). The study by Hossain (1988) on Bangladesh established that microfinance has positive impacts on social indicators such as opportunity for empowerment and decision making rights which increase confidence and self-esteem. Pitt and Khandker (1998) indicate that microfinance programs promote the poor households' investment in human capital through the choice of public versus private schooling and the contraceptive behaviour of the families. Even though it can be said that the microfinance organizations such as government institutions and NGOs started with economic solvency to the poor, this operation has several other multiplier effects (as discussed) in the lives of the poor which made these institutions more appealing in the development context. However, being positive contributors in the lives of the poor, credit providers are not equally effective or rated alike by the donors or governing bodies. For example, one noticeable change in the credit operation is the massive shift of the donor's funding channel from government to NGOs in the early 1990s. One prime reason for such shift is reported to be purely ideological, legal, and institutional method of fund delivery as it was argued that expansion of NGO involvement in development is the anti-state intervention nature of structural adjustment policy which prefers minimum government and recommended that development programs should not be totally controlled by donor and recipient governmental agencies (Schneider, 1988). The other reason behind such shift is said to be the comparative advantages of the NGOs which made them more effective than government in serving the poor in the developing countries like Bangladesh. Donors and founders of microcredit operations argued that this shift is mainly to fill the gap caused by the government's failure in addressing the root causes of poverty. For example, Yolande, Welmond and Wolf (2002) mentioned, 'A myriad of justifications and assumptions can be found throughout the development literature as to why NGOs should play a growing role in the education and other sectors, many that mirror the argument to increase the role of NGOs more generally. NGOs work at the 'community-level,' thus affecting social change where others cannot; NGOs can represent and catalyse 'civil society,' an element many consider critical to sustainability and democratization; and NGOs are simply more 'effective' than other partners'. On the other hand, research by Nunnenkamp (2008) suggests that NGOs do not provide better targeted or more effective aid than state-run development agencies. One author added, 'they do not seem to even try to outperform the latter by focussing on the neediest or by working in particularly difficult environments. The study argues against the idea that NGOs are less driven by political interest and more perceptive of poor people's needs than government-led aid agencies'. These contradictory findings raise the question about who is performing better in reducing the poverty in developing countries despite the common myth[9] in the literature of development economics that the

NGOs are more effective compared to GOs in running poverty reduction programs in developing countries.

1.1 The relative effectiveness of alternative credit-driven poverty reduction projects in Bangladesh

At the time of the liberation war in 1971, there were few NGOs that were working only for rehabilitation and giving assistance to war victims in Bangladesh. For example, *Gono Shastho Kendra* offered medical assistance to freedom fighters in 1971; *Terre Des Hommes* provided rehabilitation for unwanted children of the war in Kurigram district; and *Rangpur Dinajpur Rural Service* (RDRS) began its post-war rehabilitation in the northern part of Bangladesh. In the middle of 1970s, most of the NGOs were providing rehabilitation, education, health, sanitation, shelter, and family planning services for the people. At the beginning of the 1980s, the country experienced the success of the Grameen Bank which resulted in the wider acceptance of microfinance operations in the country. Between the mid-1980s and the early 1990s, the focus of NGOs radically shifted from rehabilitation to credit delivery. At that time, with a slight change in focus and activities, many Microfinance Institutions (MFIs) emerged in Bangladesh. The primary task of those MFIs was to offer credit with training. In Bangladesh, the founders of microcredit movement were all dissatisfied with the inability of government to take advantage of the social capital in the post-independence period to change the trajectory of poverty alleviation in the country. In addition, private sector organizations (especially, for example, commercial banks) could not operate in the remote areas because doing so would make the cost per customer much higher. Some of them operating there had their cost (pricing) structure which was beyond the capacity of the poor. NGOs, on the other hand, had comparative advantages of voluntary motivations, more resources, a larger workforce and state-of-the-art technologies which had become a popular way of delivering to the previously unmet demand for public services to the poor.

1.1.1 Government intervention in poverty reduction

The Government of Bangladesh (GoB) has been prioritizing poverty alleviation as its main development goal since 1971. To achieve this goal, the GoB formulated and implemented an interim PRSP in 2003, ‘Poverty Reduction Strategy Paper’ (PRSP, 2004), and Accelerated PRSP in the year 2005. Development expenditure by the government on housing, education, health, and family planning drastically increased from 12.88% of Annual Development Program (ADP) in the 1980s to 26.63% in the 1990s (WB, 1991 and 1995; BBS, 2002). This increase would be much greater if the special poverty alleviation projects of the GoB were included in this data.

The GoB's anti-poverty programs are divided into two broad categories: *transfer mode* programs (such as allowances for the elderly, allowances for widowed and destitute women, education stipend programs, rural maintenance programs, food for education and work, vulnerable group feeding, etc.), and *credit mode* programs (large amounts of microfinance facilities provided by ministries, nationalized banks, specialized banks, etc.). In addition, the GoB has initiated special poverty reduction projects such as fisheries, low-cost housing, poultry projects, seasonal shock unemployment reduction projects, etc. (see the detailed discussion in Chapter 3). Among these programs, it is the microfinance-driven projects that are more often employed because the other programs are believed to be beneficial mainly in short-term situations, and since they are not a source of income generation, they do not sufficiently tackle income- and hunger-based poverty. Despite such significant and diverse poverty reduction programs, the government's projects have been criticized due to, for example, perceived corruption, faulty project design, weak management, lengthy and bureaucratic processes in fund disbursement, weak coverage in rural areas, the small number of field workers, a lack of dedication by the field workers, a lack of investment in the project related infrastructure, and a lack of proper human resources practices (Sobhan, 1998).

1.1.2 NGOs as development partners in poverty reduction

Even though there are several reasons behind the proliferation of NGOs in Bangladesh, the fundamental cause is what Weisbrod (1974) terms *public goods theory*: government entities tend to provide public goods only at a level that satisfy the median voter, therefore, individuals whose demand for the goods or services may be greater than the median would not be provided for. Consequently, more NGOs arise to produce goods and services to supply this unmet demand (see Chapter 3 for a detailed discussion on the theories of non-profits). It could also be argued that to address the limitations of the GoB's microfinance-driven poverty reduction projects, particularly in relation to issues such as narrow coverage, corruption and inadequate work force, NGOs are considered the '*third channel*' by Kozlowski (1983), and the '*third sector*' by Paul (1991) and now the preferred channel for fund disbursement by the donors in Bangladesh.

NGOs have been working in Bangladesh since the 1960s, with operations increasing during the liberation war of 1971. At that time NGOs came forward with the rehabilitation programs for war victims. However, in the mid-1970s their focus gradually shifted from social mobilization, relief, and community development to service delivery and credit disbursement by the early 1980s (Zaman, 2004). The de-politicization of NGOs brought one important concept, which Wood (1997) terms the '*franchise state*'. This is where vital public services like education, health care, and banking in Bangladesh are run by NGOs but are funded by donors and the State. In order to provide these services, the number of NGOs grew at a rate of 236% during the 1990s (from 347 in the late 1980s to 1167 by the end of the 1990s), dropping to a growth rate of only 46% during the 2000s. The number of projects conducted by NGOs increased to 6781 in the 1990s and then to 9510 in the 2000s, compared to 8 in the late 1980s (NGOAB, 2010). Even though most NGOs, especially the smaller ones, are working on credit delivery with the intention of creating non-agricultural employment and enhancing women's empowerment, few NGOs have demonstrated effectiveness in providing social services like education (for instance, BRAC schools), immunization (for example, Save the Children), family planning, health care (such as *Gonoshastho kendra*) and legal services (for instance, BELA) for the poor in Bangladesh.

Despite their contribution to poverty reduction in Bangladesh, NGOs are criticized for offering credit to more solvent people, charging higher rates of interest[10], profit-oriented commercialization[11], lack of accountability in their operations[12] and fund utilization[13], political involvement[14], etc. Another major criticism as reported by Mayoux (1999) is that to gain short-term financial sustainability in microfinance-driven projects, NGOs have reduced their provision for additional services to decrease costs of particular projects. Interestingly, it was found that the amount of microcredit disbursement (NGOAB, 2010) by NGOs increased by $1069.19 million between 1991/92 and 1995/96 while rural poverty rate increased from 52.9% to 56.7%. On the other hand, between 1995/96 and 2000, the amount of microcredit disbursement decreased by $514.405 million, but at that time the rural situation had been improved with poverty reducing from 56.7% to 53.1%. The amount of credit disbursement was found to rising till 2010. However, in 2010 Bangladesh was down-graded to 'low development' countries league even though the country's ranking on the Multidimensional Poverty Index[15] (MPI) improved[16] (UNDP,

2010). All these stated findings show that credit and other social programs alone cannot make a sea change in poverty reduction rates unless customized services as demanded by the beneficiaries are provided such that the beneficiaries can utilize the credit and other supports more effectively and sustainably. Sustainability in the context of public service delivery not only means that sufficient finance or other socio-economic resources must be available to provide the services needed (Mubangizi, 2009), but it also refers to the effectiveness of the credit providers in delivering such services, in understanding the asset needs of the beneficiaries, and in exploring local priorities over an extended period of time, thus improving the services concerned.

1.1.3 The effectiveness debate and gaps in the existing literature: Introducing 'process-based' and 'outcome-based' effectiveness comparison

A study by the World Bank (cited in Narayan, 2000) using the Participatory Poverty Assessment (PPA) tool concludes that (i) the State has been largely ineffective in reaching the poor; (ii) the role of NGOs in the lives of poor people is limited; and the poor depend primarily on their own informal networks. This finding necessarily continues the debate. In quest of addressing the current debate, Government and NGO projects were compared on several grounds. Meyer (1992) and Vivian (1994) in their studies on Zimbabwe have shown that NGOs are more cost effective than government in reaching the poor. However, Hashemi (1992) in his study on several Asian countries and Carroll (1992) in his study on Latin American countries found that NGOs were more expensive in reaching the poor and maintaining popular participation. Riddell and Robinson (1992) in their work on Africa found similar result. Asian Development Bank (2003) reported that NGOs could reach only 20% of the marginal poor in Bangladesh with such a long presence in the country. Korten (1990) found that NGOs are better than government in project planning and management in social works. Meyer (1992) also reported that NGOs were more effective in delivering education and health services compared to Government in Latin America due to their better implementation capability. However, Edwards and Hulme (1996) argued that this effectiveness was by default and not by design as government lacked resources for project implementation in those countries. Hasan (1993) in his work on Pakistan found that NGOs were more effective than public sector in the sanitation programs. However, Riddell and Robinson (1992) in their study on 16 Asian and African projects (related to sanitation, immunization, etc.) found the opposite results with government's superiority. Howes and Sattar (1992) in their work on BRAC primary schooling concluded that there is no trade-off between NGO's cost effective service provision and quality of work. However, LaFond (1995) in his study has shown that long-term NGO services suffer from quality to all. Several studies reported that NGOs performed much better than public sector in innovating and delivering services like oral dehydration (Howes and Sattar, 1992) and agricultural technology development (Farrington et al., 1993a). On the other hand, Farrington et al. (1993b) found that in Latin America NGOs became less innovative when they worked as contractors to donors or government. Mahmud and Ahmed (2003) in their studies on delivering nutrition services in Bangladesh found that NGOs were cheaper in delivering the required services compared to government. Deng (2008) reported that NGOs are more likely to deliver more differentiated and customized services than bulky government units while working for rehabilitation. Edwards and Hulme (1996) also noticed that NGOs are more effective in creating and delivering social funds intended to mitigate the social consequences of economic and structural adjustment packages. However, Fernando (2006) in his study found that the effective interest rate charged by NGOs is more than 28%, which is much higher than the interest rate charged by the government credit institutions or even the commercial banks of Bangladesh. More importantly, Kelly (2008) in his study found that NGOs in Bangladesh are working as parallel government and accountable to none. In addition, Epstein and Crane (2005) in their work mentioned several other findings on issues like the number of borrowers, borrower retention rate, financial sustainability of the project, and repayment rates. However, in most cases there was no complete domination of effectiveness by either GO or NGOs.

This study compares the relative effectiveness of the stated partners (GoB and NGOs) and to ensure similarity of the projects, a decision was made to compare the effectiveness of the **'microfinance-driven projects'** of GoB and NGOs. There are two reasons behind the choice: (a) microfinance-driven projects are the only common projects run by both GOs and NGOs (there are many other projects such as food for education or work, and allowances for the elderly and widowed women allowances which are run only by GOs and NGOs do not have the same field operations); and (b) there is evidence (Littlefield et al., 2003) to suggest that poor people invest their credit and expect returns from the credit on other social needs such as health and education, making contraceptive decision, managing household emergencies, and other cash needs. Thus, microfinance has a multiplier effect and its impacts go beyond just income generation and employment creation (Littlefield et al., 2003).

In general, the 'effectiveness' of a microfinance-driven poverty reduction project is assessed based on access to and repayment rates of credit, the number of beneficiaries and the demand for loans (Kevane and Wydick, 2001; Mayoux, 1999; Goetz and Gupta, 1996). In Bangladesh the effectiveness of the major service providers in the poverty reduction programs of GOs and NGOs is also assessed on cost effectiveness (Mahmud and Ahmed, 2003), rapid response rates (McGhee, 1999), the number of beneficiaries covered (Chao, 2003), and the rate of loan recovery (Morshed, 2000). I would like to argue that these assessment methods are extremely narrow in nature. For example, repayment rates should not be used as a main indicator[17] of effectiveness in the projects concerned because beneficiaries' source of income may not necessarily be from revenue generated by productive investments. There is evidence to suggest that poor people (especially women) borrow money from one microfinance institution (MFI) to pay the debt burden from another[18] (Goldin Institute, 2007; Burra, 2005).

In addition, it was reported (Goetz and Gupta, 1996) that even though the credit is sanctioned in the name of women, it is, in many cases, used by their husbands or male members of the family which not only violates the precondition of empowerment but also questions the validity of effectiveness assessment based on the number of women reached. As can be seen, most of the stated (and available) evaluation criteria are designed from the organizational perspective and do not measure the aggregate impacts of the credit driven projects in the wellbeing of the poor – an unaddressed issue in the literature. The above studies identified that in most cases the effectiveness comparison between the partners with respect to (1) their service delivery processes; and (2) their contribution to the social, economic, cultural and political aspects of poverty, are ignored by scholars even though the need for effective service delivery and identification of specific asset requirements is well known (I will discuss this later in Chapter 2 and 3).

While addressing the first of the above two issues, the major dimensions and fields (in short called 'scale' or 'parameter') of service delivery will be identified to better target the delivery process. This aspect of development has largely been ignored by the researchers and thus there has previously been no such multidimensional service delivery scale based on the opinion of the beneficiaries available in the development literature.

In one of the chapters (Chapter-5), we will describe a method (which is new to existing literature) to develop a scale to explore different dimensions of pro-poor service delivery mechanisms. The derived and validated scale can then be utilized to compare the effectiveness of microfinance-driven projects of GoB and NGOs in delivering services to the rural poor of Bangladesh.

While service delivery is '*process-relevant*' as it doesn't indicate the outcome of the project, the second issue – contribution to different aspects of poverty, as mentioned in point 2 above, is '*outcome-relevant*' and will assess the contribution of the development partners to raising the living standards of the poor. It can be argued that the head count ratio (HCR) of poverty in Bangladesh, when based on Direct Caloric Intake (DCI) or Cost of Basic Needs (CBN) methods, reveals a change in the monetary poverty rate for the whole or regional Bangladesh, but these methods are unable to capture the variation in social, political and cultural dimensions of poverty for a specific year. This is one important limitation of the existing poverty assessment methods used in Bangladesh. Furthermore, whilst the HCR based on DCI/CBN methods offers an overall measure of the poverty situation in Bangladesh, it does not split the individual contributions of GoB and NGOs or other development partners to improving the living standards of the poor. This wider comparative study has never been performed due to the absence of any multidimensional wellbeing model for rural Bangladesh. It is important to mention that most of the poverty impact studies on Bangladesh (Refer to Table 2.5) are based on few pre-determined indicators and those studies didn't explore the customized poverty indicators from Bangladesh point of view based on the opinion of the poor beneficiaries. Sen (1984, 1993) in his Capability Approach (CA) emphasizes that indicators of capability in any assessment of poverty and wellbeing should be area-specific, and thus reflect the social values and culture of the local community. He argues that failure to design and evaluate poverty alleviation programs from the perspective of the participants can result in the total failure of the project[19]. Like Sen's (1985) human capability approach, the Sustainable Livelihoods (SL) Model (DFID, 2000) also depicts that people require a range of assets (or capital) to achieve positive livelihood outcomes (such as economic solvency or social inclusion), and no single category of asset is sufficient to ensure the overall livelihood outcome. The principles of the SL approach demand a shift in focus from outputs to people, and an exploration of poor people's own priorities (thus a customized poverty model). However, there is no methodology of listing the capabilities and livelihood assets offered by any of these approaches and no updated asset requirement list is available for rural Bangladesh[20] that can be used to understand the local circumstances and needs of the poor. Serrat (2008, pp. 4) also suggests that 'the sustainable livelihoods approach is one way of integrating a number of complex issues that surround poverty and this model needs to be customized to local circumstances and local priorities'. In addition, 'double bottom line' approach used by many microcredit agencies stressed the need for incorporating social and financial outcomes of credit lending. However, this approach like CA and SL approach has failed to offer any method of identifying the indicators of social and financial outcomes of credit lending. To address this issue, this study offers a new methodology to develop area-specific multidimensional capability, asset or capital model (see Chapter 7 for details) for rural Bangladesh by applying the CA and SL approach such that the priorities of the people in the stated area can be better understood. However, we believe that the existing criteria for institutional effectiveness comparison need to be taken into consideration too. Thus our model will incorporate economic, social, cultural, political, and religious outcomes of credit lending along with the existing effectiveness evaluation criteria such as repayment rates, the amount of borrowing, years of membership, etc – a composite model development methodology that has never been offered in existing literature.

In a later chapter (Chapter-7), we will detail a new methodology to develop and validate a multidimensional poverty/wellbeing model for rural Bangladesh by utilizing the opinion of the credit recipients and that model can capture different dimensions of poverty. We believe this model development methodology can be widely followed in exploring and customizing the poverty indicators of other developing countries. This model can then be used to compare the efficacy of various development agencies (such as GOs and NGOs) in improving the wellbeing of the beneficiaries on those dimensions.

In summary, the broad focus of the study – comparing relative effectiveness of credit-driven GoB and NGO projects – is segregated into four specific tasks as listed below:

- Proposing a new methodology to develop and validate a multidimensional service delivery effectiveness scale for poverty reduction projects in Bangladesh;
- comparing the efficacy of GoB and NGOs on the dimensions of the developed service delivery scale;
- offering a new method to develop and validate a multidimensional wellbeing model for rural Bangladesh to pin-point the specific asset needs of the poor people; and
- comparing the effectiveness of credit-driven GoB and NGO projects with respect to their relative contribution to the indicators

of developed poverty model which in turn improves the living standards of the beneficiaries.

We strongly believe that these are two different and new ways to compare the effectiveness of credit-driven GO and NGO projects which can address a significant part of the continuous debate regarding effectiveness of the stated development partners. In addition, the developed scale and model can help the policy-makers for GOs and NGOs to better target the specific service delivery issues and wellbeing indicators to achieve a higher and more sustainable poverty reduction rate in rural Bangladesh.

1.2 Organization of the book

The book is organized as follows (see Fig-1.1):

Chapter 2 describes the need for understanding the indicators, determinants and measurement of poverty and wellbeing from cross-country experiences in order to prepare a list of poverty indicators. This list can then be used to develop a customized poverty model for rural Bangladesh based on opinions of the beneficiaries. In this chapter, in addition to the existing theories, the universally-used Capability Approach developed by Sen (1984) and the DFID's Sustainable Livelihoods (SL) Approach (DFID, 1996) will be analysed to find how the indicators of poverty have been defined and measured. This chapter summarizes the scattered literature on poverty and wellbeing in one place and thus can be useful as an important source of poverty studies for future researchers.

Chapter 3 discusses the role of institutions and the need for effective service delivery in poverty reduction in Bangladesh with emphasis on the activities of Government and NGOs. In addition, the chapter explores the limitations of the existing theories in offering any effective service delivery guidelines. Moreover, this chapter details the reasons behind NGO proliferation in Bangladesh by considering the history of operations of NGOs in the country. The chapter also explains the service delivery dimension and item selection procedure, with the primarily selected items validated based on opinions of the beneficiaries so as to develop a service delivery effectiveness scale.

Chapter 4 elaborates on the methodology of the work, including questionnaire preparation, the district and village selection procedure, respondent selection, and the pilot study for administering the questionnaire.

In Chapter 5, a methodology of developing multidimensional service delivery effectiveness scale is offered and then the efficacy of microfinance-driven GoB and NGO projects are compared on the scale items.

A gender-based study on the perception of the beneficiaries towards service delivery effectiveness of GOs and NGOs can be found in Chapter 6. Findings of this chapter are new to the existing literature as this chapter will explore specific service needs of men and women and the effective delivery of those services can help the groups to better utilize the borrowed money. Existing works on women empowerment mainly focus on exploring the economic, social and political indicators of empowerment such as education, employment, participation, voice in decision making, etc (see for example the works of Kabeer, 2005; Schuler, Islam and Rottach, 2010). In addition, existing works explored the role of microcredit in creating or changing economic and social capital for women in order to reduce gender inequality (see for example, Sanyal, 2009; Hashemi, Schuler and Riley, 1996). However, we believe, a potential source of gender inequality (as well as women empowerment) can be due to discrimination in service delivery mechanism – an important yet unexplored issue in the existing literature. This chapter intends to close that gap.

Chapter 7 describes a multidimensional poverty and wellbeing model development methodology by considering rural Bangladesh as the case. It is believed that this new methodology can contribute significantly to the existing literature as other developing countries can customize their poverty indicators by using the methodology. The study then compares the effectiveness of credit-driven GoB and NGO projects with respect to their contribution to the multidimensional indicators of the proposed model.

Finally, Chapter 8 concludes with a discussion of the major findings, policy prescriptions, and guidelines for further research.

Figure 1.1: Book summary

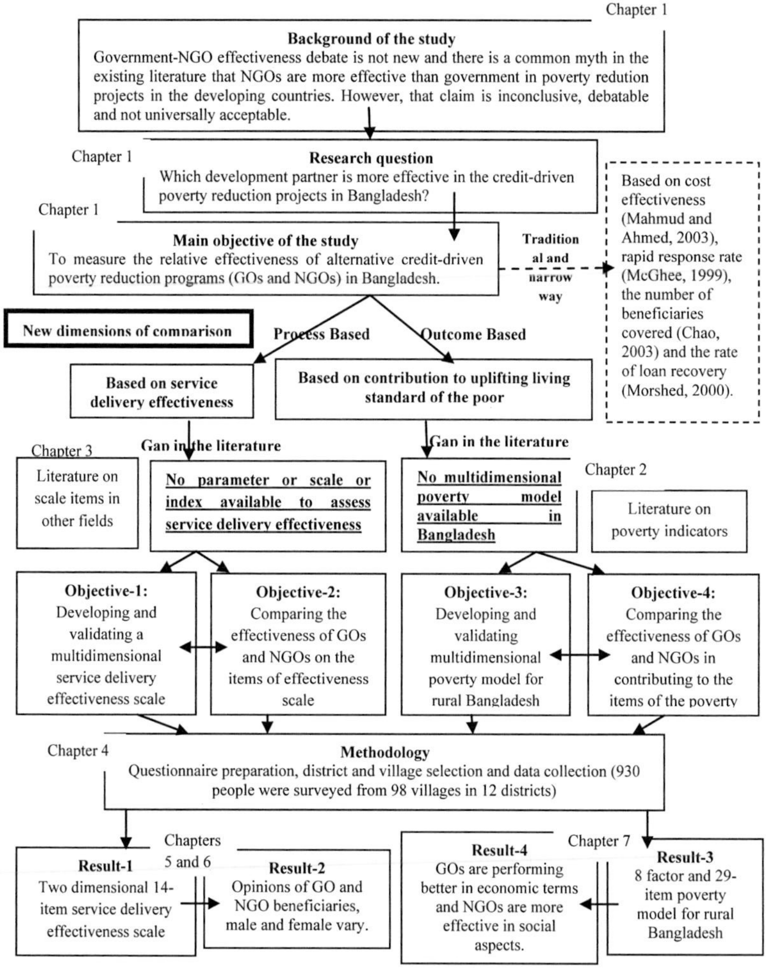

Notes

[1] Daily per capita intake of 2112 Kilo calories and 1805 Kilo calories were considered to be relative and 'hard-core' poverty respectively.

[2] The consumption expenditure data have been used to estimate the income poverty.

[3] Sen and Hulme (2004) reported that this rate was 74% for the financial year 1973-74.

[4] However, between 1991 and 2005 the total number of poor increased by 4.4 million (SUPRO, 2007).

[5] The number of 'hard-core poor' increased by 3 million between 2000 and 2005.

[6] However, UN officials also noted that the country is still struggling with seven of the other Millennium Development Goals (UNDP, 2010).

[7] Introduced in 1997, the HPI captures deprivation in longevity, knowledge and economic provision.

[8] See, for example, Sen and Hulme (2004).

[9] See, for example, Sundaram (1996); Yolande, Welmond and Wolf (2002); Jelinek (2006).

[10] Zahid (2000) in his study found that the effective interest rate charged by NGOs is more than 28%, which is much higher than the interest rate charged by the commercial banks of Bangladesh.

[11] For example, Grameen Bank has their for-profit investment in mobile communications and food businesses; BRAC has invested in commercial banking, dairy products, internet services, apparel businesses etc.

[12] See 'Growing discontent' by Annie Kelly, *The Guardian*, Wednesday, Feb 20, 2008. Kelly writes 'There are accusations that BRAC is acting like a parallel state, but one that is accountable to no one'.. .

[13] For details, see *The Daily Star,* 14 May, 2004.

[14] See, *The Independent*, 17 January, 2002; *The Daily Star*, 25 April, 2003.

[15] The HPI could not identify specific individuals, households or larger groups of people as jointly deprived. The MPI addresses this shortcoming by capturing the number of people who experience overlapping deprivations (incidence) and how many deprivations they face on average (intensity) (UNDP, 2010).

[16] The MPI of Bangladesh in 2010 was 0.29, ranking it 129th in the world.

[17] Many government projects and NGOs consider rate of recovery as one of the main criteria to assess the effectiveness of credit-driven projects. For example, PKSF, the largest credit delivery organization of the government of Bangladesh has posted the summary of credit disbursed, credit recovered and number of borrowers as the only information about their operation and success. There is no indication given about how many of their beneficiaries could break the poverty. (See:http://www.pksf-bd.org/index.php?option=com_content&view=article&id=620&Itemid=282)
Similar pattern can be found in the websites of NGOs such as in Grameen Bank (refer to: http://www.grameen-info.org/index.php?option=com_content&task=view&id=453&Itemid=527) (both accessed on March 16, 2012).

[18] According to a Goldin Institute survey (2007), it is not uncommon for families to carry as many as five loans, most used to cover old debts, rather than purchase new assets.

[19] Dasgupta (2001, pp. 32), for example, observes that 'policy evaluation techniques that were developed in the 1970s, while formally corrected, neglected to consider resource allocation in the wide variety of non-market institutions that prevail throughout the world…I have argued that the evaluation of policy changes can only be done effectively with a fair understanding of the way socio-economic and ecological systems would respond to the changes' (p. 32).

[20] There are several studies on other fields (such as fisheries, marketing, irrigation systems, urban and rural development etc.) using SL that have been done for Bangladesh. See for example, Neely, Sutherland and Johnson (2004); Ahmed (2009). SAL has been used in several other countries, however, none of those studies has developed and updated livelihood asset listing. For further reference, see Krantz, 2001.

CHAPTER TWO

POVERTY AND WELLBEING: CONCEPTS, DETERMINANTS AND MEASUREMENT

2.1 Introduction

The multidimensionality of poverty is now fully acknowledged[1] due to the advancement in poverty analysis by economists and the policy-formulating organizations[2]. The traditional definition of poverty with respect to small earning is now viewed as a narrow definition (Sen, 1982, 1983; Kothari, 1995) that bypasses other social, psychological, cultural, political, environmental, and participatory indicators. However, change is visible in the poverty analysis[3], and at least three major shifts can be observed in the literature (Shaffer, 2008):

a) the concept of poverty has been broadened from a physiological to a social model with attention focused on vulnerability, inequality, and human rights;
b) the causal variables of poverty have been enlarged by including social, political, cultural, and environmental concepts; and
c) the view on social protection vs. poverty reduction is also evolving.

But the developing countries – where poverty is more acute – have failed to undertake effective action against poverty due to their negligence in not incorporating the multiple dimensions of poverty by taking into account local circumstances (Herrera and Rouboud, 2006).

The development partners in Bangladesh (Government and NGOs) work to improve conditions for the rural poor by delivering many living-standard-enhancing services focussed on education, health care, income generation, employment creation, social mobilization, safety nets, shock mitigations schemes, water supply and sanitation, immunization, women's empowerment, etc. Although the development partners have common ground (living standard improvement) and common tools (micro-financing) to their work in Bangladesh, there has not previously been a comparative study that explores the relative efficacy of microfinance driven GO and NGO projects with respect to their contribution to raising the living standards of the poor. A prime reason behind this lacuna is the absence of any composite multidimensional poverty model to capture the different aspects of poverty from a rural Bangladesh perspective. To develop such a model, it is, at the outset, important to explore the determinants of poverty based on cross-country studies available in the literature. Chapter 2 will address these issues in detail.

This chapter is organized as follows: Section 2 discusses the causes, symptoms, and effects of poverty. Section 3 includes a conceptualization of poverty with respect to various approaches offered throughout the literature. The fourth section explores the recent development of the Capability Approach (CA) developed by Sen (1979b, 1984, 1985) to broaden the poverty indicator list as well as examine the applications of the CA in a poverty analysis of Bangladesh. The fifth section of the chapter explains the Sustainable Livelihoods Approach and its applicability in customizing the poverty indicators according to the local circumstances and priorities. Section 6 incorporates the indicators of wellbeing from cross-country experiences in order to conceptualize poverty in developing countries, and Section 7 concludes.

2.2 Causes, symptoms and effects of poverty

Studying wellbeing rather than deprivation from the perspective of those in poverty provides an opportunity for understanding what poor people have and are able to achieve. In addition to traditional wellbeing analysis, concepts of quality of life such as vulnerability, and subjective wellbeing[4] represent a novel focus on people's feelings and include their own evaluation of their living standards. Determinants of poverty and wellbeing, therefore, depend strongly on value judgments by the respective poor.

In addition to poverty indicators, it is also important to judge the severity of poverty – whether it is permanent or temporary in nature. This analysis is important for the development partners (Government or NGOs) for implementing poverty reduction strategies, since different degrees and length of time in poverty require different types of assets and services in order to get out of poverty. If someone is temporarily poor – caused by economic shock or natural calamity – he/she has an opportunity to reduce the distance from typical living standards in the society in which he/she lives. However, if the poverty trap is permanent, he/she becomes socially excluded. The reason for this is not that he/she is not able to do what others do, but rather because there is less chance [some would say no chance, see, for example, Bourgignon (1999)] that he/she can move above the poverty line no matter how much effort is put into trying to raise his/her living standards[5]. This may be so for a number of reasons, for example, what Bourgignon (1999) terms 'an unfavourable combination of skills', or in some cases he/she is born to poor parents, or due to credit market imperfection[6], or he/she hasn't had the same opportunities as children born into other social classes – all encompassed in a single term from Sen; the 'entitlement problem' (Sen, 1981a). The above discussion is summarized in Fig-2.1 where different types of poverty are identified based on their root causes rather than symptoms. A significant part of this chapter is devoted to the analysis of these types of poverty to get a clearer idea about the underlying indicators of multidimensional poverty.

Fig-2.1 outlines the root causes, symptoms and the varying effects (multidimensionality) poverty has on the lives of people. It is well known that the main symptoms of poverty are a lack of capability, lack of entitlements, inheritance problems, and general vulnerability. It is important at this point to note that our aim is not to struggle against these symptoms, but rather to address the root causes in an effort to ameliorate poverty. For instance, much of the relevant literature[7] suggests that the principal underlying cause of a lack of capability is the lack of capital (the resources or assets which may be utilized to achieve material as well as social objectives, such as, money income, training, education, and health care facilities). Therefore, in order to increase the capability of the people, we need to concentrate more on income generation, literacy, work-related training, adequate nourishment, etc. Similarly, the inheritance problem originates in child poverty and becomes inter-generational[8].

Fig-2.1 also indicates that the overall effect of this multidimensionality is the deprivation of wellbeing, which may be either visible (poor housing and clothing) or invisible (social exclusion, voicelessness). It also determines whether someone is economically or nutritionally poor or poor due to lack of participation. A person may be adequately nourished, but may be socially excluded due to being unable to exercise the right to a voice in local decision-making processes or even at home, thus he/she is poor from a social and participatory point of view. The relationships between these root causes and their multidimensional outcomes are shown with the two-directional arrow at the top of Fig-2.1.

Figure 2.1: Poverty and its relevant issues

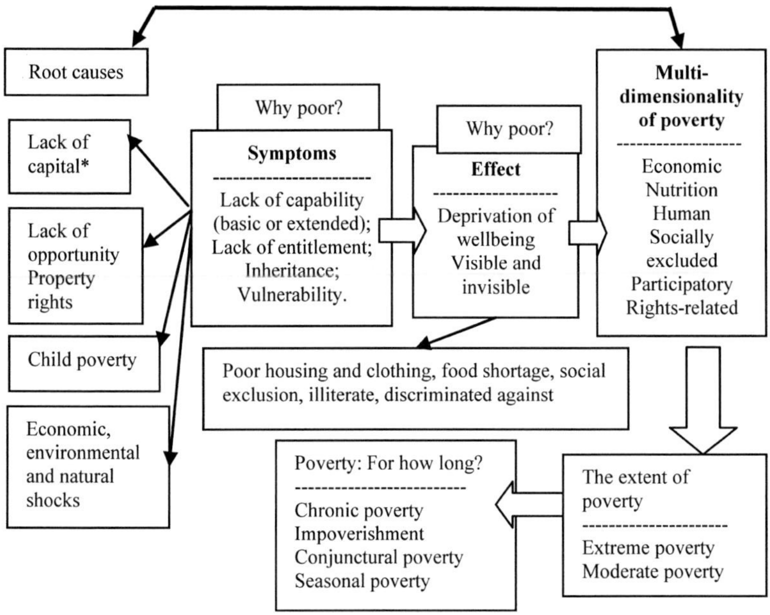

*Capital here meaning the resources or assets (financial and non financial) which may be utilized to achieve material as well as social objectives.

2.3 Poverty defined and conceptualized

To address the multidimensionality of the concept, I define poverty simply yet broadly as

> *"the inability or less capability to participate in society, economically, socially, culturally and politically"* (as suggested by Hunzai et al. and ICIMOD, 2010, pp. 2).

The evolution of this modern way of conceptualizing poverty is demonstrated in Table 2.1.

Table 2.1: Evolving approaches of poverty: From a physiological to a human rights approach

Approach	Conceptualization and limitations	Indicators in the literature
Physiological approach	Families are in primary poverty if their total earnings are insufficient to obtain the minimum necessities for the maintenance of physical/nutritional efficiency (Rowntree, 1901). Only entails the significance of income and consumption and bypasses other social, psychological, political, environmental, and participatory indicators[9]	According to Sen (1981a), starvation clearly is the most telling aspect of poverty[10]. It is claimed that the physiological approach includes both the income/consumption approach[11] and part of the basic human needs approach[12]. The income/ consumption approach relies heavily on the money metric utility where a poverty line is drawn which represents a needs adequacy level. For non-food items the problem is usually solved by assuming that a specified proportion of the food expenditure might be used for non-food. Nutrition can be used as a tool for the analysis of such calculation (Osmani, 1992).
Basic needs approach	Basic needs may be interpreted in terms of minimum specified quantities of such things as food, clothing, shelter, water, and sanitation that are necessary to prevent ill health, and the like[13].	The 'basic human needs approach' was popularized in the 1970s and came under discussion as part of the MDGs, and was illustrated in Sen (1981a, 1993) as 'basic capabilities'. Deprivation is defined as inadequate fulfillment of basic needs (such as hunger, education, child and maternal health, etc.) from food to life expectancy and mortality.

Approach	Conceptualization and limitations	Indicators in the literature
Social deprivation approaches: There are four other approaches (see the next four rows of the table) under this broad category.	Non-physiological theories of poverty argue that poverty is due to inadequacy of resources; it is important to acknowledge other forms of resources other than just income[14], for example, accumulated wealth, access to credit, family relationships, access to social networks, availability of capital.	The social deprivation concept was introduced by Sam Stouffer and his associates[15] and was formalized by Runciman (1966)[16]. Social deprivation includes indicators relevant to human rights, freedom and participation in the society[17]. A social deprivation approach uses the concepts of relative poverty[18] as proposed by Townsend (1979) who argues that poverty should be measured in terms of judgments by the members of a particular society on the way they view a reasonable and acceptable standard of living. In addition to income, decent housing, good working conditions, and caring friends or relatives are important indicators of relative poverty as well as of social deprivation.
Human poverty approach	Poverty can involve not only a scarcity of necessities for material wellbeing, but the denial of opportunities for living a tolerable life (UNDP, 1997).	Poverty as the lack of basic human capabilities resulting in illiteracy, malnutrition, shorter life span, poor maternal health, and illness from preventable diseases (UNDP, 1997). Poverty includes lack of access to goods, services and infrastructure like energy, sanitation, education, communication, pure drinking water, etc. The contribution of the human poverty approach is its concentration on the importance of information flow (such as natural disaster alert information, job, health and education related information) and infrastructures (for instance, sanitation, electricity, water, etc.).

Approach	**Conceptualization and limitations**	**Indicators in the literature**
Social exclusion approach[19]	Deprivation[20] identifies those in poverty, and social exclusion[21] is an indicator of those who are unable to participate in different spheres of social and economic life (Vinson, 2007). Social exclusion makes it harder to achieve MDGs such as reduction in poverty and hunger[22], material health and child mortality[23], universal primary education[24], gender equity[25] and combating HIV/AIDS, malaria, and other diseases[26]. It involves lack of or denial of resources, rights, goods and services, and includes an inability to participate in normal relationships and activities that are available to the majority of people in a society, whether in economic, social, cultural, or political arenas (Levitas et al 2007).	Includes such concepts as human rights, social participation (for example, members of cooperative), social integration, cultural activities and political aspects, including political participation, personal security, the rule of law, freedom of expression, and equality of opportunity[27] Discrimination can be based on ethnicity, race, religion, sexual orientation, caste, descent, gender[28], age, disability, HIV status, migrant status or where people live. It occurs in public institutions, such as the legal system[29], education and health services, as well as social institutions like households (DFID, 1992). Devicienti and Poggi (2007) and Poggi (2007a) have guided six major indicators of social exclusion that include basic needs fulfilment or not reaching a certain quality of life (having TV, telephone, paying for a week's annual holiday, having friends or family for a meal at least once a month), not having an adequate house (with sanitary toilets, enough space, enough light, heating or cooling facility), not being healthy or able to work, not living in a safe and clean environment (noise from outside, pollution, crime, industrial pollution, vandalism in the area) and having the ability to maintain social relationships (frequency of talk to neighbours, frequency of meeting people, member of any club or political association etc).

Approach	Conceptualization and limitations	Indicators in the literature
Participatory poverty[30] approach	This approach argues that the statistics on income, consumption, health care and education do not represent all the micro- and macro-level social aspects of poverty, e.g. poor women living with domestic violence, or the role of women have in family decision-making processes (Chambers, 1983). According to this framework, every person is entitled to participate in, contribute to and enjoy civil, economic, social, cultural, and political freedom.	Aspects of wellbeing and quality of life – security, self respect, justice, social life, decision-making, political participation, etc. In Southern and central Africa, the participation of the poor has been central in recent efforts to reduce poverty (Raftopoulos, 2001). It is important to view empowerment from micro- to macro-level in the decision-making process, particularly in the cases of women's and children's empowerment. Participation means that it is a person's right to be involved in decision-making, planning and reviewing an action that might affect him/her.
Human rights approach of poverty[31]	The fundamental concept of human rights[32] is the understanding that every human being has some rights and that this is not charity or even a privilege (UNDP, 2003).	Access to basic educational facilities, training and health care are fundamental rights of every citizen. Human rights-based development therefore requires: (i) participation and transparency in decision-making; (ii) non discrimination in social, political, and economic life; (iii) empowerment of the poor starting at the household level; and (iv) accountability of the actors in the poverty reduction process; the state and the private sector.

2.4 Broadening the concepts of poverty: Sen's capability approach (CA)

Amartya Sen (1993) developed[33] concepts of capability, freedom, and functioning as an alternative paradigm to the traditional economic framework of conceptualizing poverty, inequality, vulnerability, and human development. Sen argues (1981a) that utility-based evaluations of individual wellbeing might not reveal important dimensions of life and could result in misleading interpersonal comparisons[34]. Sen (1985) also observes that people and societies differ in their capacity to convert income and commodities into desired outcomes. For example, a person with a disability requires more resources (for example, wheelchairs or ramps) to achieve the same thing (moving around) than an able person. Thus, looking only to income is an incomplete measure of wellbeing (Sen, 1999). Sen's analysis of wellbeing conceptualizes poverty as '*capability deprivation*', which impedes the individual in living a valuable life and which is not caused solely by lowness of income. In particular, Sen defines poverty with respect to capabilities that are 'basic', in the sense that they satisfy primary and crucial functioning up to a certain level.

2.4.1 The conceptual framework of the capability approach

Like Adam Smith, Sen (1983) considers that economic growth and the expansion of goods and services are necessary for human development. However, like Aristotle, Sen also argues that wealth is not all we are looking for, and there is more to life than simply achieving utility (Sen, 1990). Following Rawls, Sen (1977, 1984) further demonstrates that utility cannot explore different sources of pleasure and pain. Rather, there are many other aspects of life with intrinsic value (notably rights and freedom) that are neglected by the orthodox welfare approaches (Sen, 1987, 1992, 1999). These considerations lead to the conclusion that neither income and commodity command nor utility can adequately represent wellbeing or deprivation. Sen's capability approach is based on the following major concepts:

- *Functioning*: Functioning means being and doing; it is a person's achievement – what he/she wants to do or be. Examples of functioning are: being well fed, taking part in the community, being sheltered, relating to other people, working in the labour market, caring for others, and being healthy (Sen, 1984). According to Sen (1984), functioning (like being adequately nourished) with a given commodity bundle (like, rice or bread) depends on many factors (like, body size, age, gender, location, nutritional knowledge, health status, etc.), thus it defines the social and economic standing (being poor or non-poor) of a person. Functioning n-tuple (or vector) describes the combination of doings and beings that makes a life. The functioning n-tuple emerges from the available commodity bundle. Some functionings are very elementary (basic needs), whereas others are more extended such as being happy, achieving self respect, taking part in society without shame, maintaining relationships with friends, etc.

- *Capability*: Capabilities are people's potential functioning, therefore, capability represents the ability of a person to achieve a given level of functioning (Saith, 2001). A capability set describes a person's attainable functioning. The capability set[35] is obtained by applying all feasible utilizations to all attainable commodity bundles (Sen, 1985; Saith, 2001). Sen emphasizes that capabilities reflect a person's real opportunities or positive freedom of choice between possible lifestyles (Sen, 1985, 1992, 1999). The most difficult part in the analysis is how to increase the capability of the individuals (Sen, 1999).

For the analysis of poverty, it is important to find a subset of commodities which is at least required for subsistence living or 'basic needs'[36]; Sen (1980) applies the term 'basic capabilities', meaning the ability to satisfy certain crucial functionings up to minimally adequate levels. The identification of an acceptable level of certain basic capabilities (below which people can be termed deprived or traditionally poor) doesn't simply depend on inadequacy of income which is the main basis for poverty analysis. An increase in capability is related to access to goods and services such as public transport, education or health care. Interestingly, even if these services are available, people may not have the physical capacity (due to personal handicap), the financial capacity (insufficient level of income or a large opportunity cost), or the social opportunity (due to right and freedom constraints) to be able to fully benefit from them. This means that concentrating only on income inadequacy will mislead the poverty analysis, whereas the capability approach is more comprehensive to the analysis even though Sen (1993) said, 'capability is not an awfully attractive word' (p. 33). The concepts of CA can be better explained with the aid of Fig-2.2 to see their linkage in the poverty and wellbeing analysis.

Fig-2.2 illustrates the relationship between commodities and wellbeing relating to capability and functioning. The second row in the diagram depicts how commodities and assets can be utilized to escape from poverty with respect to personal capacity. The model shown below suggests the need for specific commodities or asset endowments access to which assists in poverty reduction. However, the central theme of the model is that the degree of poverty reduction will vary depending on the capability of the individual to utilize those resources and transfer them into productive capital.

Figure 2.2: Traditional and expanded ways to conceptualize the capability approach

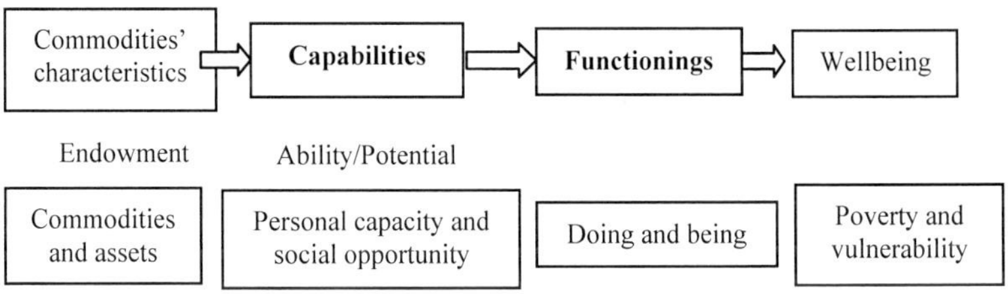

Note: Adapted from Dubois and Rousseau (2008); Clark (2005).

2.4.2 Applications of Sen's capability approach and further refinement

The capability approach has been used to investigate poverty, inequality, wellbeing, social justice, gender inequality, social exclusion, health, disability, child poverty, human needs, human rights, and human security and identity. In addition, exploration of the advantages of the CA approach has mushroomed[37]. A few of these studies (which are more relevant to my work) are shown in Table 2.2 below.

One of the major advantages of Sen's capability approach is its flexibility in that it allows researchers to use the concept in a variety of ways (Alkire, 2002). At the primary stage, the major indicators used by Sen's analysis are education (literacy), escape from morbidity, longer life expectancy, working properly, health status, political activity, enjoying positive states, etc. (Sen, 1984; Clark, 2002; Robeyns, 2002). However, Sen never subscribes a fixed set of indicators or capabilities; instead he argues that the weight of the capability depends on personal value judgments[38]. We need to consider other influential principles such as personal liberty, economic growth and efficacy. However, Sen recognizes this deficiency and states that the capability approach is open to modifications and further improvements.

Sen revised and broadened the concepts of capability by arguing that the capability set should be judged in terms of the quality and quantity of available opportunities, which he termed 'genuine choice' (Sen 1985, 1993, Crocker, 1998), and that modification was considered by many as an option of diversity (Clark, 2002). In addition, Sen (1992) stresses the concept of 'responsible choice', where intelligent choices should be made by incorporating uncertainty and social conditioning relative to the person (Kanbur, 1987). However, it can be seen that a practical application of Sen's capability approach is, as mentioned earlier, the 'human poverty approach' as forwarded by UNDP.

Table 2.2: Applications of the capability approach

Study carried out	**Indicators used**	**References**
Measurement of poverty and wellbeing (focus on functioning)	Income (opportunity), life expectancy with respect to health condition and education	Balestrino,(1996); Clark and Qizilbash (2002, 2005); Klasen (1997, 2000); Majumder and Subramaniam (2001); Sen (1992, 1999).
Capability analysis on poverty	Income, work opportunity, literacy, social exclusion	Schokkaert and Van Ootegem (1990).
Link between income and various capabilities	Income, physical capability, education, food consumption, housing, etc.	Sen (1985, 1999); Balestrino (1996); Ruggeri-Laderchi (1997); Klasen (2000).
Capability and wellbeing	Life expectancy, nutrition, literacy along the lines of gender, race, class, caste and age.	Robeyns (2003); Clark (2003); Lorgelly, et al. (2007); Alkire (2007).

In the revised version of the CA, Sen (1999) addresses the critique that in the earlier model not enough attention was paid to issues of freedom (Qizilbash, 1996). Sen further investigates the interconnection between different capabilities and freedom (Sen, 1999; Clark, 2005) and recognizes five broad categories of freedom in his newer version of the capability approach, namely political freedom, economic facilities, social opportunities, transparency guarantees, and protective security. Sen (2005) further enriches his CA by incorporating a few new indicators of human values like democracy and public participation. By aggregating all the above mentioned facts, it can be deduced that this approach views: (i) development as an expansion of capabilities and freedom; (ii) capacity as an important currency for judgments involving egalitarian justice[39]; (iii) poverty in terms of basic capability failure[40]; and (iv) lack of freedom as one main cause of poverty[41].

2.4.3 Capability list

Attempts to complete Sen's capability list are many which were applied in the fields of development studies, social science and philosophy[42]. A few works that use capability listings which can be testified in the case of rural Bangladesh are presented in Table 2.3.

2.4.4 Rationale for using the capability approach in this study

Sen (1984, 1993) emphasizes that indicators of capability in any assessment of poverty and wellbeing should be area-specific, and thus reflect the social values and culture of the local community. In fact, Sen is more conservative in the application of the capability approach. He argues that failure to design and evaluate poverty alleviation programs from the perspective of the participants can result in the total failure of the project. Consequently, one of the objectives of this study is to develop a multidimensional poverty and wellbeing model for rural Bangladesh by applying the capability approach to prioritize and better target the local needs of the poor. Incompleteness – the main criticism of the capability approach – is in effect the advantage of the concept.

Table 2.3: Building capability lists from cross-country studies

Author(s)	Items on the list	Comments
Martha Nussbaum (2000, 2003, 2005a)	(1) life, (2) bodily health, (3) bodily integrity, (4) sense, imagination and thought, (5) emotions, (6) practical reason, (7) affiliation, (8) other species, (9) play and (10) political and material control over one's environment	The list is subject to ongoing revision and should emerge through some sort of intercultural ethnic inquiry. Many commentators have criticized Nussbaum because her capability list is derived from the works of Aristotle[43]
Alkire and Black (1997)	Life, knowledge and appreciation of beauty, work and play, friendship, self integration, coherent self determination, transcendence, and being able to live with concern for and in relation to animals, plants and the world of nature.	Derived from the works of Germain Grisez et al (1987) with Nussbaum (1995). This list of capabilities is more general in nature and is, therefore, less helpful in the analysis of academic and political discussion.

Author(s)	**Items on the list**	**Comments**
Robeyns (2002)	Life and physical health, mental wellbeing, bodily integrity and safety, social relations, political empowerment, education and knowledge, social reproduction and non-market care, paid works and other projects, shelter and environment, mobility, leisure activities, time autonomy, respect, and religion and spirituality	Robeyns first proposed five criteria for the selection of capabilities: (i) the list should be made explicit, discussed and defended), (ii) when drawing up a list, we should explain how we have reached that list, that means the method of generating the list, (iii) the criteria of sensitivity to context (iv) specification aims at an empirical application and (v) the capability list should include all elements that are important
Clark, (2000, 2002, 2003). Study on both rural and urban areas of South Africa	Jobs, housing, education, income, family and friends, religion, health, food, good clothes, recreations and relaxation, safety, and economic security	He didn't term them capability indicators rather offered as perceptions of wellbeing by the poor.
Schischka, Dalzeil and Saunders (2008) Study was conducted on New Zealand and Samoa	(1) The ability to learn and apply more skills, (2) the ability to have social contact and be a part of the community, (3) the ability to lead healthy life, (4) the ability to have increased self - confidence and status, (5) the ability to earn future income (6) the ability to generate cash income from local sources, (7) the ability to support a family, (8) the ability to make goods for sale, and (9) the ability to contribute to the local church and community.	There is indeed no fixed list of capabilities rather they are culture oriented

2.5 The Sustainable Livelihoods Approach (SLA)

The Department for International Development's (DFID) sustainable livelihoods (SL) approach (Chambers and Conway, 1992) is a widely used[44] (and probably an alternative to Capability Approach) method that links understanding of the poor and vulnerable people's available endowments (asset or capital) and the importance of policies and institutions in enhancing those endowments to reduce poverty in developing countries. Like Sen's (1985) human capability approach, the sustainable livelihoods model also assumes that people require a range of assets (or capital) to achieve positive livelihood outcomes (such as economic solvency or social inclusion), and no single category of asset is sufficient to ensure the overall livelihood outcome. Thus, the multidimensionality of deprivation in poverty analysis is increasingly being recognized in the livelihoods approach. Distinctive feature of SL approach is its significant focus towards the importance of institutions in poverty reduction effort – an important yet neglected issue in other poverty models.

The sustainable livelihoods approach takes a holistic view of tackling poverty, and puts poor people and their priorities at the centre of development. The principles of the SL approach demand a shift in focus from outputs to people, and an exploration of poor people's own priorities[45]. The model states that the institutions engaged in service delivery within poverty reduction programs will formulate strategies that will ensure sustainable livelihood outcomes for both the projects and the beneficiaries. The model stresses four different types of sustainability (according to Sustainable Livelihoods guidance sheet-1.4):

- '*Environmental sustainability* is achieved when the productivity of life-supporting natural resources is enhanced for future generations;
- *Economic sustainability* for the poor is achieved if a baseline[46] level of economic welfare can be sustained;
- *Social sustainability* is gained when social exclusion is minimized; and
- *Institutional sustainability* requires that the prevailing structures and processes have the capacity to perform their functions for a longer time period'.

Two major findings can be deduced from the stated categorization.

First, according to the definition, economic and social sustainability are the livelihood targets of the poor people, whereas, environmental and institutional sustainability are the goals of institutions or development partners in the poverty reduction projects. Thus, from the broadest perspective, the assets or capital required for sustainable livelihoods can be grouped into two major categories, namely, economic and social, which are similar to the existing poverty analysis (as mentioned in Table 2.1). Second, sustainability in the case of institutions means that an institution's public service delivery not only implies the availability of sufficient finance to provide the services needed, but also refers to the overall capacity of the organizations to deliver services that enhance the living standards of the poor.

Although the model rightly points out the importance of institutional efficacy, it doesn't offer any specific set of criteria with which to assess the efficacy of the institutions or the projects. This is one of the gaps in the model that this study intends to close.

2.5.1 The different steps of the SL model and its limitations

The SL model has four distinct parts (Fig-2.3). The first part deals with 'vulnerability' issues, including natural (for instance, river erosion, cyclone, draught, epidemics, flood, sea level change, etc.), social (such as injury, robbery, disability, death of family members, etc.), economic (unemployment at calamity, harvest failure) and political shocks (political violence, strikes, governance crisis, etc.), any of which may push a large portion of rural people into poverty[47]. The second part – which is the main focus of this chapter – discusses different types of capital (usually shown with a pentagon) that are important for an acceptable standard of living such as (as quoted in Serrat, 2008, pp. 2):

- "**Human capital**, e.g., health, nutrition, education, knowledge and skills, capacity to work, capacity to adapt, etc.
- **Social capital**, e. g., networks and connections, relationships of trust, mutual understanding and support, formal and informal groups, shared values and behaviours, common rules and sanctions, collective representation, mechanisms for participation in decision-making, leadership.
- **Natural capital**, e.g., land and produce, water and aquatic resources, trees and forest products, wildlife, wild foods, environmental services.
- **Physical capital**, e.g., infrastructure (secure shelter and buildings, water supply and sanitation, energy, communications), tools and technology (equipment for production, seed, fertilizer, pesticides, traditional technology).

- **Financial capital**, e.g., savings, credit and debt (formal, informal), remittances, pensions, wages".

The model clarifies various methods for building different types of capital. For instance, to build a financial capital collateral-free credit facility, increased savings and tailored financial services are the pre-requisites. However, as mentioned earlier, there is no such livelihood asset model derived for rural Bangladesh[48] that can be used to understand the local circumstances and needs of the poor (shown as Gap-1 in Fig-2.3). The development of such a model will help the development partners to identify and better target the livelihood assets; access to which will enhance the living standards and capabilities of the rural poor, thus accelerating the rate of poverty reduction.

The next part of the model discusses structures, policies, and processes that help the poor to find out from the institutions involved available services and how to access them. This is elaborated in Chapter 3 (Section 3.4.2).

The final part of the model recommends building a livelihood strategy as the capability set for better outcomes. For instance, microfinance along with peer monitoring is a recognized strategy used to increase financial capital (by creating direct income and savings) and social capital (by organizing group meetings and involving the poor in decision-making). This part of the model includes a wide range of activities and choices that people can do and make in order to achieve their functioning[49] or livelihood goals, for example, human capability building, the use of various combinations of tools (for instance, credit, health care, education, etc.) and the choice of effective service providers.

Serrat (2008, pp. 4) suggests that 'the sustainable livelihoods approach is one way of integrating a number of complex issues that surround poverty and this model needs to be customized to local circumstances and local priorities'[50]. To address this issue, this study offers a validated multidimensional asset or capital model (see Chapter 7 for details) for rural Bangladesh by applying the SL approach such that the priorities of the people in the stated area can be better understood. The development partners will then be better able to help people become more capable of fulfilling their asset/capital needs.

Figure 2.3: DFID's Sustainable Livelihood Framework and its limitations

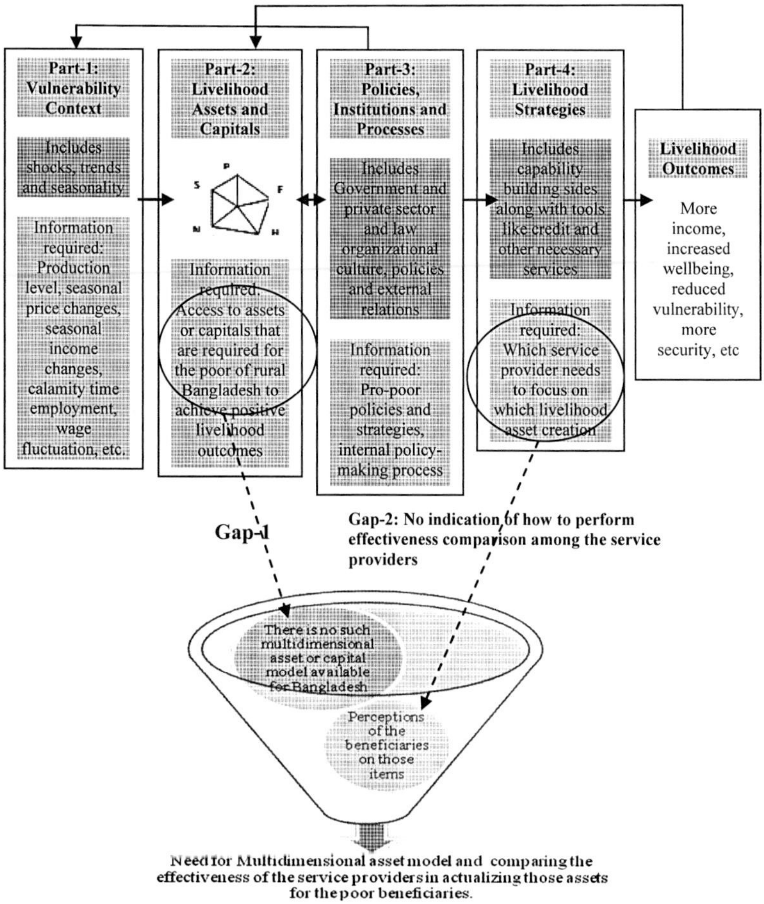

Source: Adapted and modified from DFID (1995-2000), Sustainable Livelihoods Guidance Sheet 2.1.

2.6 Wellbeing: Concepts and assessment

Both the capability approach and the sustainable livelihoods model stress the need for poor people's participation in understanding local priorities and need preferences. Moreover, the extended definition of poverty as stated below emphasises wellbeing issues:

'Poverty is a situation in which an individual or a household has difficulty in fulfilling its basic needs, lacks opportunities provided by an enabling environment to sustainably improve its **wellbeing**' (Cahyat et al., 2007, p. 3). Therefore, incorporating wellbeing in studies into poverty is to understand what the poor have and are able to do, rather than focusing simply on their deficit[51].

The literature on wellbeing is vast and continually expanding. Doyle and Gough (1991) expand on the basic needs approach by including health and autonomy, and takes this further still by adding the word 'wellbeing' in development thought (Tiwari, 2008). However, Alkire (2002) views the basic needs as pre-conditions for wellbeing. Sen (1982, 1985 and 1990) and Nussbaum (2000) have further extended the list of multidimensional indicators of wellbeing. The following are a few modified definitions of wellbeing which demonstrate the need for including wellbeing in understanding poverty:

1) According to Gasper (2002), the similar term 'welfare' means how well people live.
2) Ryan and Deci (2001, cited in Tiwari, 2008) conceives of wellbeing as happiness or pleasure and advances the Aristotelian tradition of wellbeing – not well living only[52].
3) Kagan (1994) describes wellbeing as feelings in a person's body and mind, using the term 'quality of life' in describing wellbeing instead of 'non-feeling functioning'.
4) The Human Development report[53] by UNDP defines wellbeing as having 'a long and healthy life', 'knowledge and education', and 'a decent standard of living'.

The preliminary nature of wellbeing can be seen as objective wellbeing (also called core wellbeing), subjective wellbeing, capability wellbeing and environmental wellbeing. A detailed discussion on each type is presented in Table 2.4.

Table 2.4: Types of wellbeing with assessment process and relevant theories

Concept	Definition in the literature	Assessment process	Theory/related concepts
Wellbeing (WB)	A long and healthy life, happiness and pleasure (Gasper, 2002; Ryan and Deci. 2001; Kagan, 1994; UNDP).	The UNDP's Human Development Index (UNDP, 1990-2004), Physical Quality of Life Index (Morris, 1979), the Combined Quality of Life Indices (Diener, 1995), Human Suffering Index (Camp and Speidel, 1987; Hess, 1989), Level of Living Index by UN Research Institute for Social Development (Drewnoski and Scott, 1966), Allardt's welfare index (1976).	Quality of life, living standards, human development, welfare, social welfare, well living, utility, life satisfaction, prosperity, needs fulfillment, development, empowerment, capability expansion, human poverty, and happiness.
Classifications of wellbeing			
Core/objective WB	Non-feeling features of personal life (Gasper, 2007; Doyle and Gough, 1991) (Adequate nourishment, shelter, education, security, longevity, morbidity, autonomy)	Purchasing power parity (UNDP, 2004), GDP and GNI per capita measure, Adjusted GNP method (Dasgupta, 2001), Measure of Economic Welfare (Nordhaus and Tobin, 1971; Ahluwalia and Chenery, 1974))	Objective list theory (Scanlon, 1993), Desire theories and Revealed preference theory, basic human values approach (Grisez, 1987), the intermediate needs approach (Doyal and Gough, 1992, 1993)

Concept	Definition in the literature	Assessment process	Theory/related concepts
Subjective WB	Feelings of the person whose wellbeing is estimated, also includes how people value their lives (Camfield, 2006; Diener, 1984; Myer, 1995). (Psychological health, social relationships, empowerment, social inclusion)	Human Development Index (UNDP, 1990), domains of subjective wellbeing approach (Cummins, 1996), the universal psychological needs approach (Ramsay, 1992), World Happiness Database (WHO, 1998).	Hedonism (Perfit, 1984) Eudemonia (Aristotle) Participatory Approach (WeD, 2004)
Capability WB	Wellbeing focuses on the capability of the individual to function in society (Sen, 1983, 1984) (No fixed set rather it is based on local culture)	Capability, functionings, UNDP HDI (UNDP, 1990), Central Human Capability approach (Nusbaum, 2000), Alkire and Black approach of capability dimension (1996), Gender Inequality Approach (Robeyns, 2002), participatory poverty assessment (WB, WeD)	Capability approach Sen, 1983, 1984, 1995), Functionings, entitlement (Sen, 1979, 1983)

Concept	Definition in the literature	Assessment process	Theory/related concepts
Environmental WB	Living conditions that affect both objective and subjective wellbeing (Cahyat, et al., 2007; WB, 2000; Mukherjee, 1997).	Social, political, natural and economic environment. Infrastructure and service for wellbeing fulfillment. WHO Quality of Life Scale (WHO Group, 1998), Allardt's welfare index (1976).	Participatory monitoring approach (Cahyat et al, 2007)

Recent wellbeing research focuses mainly on subjective wellbeing which is known as happiness[54]. Camfield (2006) argues that subjective wellbeing should not only be equated to happiness, rather it is connected with many aspects of life that people value[55]. Subjective wellbeing has been defined as people's multidimensional evaluation of their lives, including cognitive judgments of life satisfaction and affective evaluations of emotions and moods (Eid and Diener, 2003). Frey and Stutzer (2002) have found that happiness increases with absolute income, *ceteris paribas*, but not proportionately and at a diminishing rate. Moreover, it has been found that income explains only a small portion of the variation in happiness among people[56].

2.6.1 Indicators of wellbeing: Cross-country assessment and use in the study

The vast literature suggests a number of wellbeing indexes for developing and developed countries (Booysen, 2002; McGillivray and Noorbakhsh, 2007). Some influential indices are: UNDP's Human Development Index (UNDP, 1990-2004), the Physical Quality of Life Index (Morris, 1979), the Combined Quality of Life Indices (Diener, 1995), the Human Suffering Index (Camp and Speidel, 1987; Hess, 1989), the Level of Living Index by the UN Research Institute for Social Development (Drewnoski and Scott, 1966) and the Socio-economic Development Index (UNRISD, 1970). From as many as 20 available indices, three are particularly useful:

(a) **UNDP Human Development Index (HDI)**: This was first developed for a UNDP assessment program for the whole world. HDI is the main yardstick in this process, which primarily includes three items namely, public wealth measured by buying power per head; education measured by literacy and schooling; and life expectancy at birth. Further, the model was extended by incorporating indicators such as gender equality (measured by gender empowerment index based on school enrolment, literacy and income) and poverty (measured mainly by premature death rate, and income deficiency).

(b) **Allardt's welfare index**: Allardt (1976) proposed a wellbeing index based on his study on Scandinavian countries. The indicators included in the index are income, quality of housing, political support, social relations, health, education, being irreplaceable, doing interesting things and life satisfaction. While the index was first proposed on the basis of developed countries, it was later popularly used in developing countries as well (McGillivray and Noorbakhsh, 2007; Veenhoven, 2007).

(c) **WHO quality of life scale (WHOQOL)**: WHO developed[57] and used this model for wellbeing measurement, using as its basis the following dimensions: physical health, psychological health, social relationships and environmental conditions. In addition to these broad headlines, the index also addresses 100 questions (or indicators) to the people for their own assessment, which include pain and discomfort, sexual activity, self-esteem, mobility, work capacity, freedom, physical safety and security, work satisfaction, and financial resources. This index is also known as the World Happiness Database (WHD).

In addition to the stated generic and universally-used approaches to gathering information about wellbeing, several cross-country studies have been conducted[58] which yielded different findings. However, there has been no large-scale wellbeing identification study conducted in rural Bangladesh – a gap this monograph will address. Based on the findings of cross-country studies, the monograph will explore the indicators of wellbeing in developing countries and the applicability of those indicators will be justified by developing a customized poverty model for rural Bangladesh (see Chapter 7 for details). Table 2.5 reflects many of these indicators.

The studies presented in Table 2.5 show that wellbeing indicators vary across countries. For example, economic considerations are important in Bangladesh; in Ethiopia, Peru and Thailand, land-holding, agricultural output and livestock are more important than economic factors. Again, in Peru, access to electricity and clean water are important to the poor, whereas in Ethiopia transportation and agricultural extension services are priorities.The people of Thailand prefer to have more services to market the goods produced. Education was found to be a major indicator of wellbeing in Bangladesh, South Africa, Ethiopia, and Peru, but not in Thailand. A large-scale comprehensive study was conducted by Hargreaves (2004a) in South Africa to produce a quantitative household economic status index in which participants' criteria were used to measure the poverty, wellbeing and ill-being status so as to draw poverty lines[59]. The results of the study are given in Table A2.1 in the appendix of this chapter.

Table 2.5: Empirical studies on the indicators of wellbeing

References	Country of study	Indicators found
Moore, Choudhury and Singh (1998)	South Asia	Sources of well-being and ill-being for rural people are: having land and other assets, sufficient food, diverse sources of income, education, discriminatory treatment from public officials, gender discrimination, and having sufficient adult male family members.
Mukherjee's (1997)	Uttar Pradesh (India)	Economic and environmental security, oppression of crime and violence, protection of rights and self respects
Mahbub and Roy (1997)	Bangladesh	Eating three meals a day, being healthy, having access to health care, having children, educating children, living a peaceful life, training and development for self growth, healthy male members, and small family
Brock (1999)	Twelve countries	Food security, work and employment, having enough money and assets
Rahmato and Kidano (1999)	Ethiopia	Size of firm land, availability of livestock, access to fertilizer and agricultural equipment, and being able to feed the family year-round.
Paitoonpong (1999)	Thailand	Having enough money to save, a house, regular job or business, being mentally sound, having a good wife and loving family, living in a good environment.

References	Country of study	Indicators found
Un Nabi (1999)	Bangladesh	Savings and cultivable land, good clothing, sufficient food, ability to educate children, freedom, and a close relationship with family members
DFID and WB (2003)	Peru	Physical security, living in an environment that is free from domestic violence, gender equality.
Clark's (2000)	South Africa	Good jobs with better salaries, secure and good quality housing, and education.
Garcia (2003)	Mexico	Jobs, income, health, housing, self-esteem, and cultural identity.
Moore (1999)	Thailand	Family relationships, good friendships, religious practice, living in a clean environment, getting a good price for produce, and good appearance.

2.7 Conclusion

The multidimensionality of poverty is often neglected at the time of policy formulation or social research, which is the most telling aspect of poverty analysis. A lack of capability is cited by Sen (1984) as the main problem behind poverty, and thus, it is important to know why poor people fall behind in utilizing their capabilities. Both capability approach and sustainable livelihoods models argued that the poor have limited access to resources (or asset capital) and this hinders them in reaching their potential. Most importantly, this asset need varies across societies and communities. An understanding of the customized needs of the poor should be the starting point in formulating country-specific poverty reduction strategies, thus, there is a clear need for a multidimensional poverty model for each and every country. Heavy concentration on material wellbeing is making the poverty analysis one-sided by ignoring the growing importance of subjective aspects of poverty and wellbeing. In addition, the impact of temporary shocks (either from market or nature) is mostly overlooked, and as such the impact of vulnerability on poverty is absent from most of the studies. The impact of natural, social and political environment has also been missing from many studies even though, as we have seen, the effects of such impacts can pose a great threat to a person's standard of living in both the short and long run. It is thus crucial to view poverty, wellbeing, capability and vulnerability as integrated concepts when considering the poor.

Based on the poverty indicators found in the various studies discussed in this chapter, we have prepared Sections 2 to 8 of the questionnaire (see Chapter 4 and its Appendix for the full questionnaire) in order to explore the customized asset needs (see Chapter 7 for details of the poverty model development process) of the poor people of rural Bangladesh.

Appendix A

Table A2.1: Characteristics of different wealth groups identified in South Africa

Poorest
- Single parent, unemployed, or two parents both unemployed - Many children - Being unmarried and having no family to assist - Dependent on temporary jobs - No means of provision except by begging - Widows with many children - Insufficient and poor quality food; sometimes have to beg for food - No proper place to sleep: poor quality housing - Orphans with no parents - Inability to educate children - No clothes: almost never buy - No assets
Poor
- Temporary jobs (like farm laborer) - Have some food but struggles - Working widows and pensioners with many child - Parents dependent on working children who also have their own families in the same house sharing the same resources - Working on agricultural scheme - Many children - Unmarried and no pension - Have some type of house: not good and made of mud and show cracks - Can provide something from temporary job
Extreme poor
- Earns enough to cope daily – mostly temporary work or self employed - Those with smaller number of children to look after - Pensioners with fewer children - Widows with pension from late husband - Have a place to sleep - Unmarried - Payouts from old jobs - Children attend school irregularly - Able to buy enough food

Note: Adapted from White and Pettit (2004), p. 24

Notes

[1] For details, see the works of Booysen (2002a and b); McGillivray and Noorbakhsh (2007).

[2] See, for example, the World Bank (2000, 2001 and 2005); DFID (2005, 2002).

[3] The following two quotes depict how the World Development Report defined poverty in the years 1990 and 2000, and shows how their views have changed:

'. . . progress on poverty has been achieved by pursuing a strategy that has two equally important elements. The first element is to promote the productive use of the poor's most abundant asset – labor. It calls for policies that harness market incentives, social and political institutions, infrastructure and technology to that end. The second is to provide basic social services to the poor. Primary health care, family planning, nutrition and primary education are especially important . . . a program of well-targeted transfers and safety nets [is] an essential complement to this basic strategy' (World Bank, 1990: 3).

'The new evidence and broader thinking do not negate earlier strategies – such as that of WDR 1990. But they do show the need to broaden the agenda. Attacking poverty requires actions that go beyond the economic domain . . . Acknowledging the need for a broader agenda, this report proposes a general framework for action in three areas: (i) Promoting Opportunity: expanding economic opportunity for poor people by stimulating overall growth and by building up their assets and increasing the returns on those assets, (ii) Facilitating Empowerment: making state institutions more accountable and responsive to poor people, strengthening the participation of poor people in political processes and local decision-making and removing the social barriers the result from distinctions of gender, ethnicity, race and social status. (iii) Enhancing Security: reducing poor people's vulnerability to ill health, economic shocks, policy-induced dislocations, natural disasters, and violence, as well as helping them cope with adverse shocks (World Bank, 2000)'.

[4] See in particular studies by Rojas (2007); Pradhan and Ravallion (2000); Razafindrakoto and Roubaud (2000, 2005b); Herrera (2001); Kingdon and Knight (2004); Lokshin and Paternostro (2004).

[5] If relative poverty or social exclusion is seen as stigma by potential employers and if it is readily observable then the same argument would apply to the poor as to racial or gender discrimination. Social exclusion and long-run unemployment in some European countries might be analyzed very well in the same way – see Atkinson (1998)

[6] As very well illustrated in a model by Galor and Zeira (1993), it may be the case that poor people facing such credit market imperfection will never be able to accumulate enough collateral to get beyond it or will simply find it too hard to do so. For further information see Bardhan, Bowles and Gintis (1999) and Piketty (1999).

[7] For further information see, Sustainable Livelihoods Model of the DFID and the Capability Approach by Sen (1985).

[8] Research by the Chronic Poverty Research Centre (CPRC) suggests that the tightest possible definition of chronic poverty is that which is inter-generationally transmitted (IGT) (Moore, 2001).

[9] See, for example, Sen (1981a, 1983); Kothari (1995); Townsend (1985); Sukhatme (1977, 1978).

[10] It is a common feature in some parts of the world, but the regular face of starvation should be distinguished from the outbursts of famine that create vulnerability thus causing large scale poverty.

[11] See, Lanjouw (1997), Lipton and Ravallion (1995), Ravallion (1994), Ruggeri (2001) and Streeten (1998).

[12] See Ruggeri (2003) for a comparative analysis of the approaches to poverty.

[13] See further in Gasper (1996a, 1996b); Streeten (1981, 1984); Streeten et. al (1981).

[14] Lister (2004) argues that poverty can be defined narrowly, focusing on its 'material core' to describe situations in which the ability to consume or participate is restricted by a limited command over financial resources. She also argues that other dimensions of poverty are important, including relational deprivations associated with powerlessness, lack of voice and restricted human rights, but that these should not be confused with the core of poverty as reflecting a lack of material resources.

[15] See 'The Wartime Study -The American Soldier (1949)

[16] According to Runciman (1966), 'we can roughly say that a person is relatively deprived of X when (i) he does not have X, (ii) he sees some other person, which may include himself at some previous or expected time, as having X, (iii) he wants X (iv) he sees it as feasible that he should have X.' (page-11)

[17] See further in Mabughi and Selim (2006).

[18] Initially the concept of relative poverty was used for developed countries. However, the concept is now also widely for in less developed and developing countries (Mabughi and Selim, 2006).

[19] It is claimed that this theory was first developed in 1959 by anthropologist Oscar Lewis, and was named the 'Culture Theory of Poverty'. Lewis developed this theory from his experiences in Mexico and stated that the poor realize that they have a marginal position within a highly stratified and individualistic capitalist society, which does not offer them any prospect for upward mobility. In order to survive, the poor must develop their own institutions and agencies because the larger society tends to ignore and bypass them. Gunnar Myrdal (1962, as cited in Islam, 2005) coined the term 'underclass' for this group who in America were at the bottom of the labour market and were thus excluded from the mainstream of social life (Islam, 2005).

[20] Initially developed by British sociologist Peter Townsend (1979) and then extended by Mack and Lansley (1985); Gordon and Pantazis (1997); Gordon and Townsend (2000); Levitas et al. (2007). Also defined as enforced lack of socially perceived necessities (Mack and Lansley, 1985).

[21] First applied in the French welfare system in 1970 to describe the process of marginalization and deprivation. Bergham and Magnusson (1995) developed a framework in which social exclusion is seen as the outcome of a dynamic process that is triggered by deprivation.

[22] 'In Vietnam the government estimated that by 2010, 90% of the poverty in the country will be among ethnic minorities. In Tanzania, households with disabled members are 20% more likely to be living in poverty' (DFID, 2005).
[23] DFID (2005) quoted that, 'in Guatemala, the number of children dying before they reach their fifth birthday is 56 in every 1000 for children of European descent, compared with 79 in every 1000 in the indigenous population. In India, it is estimated that discrimination against girls increases the total rate of child mortality by 20%'.
[24] According to DFID (2005), 'in Siberia and Montenegro, 30% of the Roma children have never attended primary school. In the Indian states of Uttar Pradesh and Bihar, primary school enrolment for scheduled caste and scheduled tribe girls is 37%, compared with 60% for girls from non-scheduled caste. Among boys from non-scheduled caste, 77% are enrolled'.
[25] A study in Namibia found 44% of widows lost cattle, 28% lost small livestock, and 41% lost farm equipment in disputes with their in-laws after their husbands died (FAO, 2003).
[26] 'In China, although ethnic minorities make up less than 9% of the population, they account for 37% of known cases of HIV. In Guatemala, 87% of children of European descent are vaccinated against measles, compared with 70% in the indigenous population', according to DFID (2005).
[27] See further in Bhalla and Lapeyere (1997); Tilly (2006); Hickey and Bracking (2005).
[28] In Lesotho, women have until recently been disadvantaged through the law. They could not inherit land or property, get a job or sign a contract without the permission of their husbands (DFID, 2005).
[29] 'In Pakistan, the evidence in court of a Muslim woman is worth half that of man' (DFID, 2005).
[30] This is not similar to the concepts of participatory poverty assessment, which is a way to collect information about wellbeing indicators from the poor.
[31] 'I was often asked, what is the most serious form of human rights violations in the world today, and my reply is consistent: extreme poverty' – Mary Robinson
[32] 'The Universal Declaration of Human Rights recognizes human rights as the foundation of peace, justice and democracy. Within this UN normative framework, UNDP in 1998 adopted its policy of 'Integrating Human Rights with Sustainable Human Development'. Subsequently, in 2000 and 2002, the Human Development reports affirmed that human development is essential for realizing human rights and human rights are essential for full human development' (UNDP, 2003).
[33] Beginning with the Tanner Lecture 'Equality of What?', first delivered at Stanford University in 1979.
[34] According to Robeyns (2002), 'for instance, a person may be in a desperate situation with little food and poor shelter, and still be contended with life if he/she has never known any different. A utilitarian evaluation will only assess his/her satisfaction, and will not differentiate between a happy healthy and well sheltered person, versus an equally happy, but unhealthy and badly sheltered person who has mentally adapted to the situation'.

[35] Sen defines capability in a broader sense, which comprises a large set of functioning and is why capability in most cases is used as a synonym to 'capability set' (Qizilbash, 2005).

[36] The literature on basic need is extensive. For primary concepts, see Streeten et al. (1981).

[37] See the contributions of Romer (1982), Dasgupta (1993), Helm (1986), Zamagni (1986), Basu (1987), Brannen and Wilson (1987), Hawthorn (1987), Kanbur (1987), Nussbaum (1988, 1990), Griffin and Night (1989a, 1989b), Cohen (1993), Steiner (1990), Sugden (1986), Broome (1988), Stewert (1988), Suzumura (1988), Goodin (1988), Hossain (1990) and Outegem (1990). Cited in Clark (2003, 2005); Robeyns (2002, 2003); and Alkire (2007).

[38] The capability approach differs from standard utility-based approaches in not insisting that we must value only happiness or only desire fulfillment (Sen, 1993).

[39] See, Sen (1990a and 1992).

[40] See, Sen (1983 and 1985c).

[41] See, Sen, (1999, 2000).

[42] See, for example, Alkire (2002); Clark (2002); Saith (2001); Alkire and Black (1997); Alkire (2002); Clark (2002 and 2003); Desa (i1995); Nussbaum (1995, 2000 and 2003); Robeyns (2003) and Schischka, Dalziel and Saunders (2008).

[43] See for example, Stewart, 2001, pp. 1192; Clark, 2002.

[44] For a list of works, see Neely et al. (2004); Scoones (1997).

[45] This is termed in the model as people-centered and participatory (DFID, 2000).

[46] Currently a $1 per day baseline.

[47] Discussion on vulnerability in the context of Bangladesh can be found in the study of Twigg (2009).

[48] There are several studies on other fields (such as fisheries, marketing, irrigation systems, urban and rural development etc.) using SAL that have been done for Bangladesh. See for example, Neely, Sutherland and Johnson (2004); Ahmed (2009). SAL has been used in several other countries, however, none of those studies has developed and updated livelihood asset listing. For further reference, see Krantz, 2001.

[49] Functioning is an achievement either by a person or by an organization (Sen, 1985).

[50] Sustainable livelihoods guidance sheets also recommend that the asset or capital requirement should be investigated case by case.

[51] Researchers in the field of international development have intensely explained the relationship between wellbeing and poverty. For example, see Morris (1979); Sen (1982); Streeten (1984); UNDP (2005); WeD (2004-2007).

[52] According to Ryan and Deci, well living can become denigrated as an elitist notion (Tiwari, 2008). Gasper (2003) describes well living as well becoming and well dying. Jennings (2003) argues that quality of death should be seen as a part of quality of life, including decline, fade-out and departure.

[53] The approache to wellbeing by the UNDP is the contribution of Sen and Haq. They used three basic dimensions of human development – a long and healthy life, knowledge and a decent standard of living captured through life expectancy at

birth, adult literacy rate, and the combined primary, secondary and tertiary gross enrolment ratio and GDP per capita to calculate the HDI.

[54] Despite recent research concentration, the subjective wellbeing in fact originated in the USA. Influential studies have been published by Campbell (1975) and Andrews and Withey (1976). This approach was further refined in the German Welfare Studies (Glatzer and Zapf, 1984). Specializations have been developed on subjects such as perceived poverty (VanPraag, 1980), values (Inglehart, 1990) and happiness (Veenhoven, 1997). See for details, Easterlin (2001).

[55] Diener and Fujita (1995) show that, 'people are happier when they have the resources needed to reach their particular goals. Therefore, it is likely that a long-lasting sense of happiness comes at least in part from achieving our values and goals'.

[56] For example, Veenhoven (1991) found that the relationship between income and happiness is weak beyond a fairly low international level of income per capita.

[57] WHOQOL Group (1998).

[58] Among the vast literature on wellbeing the most notable studies are, the study conducted by Cooke and Kothari (2001), White and Pettit (2004), Laderchi (2001), Camfield and McGregor (2005), Moore and Choudhury and Singh (1998) with the help of DFID-UK, research by UNDP (1998), extensive work by the World Bank in three volumes (Volume one –'Can Anyone Hear Us?', Volume two –'Crying Out For Change', volume three –'For Many Lands') and finally the works by ESRC Research group on Wellbeing of Developing Countries (WeD).

[59] The study was conducted on small reference groups of villagers for a microfinance program. The numerical data collected through this process proved to be highly accurate in identifying the poorest families (Simanowitz, 2000).

CHAPTER THREE

THE ROLE OF INSTITUTIONS AND THE NEED FOR EFFECTIVE SERVICE DELIVERY IN POVERTY REDUCTION

3.1 Introduction

This chapter outlines the role of institutions in poverty reduction programs in developing countries, and the need for effectiveness in these institutions. The chapter argues that increased access to capital resources is necessary for development, but is not in itself sufficient for sustainable poverty reduction, while institutional service delivery processes are ineffective and not pro-poor. The need for effective institutional arrangement is well recognized in the literature[1]; however, although some theories or models point out the need for effectiveness in delivery processes, they fail to address the dimensions of service delivery effectiveness from an institutional view point. This chapter intends to highlight those issues.

In his capability approach, Sen (1999) stresses the need for institutions and states that 'Individuals live and operate in a world of institutions. Not only do institutions contribute to our freedoms, their roles can be sensibly evaluated in the light of their contributions to our freedom' (p. 142). Two major issues can be extracted from this statement, and these are central to poverty reduction:

a) effective functioning of the institutions; and
b) evaluation by those who are direct beneficiaries of that functioning.

These two issues lead directly to two major propositions:

c) successful institutions are 'demand driven', meaning that the poor themselves shape initiatives and identify what types of services the institutions should offer; and

d) the first goal of poverty reduction and development should be to help the poor to develop their capabilities. This requires not only a resource commitment (such as microfinance), but a willingness to build administrative and additional support in the field. We call these the 'effectiveness' dimension of an institution.

Once the importance of an institution is recognized[2], the next task would be to answer the question: What is the role of institutions in poverty reduction programs, and how can we define and quantify the effective functioning of those institutions?

3.1.1 Institutions in poverty reduction programs defined

A broader definition of institutions is '…the humanly devised constraints that structure political, economic, and social interactions' (North, 1991, p.1). From this it can be inferred that institutions could be state or non-state. State institutions cover many aspects of the public provision for basic education and health services, public order and safety, and infrastructure (Deolalikar et al, 2002). On the other hand, non-state institutions are social institutions, comprising social values and norms. In this study, the institution is defined as:

> "those organizations that help citizens access the resources or conditions required for actualizing the necessary capacities to break poverty, and is exemplified by Government and other social non-profits and Non Government Organizations (NGOs)".

It is worth noting that even though public (GO), private (profit-based commercial banks), and third-sector (other non-profits) coexist in Bangladesh, the poverty reduction programs are directly run by the public and third-sectors only (see Section 3.2.1 and 3.2.2 for details). Thus, while comparing the effectiveness of poverty concerned projects, we are specifically making a comparison between government and third sector, which includes NGOs, microfinance institutions (MFIs), and cooperatives, but civil societies are excluded. The fundamental difference between NGOs and MFIs is that although both work with microcredit, NGOs[3] offer credit only, whereas MFIs offer training along with credit[4]. However, in order to gain financial sustainability, most of the MFIs in Bangladesh have reduced other social services such as training in order to reduce the cost of their operations (Mayoux, 1999). Thus, it can be argued that both NGOs and MFIs behave and function similarly. In this study, the terms NGOs and MFIs are used synonymously and interchangeably[5] as the third sector as opposed to the government sector.

3.2 The role of institutions in poverty reduction

The role of institutions and their policies are crucial for the three pillars of the Asian Development Bank's poverty reduction strategy[6]: pro-poor, sustainable growth with social development and governance. To formulate country-specific poverty reduction strategies, an analysis of the nature of these institutions and their policies will be helpful.

3.2.1 Role of government in poverty reduction

The economics of government can be seen as an extension of welfare economics. Governments with power and responsibility take action and policy measures on behalf of the whole society, with the privilege that they are elected by the citizens of the country and thus people's voices (the public interest) are reflected in their activities. As the government is responsible for the welfare of the society as whole, the objectives of the government's economic policies, therefore, are to promote effectiveness (to solve market imperfections) and equity (fairness).

Greenwald and Stiglitz (1986) show that whenever information is imperfect in the market, government interventions could make everyone better off. Government is responsible for ensuring that adequate safety-nets are in place or can be provided quickly. This cannot be expected from a market that operates only to satisfy their target customers. That's why, whenever there is a need for mass intervention (such as poverty reduction or infrastructure building), government remains the most appropriate sponsor/partner.

Even though government organizations in developing countries are sometimes perceived to be slow, ineffective and corrupt (Macchiavello, 2008), the East Asian economies have demonstrated that government can be highly adaptive and the only actor for development. In those countries, government acts as the facilitator for the markets which in turn helps the economy to grow in a controlled and equitable way.

The major comparative advantages of governments are their relatively large scale (may not be quite large enough to reach 100%) and the resources they control which provide additional sources of strength and capability. These are important in the sense that to enhance the capabilities of the people to fight poverty, institutions should also be capable with adequate resources and effective processes. In general, the government plays major roles in poverty alleviation such as providing:

(a) a stable macro environment
(b) social and physical infrastructure with public health
(c) education and training
(d) technology transfer
(e) environmentally sustainable development
(f) support to private sector
(g) prudential regulation of financial sector

The main comparative advantage government has in providing those services is in its long-standing experience and specialized skills. However, when it comes to the matter of 'effectiveness', even if government is endowed with enough resources, there may be a need for market or third-sector[7] interventions in delivering the services more effectively (this case is more applicable to developing economies). But this proposition should not suggest 'no government'; rather it exhibits government as necessary pre-condition for development.

In the MDG context, government (according to Brinkerhoff et al, 2007):

- may consider MDGs their national agenda and support the community in fulfilling them through administrative and technical support along with delivering required services such as training, education, health care etc, efficiently;
- can use their institutional longevity to heavily influence other stakeholders to act and support collectively for equity;
- can promote participation by the development actors through engaging citizens in the participatory process; and
- can help needy people by way of wider safety net programs

Even though government is assumed to be the most powerful (may not be the most effective) actor in the economy, it is accountable to those who elected them – the citizens. Thus it is important that the citizens assess the performance of the activities of government in attaining MDGs such that the refined or suggested policies would become more pro-poor.

3.2.1A Poverty and development plans in Bangladesh: Government's effort

Since the country's inception in 1971, several poverty models have been tested. Even when those models had different goals and strategies, poverty alleviation has always been the ultimate objective of those diverse projects. In the course of time the policies of the Government of Bangladesh (GoB) have been shifted from only basic needs fulfillment at the beginning of 1970s to addressing the broader social needs of the poor. The percentage of the budget allocated for poverty reduction is 57.50% in 2010-11, slightly more than the 55.92% in the revised budget of 2009-10 (MOF, GoB-2011). For gender awareness or women's empowerment, the GoB has allotted 25.96% and 24.65% of the annual budget in the years 2010-11 and 2009-10 respectively (MOF, GoB-2011). The Five-Year Plans of Bangladesh have always put poverty reduction at the centre as can be seen below:

- The first Five-Year plan (1973-78) put more emphasis on economic restructuring through a socialistic approach and thus at that time poverty policies were focused towards equitable distribution of resources. However, in that plan preference was given to infrastructure building and basic needs (especially food and shelter) fulfilment.
- The Two-Year plan (1978-80) was formulated to fulfil the objectives of the first five-year plan and to provide future economic direction with negligible change in poverty reduction strategies.
- The second Five-Year Plan (1980-85) included renewed effort for poverty reduction with a focus on a basic needs approach through promotion of the market economy or private sector. This plan was criticized by many who believed that it was an attempt to reduce socialistic psychology (Aminuzzaman, 2000) in the country, and that this might have an adverse effect on the equitable distribution principle of poverty reduction.
- The third Five-Year Plan (1985-90) had particular characteristics due to its major concern on aid conditionality by recognizing that poverty, unemployment, population growth, malnutrition, illiteracy are all interrelated concepts that require simultaneous attention.
- The fourth Five-Year Plan (1990-95) gained a special place in the poverty study of Bangladesh as at that time human resource development was considered the main arsenal against poverty, and in addition, structural improvement through land reform was prioritized. This was the first national plan that recognized the

importance of a 'safety net' even though this was a major strategy from 1971. This plan also declared the importance and institutionalization of NGOs in poverty reduction programs in Bangladesh.

The remaining plans also focused strongly on poverty alleviation and in 2000s the national plans incorporated two important poverty issues – participation and women's empowerment. However, this too was criticized because in most cases, no serious attempts have been made to translate the policies of the national plan into concrete programs and projects within a coherent institutional framework (Aminuzzaman, 2000).

3.2.1B Poverty reduction strategy papers (PRSP) by the GoB

In September 2000, Bangladesh was one of the 189 nations that signed the Millennium Declaration at the Millennium Summit with the objective of achieving eight specific goals called the Millennium Development Goals[8] (MDGs). To comply with the new rules[9] of fund disbursement by the World Bank (WB) and the International Monetary Fund (IMF), in 2003 Bangladesh for the first time prepared and implemented the Interim Poverty Reduction Strategy Paper[10] (i-PRSP) with an eight-point strategy: employment creation, nutrition, quality education (particularly in primary, secondary and vocational levels with a strong emphasis on the education of girls), local governance, maternal health, sanitation and safe water, criminal justice and monitoring. After just one year in 2004, Bangladesh launched its first PRSP with its major objective being to reduce poverty by half (29%) by 2015.

In 2005, a Three-year Rolling Investment Program (TYRIP) was implemented in an attempt to make the Poverty Reduction Strategies and the MDGs operational for the period FY05 to FY07, and this was renamed as the Accelerated PRSP[11] (APRSP). APRSP was based on five strategic blocks: macroeconomic environment for pro-poor economic growth, critical sectors for pro-poor economic growth, infrastructure building to support poverty reduction, effective social safety-nets, and targeted programs and human development.

An overview of the Annual Development Program (ADP) allocation shows that despite the relatively higher importance of poverty reduction, allocation to poverty reduction never exceeded 14% of total ADP over the years between 1985 and 1994 (Gafur, 1994). The trend still continues and in recent years (2010-2011) the rate is around 9.7%; a fall from 9.95% in 2009-10.

3.2.1C The GoB's anti poverty programs: Historical part

Bangladesh has a long history of implementing poverty reduction plans dating back to the 1960s. In the mid-1960s, the *Comilla Model* received international recognition for rural development (Aminuzzaman, 1985). However, this model was out of the picture in the post-independent Bangladesh due to changed political and socio-economic realities. After the devastating famine in 1974, the GoB opened *Langarkhanas* (gruel kitchens) as temporary relief from the circumstance (Asaduzzaman and Huddleston, 1983). In 1975, with the assistance of the World Food Program (WFP), the GoB started another food assisted program called Vulnerable Group Feeding (VGF) aimed especially at destitute women. This program was renamed Vulnerable Group Development (VGD) in 1980 with its aim re-focused towards development. At that time, the GoB concentrated more on humanitarian and other aids with three major objectives:

1) Direct capability-building projects through investment in social sectors such as health and education with the intention of enhancing living standard indicators.
2) Growth oriented projects aimed at higher GDP and macroeconomic stability through a 'trickle down' mechanism.
3) Targeted special employment schemes in rural areas called Rural Public Works Programs[12] (RPWP), sometimes is classified as 'Safety Net' in rural Bangladesh which is an ongoing project of the GoB.

3.2.1D Recent and continuing anti-poverty programs of the GoB

Recent anti-poverty programs of the GoB can be classified as two broad categories, namely *transfer mode* and *credit mode* programs (see Fig-3.1). In those programs there is a large investment in safety nets[13] (in 2009-10 the total allocation was 17.62% of the budget). The anti-poverty activities of the GoB are summarized in Fig-3.1.

Under **transfer mode** programs the largest budget is for the 'cash transfer program' (allotment was 61122 million Taka in the annual budget for 2010-11), which includes allowances and honorarium for needy people (see Fig-3.1 for details). The safety net through the food transfer program had an allotment of 57262 million Taka (MOF, GoB-2011) which included projects like food for work, food for education, test relief, VGD, and VGF. The budget of 2010-11 included an allocation of 41118 million Taka for social protection and empowerment programs. This includes funds for income generation for the ultra-poor, climate change, funds for small farmers, training, rehabilitation of beggars, etc. A large amount is allotted (33953 million Taka) for social development programs that include stipend and nutrition projects. Finally, there are several special poverty alleviation programs such as poultry, livestock and fisheries programs, ASRAYAN (housing) projects, funds for mitigating natural disasters and economic shocks[14], seasonal unemployment reduction programs in *Monga*[15] areas etc.

Figure 3.1: Poverty alleviation projects of the Government of Bangladesh

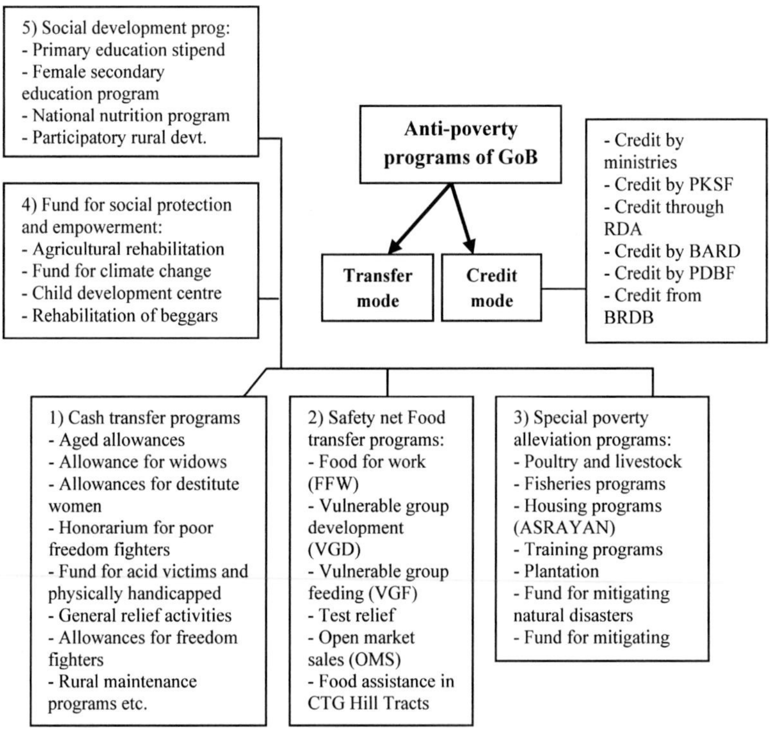

Credit mode programs of the GoB are operated by ministries, nationalized commercial banks, specialized commercial banks, and several specialized institutions. Table 3.1 summarizes the activities and credit disbursement of the GoB institutions.

Table 3.1: Summary of the activities of the major credit-driven institutions of the GoB

Institution (project)	Activities and purposes	Credit delivery status
Palli Karma Shahayak Foundation (PKSF)	(a) rural microcredit (b) urban microcredit (c) microcredit for the poorest of the poor (d) micro-enterprise-credit and (e) seasonal credit (f) agriculture sector microfinance (g) program initiatives for 'Monga' Eradication (PRIME) to manage microcredit in greater Rangpur district and (h) credit facilities for the poor- friendly program, initiating 'Learning and Innovation Fund to Test New Ideas (LIFT)' program	As of June 2010, PKSF disbursed a cumulative amount of loans amounting to Tk. 7,007.43 crore to its 257 partner organizations (POs) (MOF, GoB-2011). By revolving this amount, the POs have distributed Tk. 4,3358.37 crore. The number of borrowers at the field level is 8.3 million; 91% are women.
Bangladesh Rural Development Board (BRDB)	1) Rural Livelihood Project (RLP); 2) Poverty Reduction through Minor Crop Production, Preservation, Processing and Marketing Program; 3) Integrated Poverty Alleviation Program (IPAP); 5) Women Development (W/D) Program and Revolving Agricultural Credit Program; and 6) Employment Guarantee Scheme for the Hard Core poor of the Northern Region.	Up to December 2009, BRDB disbursed 7750.84 crore Taka among 5.3 million members with a recovery rate of 94% (MOF, GoB-2010).
Palli Daridra Bimochon Foundation (PDBF)	Capability building, women's empowerment, on and of-farm activities, leadership development, social mobilization etc.	Up to 2008, cumulative disbursement was 2292.41 crore Taka only. In 2010, total credit disbursement was 376 crore Taka.

Institution (project)	Activities and purposes	Credit delivery status
Different ministries	Employment creation, women's empowerment, off-farm employment, small business development, etc	Up to December 2009, different ministries all together disbursed cumulative amount of microcredit amounting 61628.23 crore Taka.
Nationalized[16] and specialized banks[17]	Employment creation through small business development, agricultural credit schemes, poultry and livestock, destitute group development etc.	Through nationalized banks, 16699.59 crore Taka up to December, 2009

3.2.2 NGO's contribution to poverty alleviation

In developing countries, due to the shortage of resources, expertise, political will[18] and human capital (in short, public sector failure), the public sector could not reach the remotely located poor. Thus, the poor remain deprived of public facilities such as hospitals, health centres and schools. In addition, private sector organizations (especially, for example, commercial banks) do not operate in those areas because to do so would make the cost per customer much higher and even if some of them are operating there, their cost (pricing) structure is beyond the capacity of the poor. NGOs, on the other hand, have comparative advantages with voluntary motivations, more resources, a larger workforce, and with state-of-the-art technologies, have become a popular way of delivering to the previously unmet demand for public services to the poor. The proliferation of NGOs was in response to the gaps (Bebbington and Farrigon, 1992) left by public and private sector failure, and this abundance has largely been patronized by the donors[19]. NGOs are defined in this study as,

> "autonomous non-profit and not politically attached organizations that work for social welfare in the public interest. Hence the concept of NGO is generally restricted to social, cultural, legal and environmental advocacy having non commercial vision in public works".

NGOs began their operations with a focus on care and welfare (such as service and delivery, mobilizing resources, human resource development, public information, etc.). This motivation gradually expanded (in some cases shifted) to development and change (such as welfare organizations, development organizations, environmental organizations, women's organizations, human right organizations, environmental groups, income generating projects, job creation programs, workers' organizations[20]). Importantly, these two sets of functions are not mutually exclusive and thus, most NGOs are said to be multi-functional. However, the literature suggests[21] there are three broad categories of NGOs. Their focus on the beneficiaries is described in Table 3.2.

Table 3.2: Broad categories of NGOs and their activities

Type of NGO	Definition/objectives	Examples
Service provider NGOs	Initiate livelihood, credit, health projects, and training and education activities among others.	Balochistan Community Girls school project, School for Life program in Northern Ghana, NGOs training doctors in Cambodia, Training volunteer community family planning workers: CARE in Ethiopia, Water and sanitation programs by Orangi in Pakistan, Hygiene Education by Oxfam, Maternal and child health services by BRAC, Health support by Partners for health in Haiti, Health Shebika program for oral rehydration by BRAC in Bangladesh, need for Kwashiorkor by Africare Food Security initiative, Uganda and Burundi, BRAC Bangladesh, Coptic Orphans valuable girl project in Egypt, UNICEF funded informal education in Cambodia

Type of NGO	Definition/objectives	Examples
Empowerment NGOs	Aim to transform the socioeconomic system by addressing the structural causes of poverty and by transferring power into the hands of the poor people	Project Hope in Malawi, Self-employed women's association in India, Mother child Day care centres in Uganda, Gram Vikash rural health programs in India, world conference on women's health addressing UN issues, advocacy by Partners for Health in Haiti, Russia and Peru, Vidayak Sansad in India, CAMFED in Zimbabwe and Ghana, Haki Elimu in Tanzania, FENU in Uganda, IUCN's wok on biodiversity, BELA Bangladesh, LICADHO Cambodia, ICRW, Gender Action in Ghana, Better life pro-actions for girls model, Asian women in politics
Development NGOs	These NGOs perform the activities of both service provider NGOs and empowerment NGOs by making a balance between short and long-term poverty reduction goals while addressing the issues of empowerment	Credit programs by Grameen Bank, ASA, PROSHIKA and BRAC in Bangladesh, Aga Khan projects in Pakistan, CARE, Roundabout Play pumps in South Africa, Mozambique and Zambia, Health insurance programs by SEWA, BRAC and Grameen, freedom from Hunger credit with education in Ghana, Project hope in Ecuador and Honduras, Prosalud in Bolivia, Lao Youth Organizations in Lao PDR, Guinea worm eradication in Africa, NGOs in Ethiopia like REST, APDA, Forum on street children

Besides flexibility, quality assurance (through skilled workers) and their holistic nature, NGOs are often preferred because they work more closely with the individuals and community where public and community goods are concerned. Direct communication with the members (which government usually can't do) has at least two major implications. First, the

NGOs can design and offer a well-suited and an appropriate mix of public goods, and second, by engaging the people in the process, the NGOs can help the beneficiaries in building required capabilities, and this is seen as a response to service delivery failure (Brinkerhoff and Brinkerhoff, 2002). In addition, NGOs' comparative advantage in reaching the marginal poor is well appreciated, with this relationship with the people being attributed to NGOs' public legitimacy (Hulme and Edwards, 1997). Moreover, NGOs have become so powerful nowadays that their intermediary abilities, such as in brokering interactions between and among local communities, other NGOs, civil societies, government agencies, other private organizations and donors are well recognized. NGOs' experience in working with such diverse communities is considered the reason for their broader understanding of various operating procedures. NGOs' role in and contribution to sectors of development, particularly in poverty reduction and social mobilization are also well recognized[22].

3.2.2A Failures of the NGO sector in poverty reduction

Even though the NGO sector potentially makes a greater contribution to achieving the MDGs and reducing poverty, this contribution should be tested according to local circumstances and by considering the potential failures of the NGO sector. It is argued that the theoretical comparative advantages of NGOs may not hold true for all NGOs universally (Brinkerhoff et al. 2007). Two frameworks have been suggested in favour of this claim as shown in Fig-3.2.

It has also been pointed out that:

- NGOs could not reach the marginal poor who are in need of the services most[23].
- NGOs sometimes duplicate government services and cause confusion among people, and many of those NGOs have created mechanisms for tapping into government or donor funds (ADB, 2001).
- Unlike the democratic governments, NGOs are not elected and so they don't receive (or may not like to get) immediate feedback from the beneficiaries like other private organizations.
- Even though the NGOs work for empowerment, collecting evidence and incorporating the suggestions and feedback from the beneficiaries into the decision-making process are rare.

A potential source of ineffectiveness, therefore, lies in this process as NGOs do not usually upgrade or update their service delivery process according to the needs of clients. Based on this evidence, it can thus be argued that like public and private sector failure, there could be a 'third or voluntary sector failure' unless an effective and pro-poor service delivery system is developed.

Figure 3.2: Theoretical arguments for NGO failure

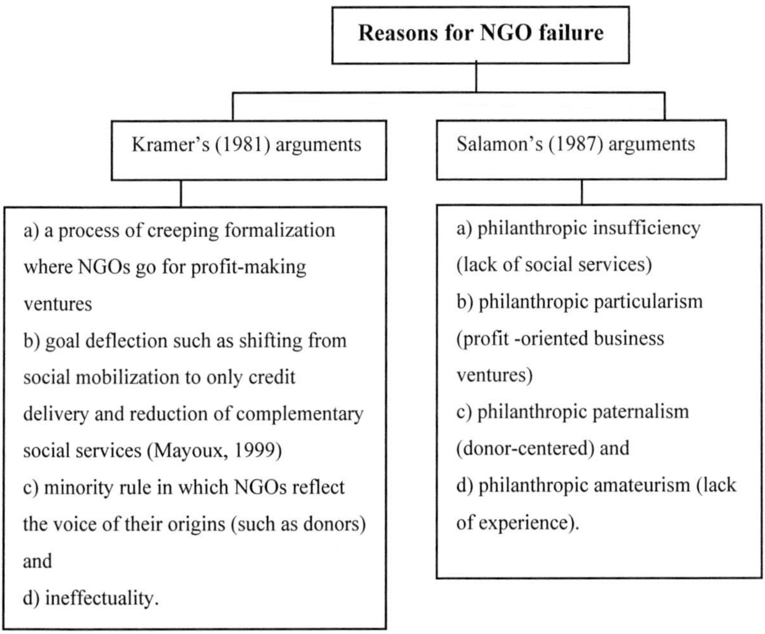

3.2.2B NGO proliferation in Bangladesh: History and theoretical justification

The rapid growth of NGOs in Bangladesh has a long history and theoretical justifications. Recognition of NGOs in the fourth Five-Year Plan can be considered a main reason behind NGO proliferation in the credit and service delivery mechanism in Bangladesh. At the time of the liberation war in 1971, there were few NGOs which were working only for rehabilitation and giving assistance to war victims. For example, *Gono Shastho Kendra* offered medical assistance to freedom fighters in 1971, *Terre Des Hommes* provided rehabilitation to unwanted children of the war in Kurigram district, Rangpur Dinajpur Rural Service (RDRS) began its post-war rehabilitation in the northern part of Bangladesh and at that time Bangladesh Rural Advancement Committee (BRAC) also had limited rehabilitation activities for the war victims. It is claimed (Zohir, 2007) that *Swanirvor Bangladesh* is the first NGO (in 1975) that worked for agricultural production, youth mobilization and rural development rather than solely rehabilitation. At that time PROSHIKA was formed as a local NGO that ran local training programs for the Canadian University Students' Organization (CUSO). Decades of NGO sector expansion in Bangladesh can be summarized as:

- In the 1970s, most of the NGOs were providing rehabilitation, education, health, sanitation, shelter, and family planning services for the people.
- At the beginning of the 1980s, the country experienced the success of the Grameen Bank which resulted in the wider acceptance of microfinance operations in the country.
- Between the mid-1980s and the early 1990s, the focus of NGOs radically shifted from rehabilitation to credit delivery. At that time, with a slight change in focus and activities, many Microfinance Institutions (MFIs) emerged in Bangladesh. The primary task of the MFIs was to offer credit with training. However, there were many NGOs still operating in social services such as education (BRAC schooling), health care (Gono Shastho Kendra), sanitation and water supply (CARE, DANIDA, OXFAM) etc.

Since the inception of NGO Affairs Bureau (NGOAB) in 1990, NGOs have been required to be registered as social and voluntary organizations to access foreign funds. In this study, we consider NGOs those organizations which are beyond the control of the GoB and semi-GoB agencies, and are classified as NGO-MFIs by the Microcredit Regulatory Authority[24] (MRA) and can offer financial or non-financial services to their beneficiaries. At present, according to the NGOAB (2011), the total number of registered NGOs in Bangladesh is 2040 and according to the MRA, of that number, 560 are NGO-MFIs. However, it has been reported that at present around 20,000 credit and social service delivery related NGOs are operating in Bangladesh (ADB, 2002).

This massive expansion of the NGO-MFI sector was, in fact, derived from the interest of government, donors, society, and beneficiaries. Table 3.3 summarily demonstrates the linkage of NGO proliferation in Bangladesh with the theories of non-profits.

Table 3.3: Theories of non-profits and their relation to NGO proliferation in Bangladesh

Theories of non-profits	Definition	Rationale of the theory for the NGO proliferation in Bangladesh	Limitation	References
The Public Goods Theory	Governmental entities will tend to provide public goods only at the level that satisfies the median voter.	**Supported by donors and Government:** There must be some unsatisfied individuals whose demand for the goods or services may be greater than the median. Non-profit organizations arise to produce and supply this unmet demand (fourth Five-Year Plan)	(1) The theory doesn't explain why non-profit, rather than for-profit firms arise to fulfil the unmet demand. (2) The theory doesn't discuss what type of non-profit is more suitable for public policy (3) The theory doesn't explain how to measure efficacy of the non-profits	Weisbrod (1975, 1977), Hansmann (1980), Powel (1987), Salamon (1987)
The Contract Failure Theory	The theory is defined as the inability of consumers to police producers (especially the for-profits) by ordinary contractual devices and represents a particular kind of market failure.	**Supported by donors:** A non-profit firm, by contrast, offers customers the advantage by owing the non-distributional constraint and has got no chance (by definition) to take advantage of the customers. Explains the limitations of the earlier theory.	(1) The theory offers no solution to the agency problem. (2) There is no explanation as to why individuals may want to make donations that bring benefits to individuals with whom the donors have no connection. **(3) No guidelines offered about how to police and assess the performance of the organizations**	Nelson and Krashinsky (1973), Hansmann (1980, 1987), James (1986).

Theories of non-profits	Definition	Rationale of the theory for the NGO proliferation in Bangladesh	Limitation	References
The Consumer Control Theory	Stronger consumer control may be necessary to guarantee that products offered by firms are of sufficiently high quality.	**Supported by the beneficiaries:** It is important to establish the strong consumer control over the firm to monitor and control the activities of the firm in case of market failure.	(1) It is mostly applicable for mutual non-profits (for example, clubs or cooperatives) where patrons have the right to control the activities of the firm (2) The theory has limited empirical support and doesn't distinguish between the non-profits and other forms of limited-profits firms (3) No indication has been given about what are the parameters to judge higher quality of the services. No idea has been offered about how to compare the quality factor among the non-profits.	Ben-Ner (1986), Hansmann (1987:34)
Subsidy theory	Large-scale expansion of non-profits is due to the subsidies provided by the state.	**Government's support:** Non-profits benefit from different types of explicit and implicit subsidies, including exemption from tax, special postal rates and favorable treatment under unemployment tax system.	The theory doesn't explore what might be the probable rate of tax exemption required to have the optimal social effect from the various kind of non-profits	Fama and Jensen (1983), Hansmann (1985a)

Theories of non-profits	Definition	Rationale of the theory for the NGO proliferation in Bangladesh	Limitation	References
Entrepreneurship theory	Social entrepreneurs differ from business entrepreneurs in a way that instead of creating monetary or economic value for the firm, they create social values by adopting a mission of creating social values.	**Social reasons:** Social entrepreneurs maximize non-monetary returns such as faith, number of believers or members, adherents, etc.	The theory ends up without any explanation for the solution to the agency problem and **measuring efficacy of the non-profits.**	Ackerman (1996), Dennis Young (1983)

3.2.2C Major activities of NGOs in Bangladesh

Although NGOs are now providing service delivery in social areas such as, health, education, sanitation and clean water supply, for many NGOs/MFIs their role is limited to financial services – microcredit delivery. NGOs/MFIs consider credit the main tool with which to encourage employment generation and women's empowerment. However, this motive in particular has reduced the NGOs' contribution to social mobilization because of the belief that financial sustainability is the major indicator of a project's effectiveness, and social mobilization might incur additional costs which are hard to recover (Mayoux, 1999). Recent additions to the activities of NGOs are in advocacy, research and environmental conservation works. Several NGOs (such as BELA) in Bangladesh offer free legal assistance to the poor especially to women. This section will discuss a few noticeable activities of NGOs in Bangladesh that are relevant to poverty reduction.

a. **Access to credit with peer lending/monitoring:** The trend of delivering microfinance with a peer monitoring process began after the success of the Grameen Bank in the early 1990s. However, it is claimed that group-based lending (to as many as 30-40 people) was first introduced with limited practice in the late 1970s through government funding (Zohir, 2007). Since the credit is peer monitored, there is no need for collateral. The use of microfinance initially was limited and the process was slow however, with the inception of the Palli Karma Sahayak Foundation (PKSF) in the early 1990s, many small and large NGOs/MFIs started to operate throughout the country. The trends in microfinance disbursement show that in 2004 cumulative credit disbursement was 20000 crore Taka ($3500 million), whereas, in 2009, a total of 26000 crore Taka ($4400 million) was disbursed by only 21 large NGOs/MFIs[25] (MOF, GoB-2011). Until December 2009, the cumulative credit disbursement was more than 73000 crore Taka ($12300 million). This value would be much higher if data from other small and non-registered NGOs/MFIs could be included. This rapid credit disbursement growth demonstrates the NGOs/MFI's major focus towards credit. At the end of 2009, the total number of beneficiaries of the NGOs/MFIs was 2.65 crore with savings of 11879.99 crore Taka'($1900 million) (MOF, GoB-2011).

Loan sizes from NGOs/MFIs are usually less than 10000 Taka (around US$137) [26] but with a successful repayment history the next credit can be up to 90000 Taka (US$700). In addition to these microfinance schemes, several NGOs/MFIs offer microenterprise credit ranging between US $700 and $7000. According to the Microcredit Regulatory Authority (MRA, 2011)[27]:

- Maximum interest chargeable was set at 27 (twenty seven) percent per annum.
- Interest on loans to be calculated on a Declining Balance Method.
- Minimum number of instalments (weekly) on general loans must be 50.

Due to its micro nature and easy weekly instalment process, micro-financing is claimed to be replacing traditional rural money lenders (*Mohajon*) in Bangladesh. However, it is also claimed that excessive use of microcredit without proper training and monitoring can cause adverse effects in society (Goldin Institute, 2007). For instance, possibly due to the lack of monitoring, the credit is usually used by the male family member, and this goes against the concept of women's empowerment – one of the primary goals of microcredit. A lack of proper consultation and training in utilizing the loan creates waste in society through beneficiaries not making use of the loan effectively, causing them to default and so remain trapped in chronic poverty. Thus, we believe large-scale microcredit disbursement cannot make a sea change in the poverty rate unless proper services – customized to the needs of beneficiaries – are provided along with the credit. Thus, effectiveness of the microfinance driven projects largely depends on service delivery mechanisms – the issue that has always been neglected.

b. **Social intermediation and women's empowerment:** One of the major activities of the NGOs nowadays is considered to be women's empowerment. It is believed that making credit available to women would create their economic solvency thereby enhancing women's voices in the family and society at large. With that view in mind, most of the NGOs/MFIs consider women their main target market and beneficiaries. The concept of group meetings (social intermediation) which increase awareness among women is widely recognized one in the development literature. In Bangladesh, more than 92% of the borrowers of NGOs/MFIs are women. Several studies (for example, Morshed, 2000) have identified that domestic violence in Bangladesh has declined due to the use of credit by women. Several other studies (Pitt et al., 2006; Khandaker et al., 1998) found positive impact from the use of credit on family life, consumption, decision-making, etc.

c. **NGOs as social service delivery agents:** NGOs are considered an alternative delivery channel for social services like education, health, sanitation, immunization, etc in Bangladesh. BRAC has operated their informal education system since 1985 and currently it has 3200 primary schools from which 3.80 million students (65% girls) have graduated. In addition, BRAC operates 20140 pre-primary schools, numerous multi-purpose community learning centres, and it has partnerships in the primary and secondary education system in Bangladesh. NGO involvement in health care is appreciable. For instance, *Gono Shastho Kendra* has many clinics in both rural and urban areas; BRAC and Water Aid helps with sanitary and water supply in rural areas; CARE-Bangladesh assists in immunization programs (Extended Immunization Program by UNICEF) throughout the country, and other satellite clinics (such as *Sobuz Chata*, *Surzer Hasi* guided by the UN) and nutrition programs (Bangladesh Integrated Nutrition Projects) run by NGOs are remarkable.

3.3 The need for effective service delivery in poverty reduction projects in Bangladesh

After the inception of Bangladesh in 1971, donors used to channel funds for social work through government organizations. However, that changed in the early 1980s because it was claimed that government was less effective in reaching the poor due to GOs' small workforce and large bureaucratic processes. Thus, NGOs emerged as the new channel for credit delivery. From this argument it can be deduced that at the initial stage the determinants for organizational efficacy measurement were 'area coverage' and 'commitment to social work'. After that when the coverage of the development partners (GOs and NGOs) increased significantly (as stated earlier), efficacy-determining criteria evolved. In the course of time, these service providers were assessed and compared based on cost effectiveness (Mahmud and Ahmed, 2003), rapid response rate (McGhee, 1999), resource utilization (Ahmed, 2001), employment creation (Ahmed, 2001), sustainability of the projects (Ahmed, 2001) and the rate of loan recovery (Morshed, 2000). Among these common criteria, the repayment rate is now considered as the yardstick that is most appealing to the donors. Therefore, most of the GO and NGO/MFI projects highlight this rate on their websites or annual reports to attract more funds. We argue that this is a narrow and mis-targeted method of measuring the effectiveness of the service providers. A study by the Goldin Institute (2007) found that beneficiaries take credit from one service provider to repay the debt burden from another. So the money that is repaid might not be necessarily be generated from any productive venture. This process may increase the repayment rates of certain GO and NGO/MFI projects. But this multi-credit lending process has created a macro-trap for many poor beneficiaries who moved from being a temporary poor status to a chronic or permanent poor as they became defaulters in a number of credit schemes. This argument against using repayment rates as a measure of effectiveness is further supported by the studies of Hossain (2009) and Azam and Katsushi (2009). Their studies show that even after posting high repayment rates, poverty and vulnerability to poverty increased in Bangladesh. It can thus be argued that effective functioning of institutions should not be judged in terms of the organization's benefit (such as high return rate) as this does not necessarily represent the need preferences of the beneficiaries.

Between 1991/92 and 1995/96, microcredit disbursement (NGOAB, 2010) through NGOs[28] increased by $1069.19 million, while rural poverty increased from 52.9% to 56.7%. Moreover, between 1995/96 and 2000, microcredit disbursement reduced by $514.405 million but at that time the rural poverty situation improved as it reduced to 53.1% from 56.7%. These observations support the argument that large credit disbursement and higher repayment status cannot make a significant change in the poverty reduction rate unless proper services are provided to enable the poor beneficiaries to best utilize the credit in order to get higher return from their investments. This higher return (both economic and non-economic) can help them to get out of poverty within the desired timeframe. However, there is no such comparative study available that focuses on the effectiveness of service delivery in GO and NGO poverty reduction projects. It has been widely noted that failures of the management are common in public and social production of services due to a lack of focus on effective service delivery processes (Macchiavello, 2008). Fig-3.3 outlines that success of service providers in social works mostly depends on efficacy in service delivery.

As shown in Fig-3.3, at the initial stage of the micro-financing process most credit providers face a similar environment in which they look for funds from donors and they are accountable to society and civil organizations. There may be a few differences with respect to organizational cultures, structures, and policies; however, as credit-driven organizations, they all strive for the ultimate goal of poverty reduction. Outcomes for the development partners vary at this stage of service delivery (or process) because there may be variations in organizational effectiveness. For instance, in Fig-3.3, the dotted flow shows ineffective delivery and dotted boxes demonstrate the outcomes of this delivery; whereas the solid flow and boxes describe the opposite. Moreover, the diagram also demonstrates that in the case of ineffective delivery processes (inappropriate organization), participation of the beneficiary in the decision-making process of organizations is minimal or nil. This results in an organization-oriented service delivery that leads to wider and greater distribution of credit without targeting pro-poor growth with fair distribution of credit. This phenomenon leads to multiple unproductive credit schemes by a single beneficiary due to poor utilization of the credit seemingly caused by ineffective non-customized services. Therefore, with multiple credits, organizations get financial sustainability (final dotted box) with no improvement for the clients.

Figure 3.3: Relationships between institutional policies, processes and poverty reduction

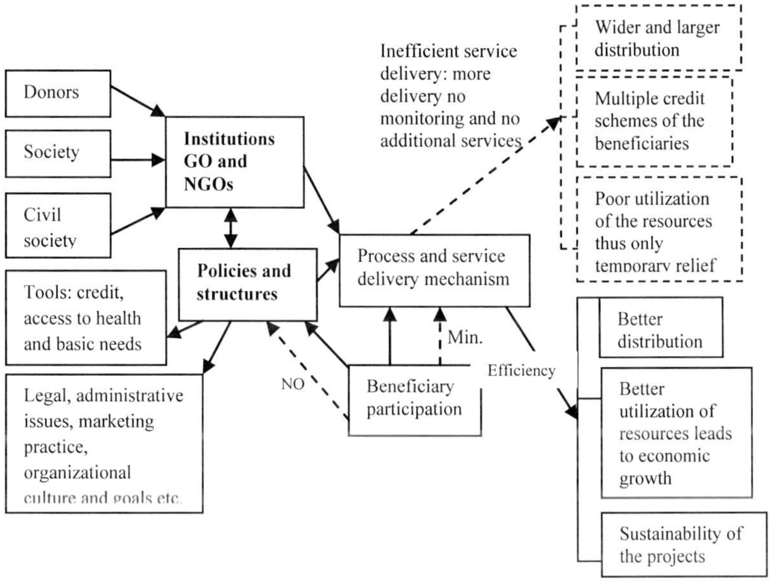

Note: Dashed arrows show the existing practices which result from poor utilization of credit. Solid arrows show the effective way of utilizing the credit that result in pro-poor growth and beneficiary satisfaction

This process could be reversed with significant beneficiary participation (indicated by the solid arrows in Fig-3.3), and thus customized and effective service provision leads to better utilization through better consultation, training, monitoring, etc., and consequently to better returns from the project. The greater return would have two impacts:

a) enhanced beneficiary living; and
b) improved sustainability of the projects.

3.4 Why is effective service delivery important for non-profits? Theories and realities

In a profit-oriented business environment, the role of the customer is altering the paradigm, resulting in service quality becoming a priority in these industries (Prahalad and Ramaswamy, 2000). In traditional marketing (for profit), a customer-focused strategy is now the means by which an organization can gain competitive advantage and survive. Even though Albrecht and Zemke (1985) emphasized that the capacity to serve clients effectively and effectively is an issue every organization must face – whether it's a manufacturer and traditional service provider, profit making or non-profit organization – however, this practice is still understated in the provision of social services especially to the poor who as a group suffer from a lack of voice and freedom in society. There are two important reasons for effective service delivery:

1. If we consider the actors in poverty reduction programs (GOs, NGOs, MFIs, cooperatives etc.) a single industry, then it can be seen that at the macro level these organizations (especially GOs and national NGOs) are in competition with each other to get funds from external donors, and at micro level they (local NGOs and cooperatives) are again in competition with each other for limited public and private (from national NGOs) funds. A social work organization cannot claim to be the single provider of services in a specific area (for instance, in education, health care or credit delivery), because there are other social organizations that do the same. For this reason, non-profit and social work managers should know that the only way to differentiate their organizations from the competitors is providing quality services. Donors can now make better-informed decisions about delivering funds to the organizations that maintain a certain quality standard in delivering services to the beneficiaries.
2. Like profit-oriented organizations, the service delivery effectiveness of the social organizations will be assessed by their respective customers or beneficiaries. As a participatory poverty approach (PPA) is considered by world organizations (such as the World Bank, ADB, etc.) a strategic step in the decision-making process in poverty reduction programs, taking beneficiaries' opinions on service quality would be the most appropriate strategy. The inclusion of beneficiaries in this process is shown in Fig-3.3 (see the box labelled as beneficiary participation and the arrows).

The need for effective service delivery is well recognized in the literature. Mathur (in Mubangizi, 2009) attributes the failure of development and poverty reduction programs to the ineffectiveness of the administrative and delivery systems. Braathen and Palmero (Wilson et al., 1989) have argued that poverty should not be seen as a problem itself. Instead, they advocate for a focus on administration, accountability, and budget management along with desired service delivery.

3.4.1 The capability approach, institutions and service delivery

Sen's Capability Approach (CA) (as discussed in Section 2.4 in Chapter-2) is an alternative and widely recognized way of framing poverty, inequality, and human development issues. Applications of CA can be found in countless articles and several books (Clark, 2006). In short, Sen (1984) outlines the need for having assets, commodities, a sustainable livelihood, and services for an acceptable standard of living. The inability to acquire the stated requirements is the main cause of poverty. As stated in the CA, the main role of government (GOs) and other development actors (for instance, NGOs) is to endow citizens with the required conditions for actualizing the necessary capacities and opportunities. To achieve this, development organizations (GOs and NGOs) utilize microcredit as an important tool for helping the poor to invest borrowed money in productive work (for example, small business, poultry etc.) which will in turn generate income (ability factor). This income can then be used for several purposes, such as paying the loan instalments, saving for further investment or asset-building (like buying a land or home), and most importantly for buying commodities (from food to non-food items, and other social commodities like education and health care). In addition to micro-financing, several policies may be useful in creating such abilities in poor people. For instance, policies that can increase poor people's control over land will help them to adopt farming practices that can drive up their income. This income can, in turn, be used for the above stated purposes. This is how the Capability Approach and its associated tools aid the creation of assets, commodities and some aspects of sustainability issues.

However, as seen from the above study, the CA focuses on the end results and not on the management process or the service delivery mechanisms that lead to the provision of these capabilities. Microcredit can generate income and help reduce poverty at a rate that will certainly vary depending on the degree of efficacy in utilizing the borrowed money. A beneficiary receiving proper training along with other services must be more capable of utilizing the loan amount effectively compared to the beneficiary receiciving money but no associated training or services; thus their capacity to fight against poverty would be low. This is the reason for the prevalence of significantly high rural poverty in Bangladesh despite large credit disbursement. It can thus be argued that capability enhancement of the poor beneficiaries largely depends on the capability of the institutions or service providers.

3.4.1A How institutional capability building can help?

In public policy, micro-level policy action (such as food for work or food for education programs in Bangladesh) focuses on selecting beneficiaries for public works, welfare payments or microfinance projects[29] (Dreze and Sen, 1989; Alkire, 2002). In these programs, it is difficult to identify and classify beneficiaries with respect to their relative efficacy of conversion function by using CA. There are people who need less money than others to avoid capability failure, and who can use the credit or support more effectively in generating income or wellbeing. The capability approach doesn't indicate how to manage this variation of need in order to reduce undesirable distributive consequences. As a result, the MFIs charge uniform interest to everyone despite the fact that returns from different projects vary. This, in turn, causes many beneficiaries to default due to the higher interest burden compared to the returns of their respective projects. Those who can manage some return cannot save anything after repaying the instalment. This is the reason behind high repayment rates in GOs and NGOs. It can thus be argued that the high default rate is mostly due to the lack of capability in the service providers for enhancing the potential of the beneficiaries.

This problem can be solved by creating 'capability' in the organizations involved in poverty reduction programs. For example, a system developed by someone may include one-to-one consultation between the official and the beneficiary before approval of the loan so that officials can identify the beneficiaries who are more capable of utilizing the loan (based on educational qualifications, previous experience, expertise on a specific job etc.) or the expected return from the proposed project. This system can necessarily solve at least three major problems: a reduction in undesirable distributive consequences, the arrangement for a customized rate of interest, and guaranteed repayment with some savings based on expected or calculated returns. There may be many such strategies that can be implemented to enhance the capability of the service providers which in turn will enhance the capability of the beneficiaries to fight poverty. However, the CA doesn't provide any indication about how to manage the capability of the service providers

3.4.2 The sustainable livelihoods approach and service delivery

In order to understand the organizational process and service related issues in poverty reduction programs, the capability approach was further expanded and a schematic model called 'sustainable livelihoods' was developed by Chambers and Conway[30] (1992), and further popularized by

Department of International Development (DFID), UK. This approach not only stresses the need for a customized poverty model (as mentioned in Section 2.5), but also emphasizes the importance of understanding institutions by mapping the institutional framework and linking the micro to the macro and the formal to the informal sectors.

3.4.2A Understanding of the sustainable livelihoods model and its limitations

The model has four distinct parts (Fig-3.4). In the first part it deals with the 'vulnerability' issues that include natural, social, economic, and political shocks which may push a large portion of rural people into poverty. The second part (livelihood assets and capital) discusses the different types of capital that are important in maintaining an acceptable standard of living. An explanation on vulnerability and capital is given in Chapter 2 (Section 2.5.1). The next part of the model discusses institutions, structures, policies, and processes that make the poor people aware of the available services and how to access them.

Two powerful sectors act in this process: (1) the public sector and (2) the private and third sector which includes NGOs, civil society, commercial organizations, membership organizations etc. This sub-section which comprises public and private sectors is termed a 'structure' as these institutions make the processes function. The second sub-section of this part of the model describes 'processes'– the way structure and beneficiaries should interact. Several recommendations are made for improving the process, for example providing information to support more pro-poor policy-making processes, strengthening the contact between the poor and the institutions, supporting a participatory process, promoting a fair and competitive market, etc. (similar to what is suggested in Fig-3.3). One of the most common problems in development is that the transforming of structures and processes do not work to the benefit of the poor. It is a deliberate outcome driven by the failure of prevailing service arrangements. In the existing process, the poor play a very small part. The model suggests that external support can help solve these problems through building a structure for the poor. However, structures on their own – without accompanying effective processes – have only potential or option value; the two aspects must be considered together as a leading role in the process. In such circumstances the primary or at least simultaneous focus must be on processes, ensuring that these work to the benefit of the poor. With this justification, the model offers several guidelines (as of guidance sheet-1.4):

a) building structures that represent the poor;
b) promoting reform in structures and processes which will be pro-poor;
c) promoting private sector organization along with government.

While ‘structure of the organizations’ and many parts of the ‘process’ are explained through the model, the internal dynamics of institutions, a beneficiary’s required fields of effective service delivery and the process of strengthening the service delivery by organizations have largely been ignored (indicated as gaps 3 and 4 in Fig-3.4).

The final part of the model recommends the building of livclihood strategies as the capability set to get better livelihood outcomes. For instance, microfinance along with a peer monitoring approach is a recognized strategy to create financial capital (by creating direct income and savings) and social capital (by organizing group meetings and incorporating the poor in the decision-making) to fight poverty.

In the final part, the model discusses the range and combination of activities and choices that people can make in order to achieve their functioning[31] or livelihood goals. This includes human capability building, the use of different combinations of tools (for instance, credit, health care, education, etc.), and choosing effective service providers. However, in the absence of any standard scale/index to measure service delivery, we cannot compare the effectiveness of various service providers. Like the capability approach, this is a major limitation of this model.

Figure 3.4: DFID's sustainable livelihood framework and its limitations

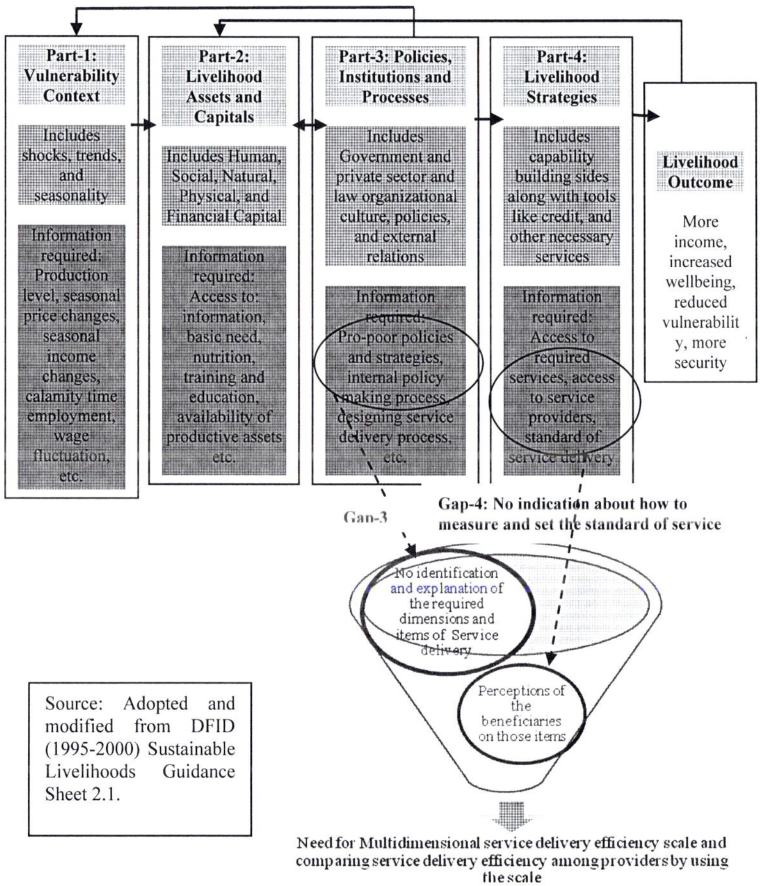

3.5 The dimensions of effective service delivery for non-profits

In this section, we will highlight the major dimensions and their underlying items that are required to ensure quality service delivery. This aspect has mostly been ignored in the development economics literature. It is also important to mention that the usual 'performance scale' or 'service quality scale' of for-profit firms are supposed to be different from the 'effectiveness scale' of non-profit firms. Thus, we will address issues in effectiveness according to the characteristics and need preferences in service delivery in poverty reduction programs. The performance scales often applied to for-profit organizations are not compatible with an analysis of non-profit GOs and NGOs for the following reasons:

- First, in the case of non-profit projects such as poverty alleviation programs, social welfare rather than financial objectives drive the organizations' strategies. Thus, non-profits tend to focus more on fundraising and volunteer management (McNamara, 2010). For instance, in poverty alleviation programs field workers are in direct contact with their beneficiaries (door-to-door) at no cost, whereas in the case of for-profits there are charges for the services provided. Thus, the issue of volunteerism needs to be addressed in the performance scale of non-profits.
- Secondly, in poverty reduction programs the most important roles are played by field workers who travel door-to-door (note that the motivation of sales agents is very different from that of social workers). Thus, there are different yet important issues in the performance scale relative to the skills, service knowledge, and timing of inspections by field workers from the non-profits compared to those working in for-profit organizations.
- Thirdly, in for-profits, promotional activities like advertising are performed for target customers, whereas in non-profits such activities are performed for potential donors and sponsors and as such it is unnecessary to include them in the performance scale of non-profits.
- And finally, the socio-economic characteristics of the respondents in our scale (less able poor people) are quite different from those of a performance scale used in for-profit organizations.

For this study, effectiveness and quality in service is defined and measured by the beneficiaries through overall assessment of the services. These include administration, management, technical support of the workers, the skills and knowledge of the front-line workers and managers, problem solving efficacy, speed of the process, inclusion of the beneficiaries in the decision-making process, service reach to the beneficiaries, welfare focus, understanding of needs, liaison with other organizations, etc.

There is vast literature on performance measurement in for-profit organizations. Two popularly used models are the Service Quality Model (SERVQUAL) and the Performance Only Index (SERVPERF). The SERVQUAL model has been used in a variety of profit-motivated industries across different cultures. In several studies, the reliability of the model has been assured (Babakus and Boller, 1992; Brown and Swartz, 1989). However, there are other studies that have criticized the scoring methods and the specific application of the model to several other industries. Cronin and Taylor (1994) have offered SERVPERF which has received strong support from different studies (Teas, 1993; Brown et al., 1993). Even though this type of scale is not found in the development literature, Leonard and Marshal (1982) made several points for a successful poverty-oriented organization, and used the term 'linkages' to describe the positive aspects. These include:

- Representation (for example, formal and informal participation in planning and implementation);
- Technical and personal assistance (for instance, in service training, management and program advice);
- Regulation and monitoring (such as, audits, administering market price, registration of local organizations, etc.);
- Finance (such as credit, grants, and savings).

Parasuraman et al. (1985) offers three main principles for ensuring quality services.

- The **first principle** is in making service quality part of employees' main responsibilities. This means that organizations need to understand the need for effective service delivery for their own growth and betterment of the beneficiaries. This needs to be incorporated in the organization's policies and regulations.
- **Second,** effective service delivery effort should be in line with organizational credibility, trust, fairness, and welfare concerns. And in delivering better services, organizations need to focus on surrounding environmental changes. Moreover, this quality assurance process should be ongoing and subject to periodic survey.
- **Third,** people (beneficiary and employee) involvement is a critical component.

Based on the vast literature[32] and the discussion made in the above section the determinants of effective service delivery can be found from the expected interactions between beneficiaries, managers, and field workers, and from their individual roles in the whole delivery process as depicted in Fig-3.5.

Figure 3.5: Service delivery interaction among beneficiaries, workers and organization

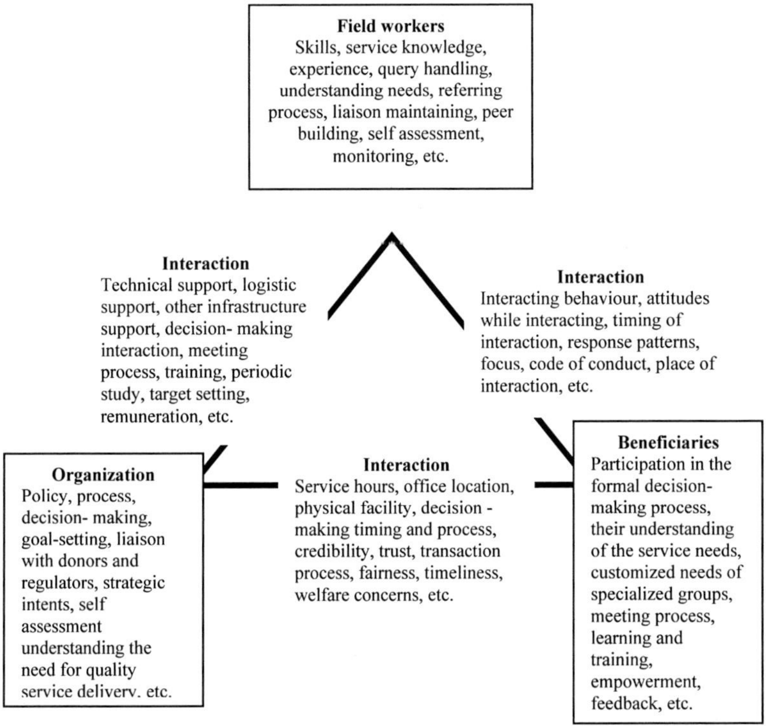

In light of the issues shown in Fig-3.5, and by comparing these with the existing dimensions of the 'performance scale' and 'service quality scale', at this initial stage we propose the following five dimensions of effective service delivery:

- *Credibility*: Measures the reasonable grounds for being believed. That means the items of this dimension will measure the degree to which people can rely on the activities of the service provider. Thus, issues such as timeliness and speed in decision-making, sincerity in operations, fairness in decision-making processes and ways of treating people, timely information sharing, etc. are the main determinants of credibility.
- *Reactive dimensions*: This measures the way and the depth of the service provider's response to the queries from the beneficiaries and the approach they take in solving them. Items that belong to

this group are: the responsiveness of managers and workers, the attitude of the workers and managers while interacting with beneficiaries, feedback processes, query handling methods, technical support in response to any queries, etc.

- *Confidence dimension*: The term confidence is defined as how beneficiaries feel about the services of the support organization and whether they are confident enough to refer this provider to other potential beneficiaries. In short, this is the trust factor for the organizations and these issues focus on transparency in transactions, consultation and guiding ability of the workers, the promise-keeping attitude of the organizations, professionalism, knowledge and skills of the workers, etc.
- *Empowering dimension*: This dimension is specifically used to measure the focus of the organizations towards beneficiaries in order to see to what extent the organizations value the suggestions of their beneficiaries. Determinants of this dimension include: attention of the workers and the organization to the welfare of the beneficiaries, group meeting processes, listening and incorporating suggestions from the beneficiaries in the organizational plans and strategies, a caring attitude, degree of participation of the beneficiaries in service delivery process, etc.
- *Accessibility dimension*: This dimension is particularly used to measure the communication facilitation system between beneficiaries and the organization. As the coverage and reach of the service provider is an important factor in degree poverty reduction, this dimension thus includes items such as location of office, business hours, timing of the visit by the workers, areas covered, technology used in communications, etc.

Chapter 5 of this book develops a two dimensional service delivery effectiveness scale using the five dimensions discussed above (the items under these five dimensions are given in Section 9 of the questionnaire in the Appendix of Chapter 4).

3.6 Conclusion

This chapter explored the need for and the contribution of appropriate institutions involved to poverty reduction in Bangladesh. The chapter linked the theoretical perspective with a practical scenario of Bangladesh to explain the standing of government and the emergence of NGOs. It also explored the notion that despite the remarkable contribution by the

Government of Bangladesh and the NGOs, the country's poverty rate remains alarming. From the application of the Capability Approach (Sen, 1984) and the sustainable livelihoods model, the chapter argues that service delivery effectiveness is a requirement for better outcomes from poverty reduction projects in Bangladesh. However, due to the absence of any such a parameter to assess the effectiveness of service delivery, this important aspect of the policy package has largely been ignored. In general the effectiveness of the institutions is assessed through the repayment rate of credit, area coverage, loan disbursement, response rates, etc. It is believed that comparing the institutions concerned with poverty with respect to service delivery effectiveness will help the donors find better channels for fund delivery in future. This is the rationale of Chapters 5 and 6. It is thus argued that moving from the traditional to more appropriate institutions largely depends on their contribution in delivering customized services to the beneficiaries.

Notes

[1] For instance, see Sen's (1999) Capability Approach and the DFID's Sustainable Livelihoods Approach.

[2] The World Bank's Annual Review of 2000 Evaluations (1988) found, 'investment in institutional development to be the single most important determinant of a poverty reduction project's sustainability'.

[3] In Bangladesh, 'the term NGO refers to all such organizations and institutions that are registered with the Government under the Voluntary Social Welfare Agency Ordinance of 1961 and the Foreign Donation (Voluntary activities) Regulation Ordinance of 1978. NGOs can thus be defined as those institutions that are registered with the NGO Affair Bureau (NGOAB), Bangladesh'. For a detailed list see, http://www.ngoab.gov.bd/Files/NGO_LIST.pdf

[4] Hoque (2010) found that 89% of the borrowers did not receive any training from MFIs in Bangladesh. However, the study by Cheston and Kuhn (2002) on several countries has shown that MFIs offer different types of training such as, business training, civil society participation training, political and social awareness training, rights training, marketing and selling training, customer care training etc. They have quoted 'by giving women access to working capital and training, microfinance helps mobilize women's productive capacity to alleviate poverty..' (p. 7).

[5] A similar approach is used by the Microcredit Regulatory Authority, Bangladesh. See, for instance, http://www.mra.gov.bd/index.php?option=com_content&view=category&layout=blog&id=29&Itemid=80

[6] 'Since poverty causes and characteristics differ from country to country, the starting point must be a comprehensive examination of the constraints and opportunities for poverty reduction in each country... This will require understanding the nature, intensity, and spread of poverty; the distributional effects

of macroeconomic policies; the focus and efficiency of public expenditures; and the effectiveness of government programs and institutions' (ADB 1999a, pp. 15)

[7] Third sector includes NGOs (Kozlowski, 1983 and Paul, 1991), microfinance institutions (MFIs) and cooperatives, but excludes civil societies.

[8] The MDGs comprise 8 targets with 48 indicators. The targets are to be achieved by 2015 with the comparison point being 1990. In addition, Bangladesh signed the Conventions on the elimination of all forms of discrimination: racial, gender and child discrimination.

[9] 'In September 1999, the World Bank Group and the IMF decided that nationally-owned participatory poverty reduction strategies should provide the basis for all their concessional lending and eligibility for debt relief under the enhanced Heavily Indebted Poor Countries (HIPC) Initiative. This approach, building on the principles of the Comprehensive Development Framework (CDF), has led to the development of Poverty Reduction Strategy Papers (PRSPs) by country authorities for submission to the World Bank and IMF Boards' (WB and IMF, 1999).

[10] Bangladesh's I-PRSP is titled 'A National Strategy for Economic Growth, Poverty Reduction and Social Development'.

[11] This is titled 'Unlocking the Potential: National Strategy for Accelerated Poverty Reduction'

[12] Started in 1984 and was known initially as Rural Poor Projects (RRP).

[13] It was reported that there are 27 safety net projects[13] run by the GoB (MOF, GoB-2010).

[14] To combat the economic crisis in 2008-09, GoB increased the food allotment for VGF from 2.7 lac metric ton to 5.5 lac. In the same year, allotment for Test Relief increased to 4 lac metric ton from 3.6 lac.

[15] *Monga* is seasonal food insecurity in ecologically vulnerable and economically weak parts of north-western Bangladesh, primarily caused by an employment and income deficit before Aman (Rice grown in monsoon) is harvested. It mainly affects those rural poor, who have an undiversified income that is directly or indirectly based on agriculture.

[16] These are Sonali, Janata, Agrani, Rupali, Bangladesh Krishi and Rajshahi Krishi Unnayan bank.

[17] Anser VDP Bank, Social Islami Bank, The Trust Bank, Basic Bank, Uttara Bank

[18] Corruption, eclecticism, cronyism, political patronage and pervasive institutional weakness are manifest in those political systems (Brinkerhoff et al., 2007).

[19] NGO expansion is seen as complementing the counter-revolution in development theory that underpins the policies of liberalization, state withdrawal and structural adjustment favored by official donors. NGOs are viewed as the 'private non-profit' sector, the performance of which advances the 'public-bad', and 'private good' ideology of the new orthodoxy (Hulme, 1997).

[20] Source: CWF (1994, p. 8).

[21] ADB (2002).

[22] For details see, Brinkerhoff et al. (2007); Edwards and Hulme (1997).

[23] NGOs cover more than 80% of the villages in Bangladesh. However, it was argued that these NGOs cover only 20% of the rural marginal poor (ADB, 2003).

[24] See for instance, http://www.mra.gov.bd/index.php?option=com_content&view=category&layout=blog&id=29&Itemid=80

[25] According to the Ministry of Finance (2010). 'Some of them are BRAC, ASA, PROSHIKA, Swanirvor Bangladesh, Shokti Foundation, TMSS, SSS etc'.

[26] As of May 24, 2011 by using an online exchange rate calculator.

[27] The following clarifications are given for the stated issues: 'In Bangladesh interest on microcredit is calculated on a flat-rate which leads to misunderstanding and confusion about the effective rate of interest. Due to this method of calculation the effective rate of interest charged apparently at 15% goes up to a minimum of 30% which is not clear to many including the clients. Under this method, if a client borrows Taka 1,000 at 15% per annum, the total amount to be paid back at the end of the year is calculated first, which works out to Taka 1,150 (Principal 1,000 + Interest 150). If the MFI recovers this total amount in 50 installments, each installment is calculated to be equal to Taka 23 (Taka 1,000 divided by 50 = Taka 20 against the principal and Taka 150 divided by 50 = Taka 3 against the interest). This in effect means that at the time of repayment of each installment, interest is still calculated on the original principal of Taka 1,000. For example, when the 50th installment is paid, the principal amount outstanding is only Taka 20, and the interest at 15% per annum should be equal to Taka 0.108 instead of Taka 3 that is charged under the system. This results in the effective rate of interest increasing to as much as double the original rate i.e., 30%'.

[28] A similar finding is true for Government agencies.

[29] Different NGOs and GO agencies follow different criteria for targeting beneficiaries.

[30] Livelihoods thinking date back to the work of Robert Chambers in the mid-1980s.

[31] Functioning is an achievement either by a person or by an organization (Sen, 1985)

[32] For details see, Khan, 2010; Van Niekerk, 1996 and Parasuraman, 1988.

Chapter Four

Methodology: Development of Questionnaire and Data Collection

4.1 Introduction

This chapter discusses the multi-stage district, village and sample selection process. A formal questionnaire[1] containing 97 questions (derived from Chapters 2 and 3) has been used to collect data during the period August 20 to December 5, 2009. As the main objective of this study is to explore and compare the real impact of microcredit-driven GO and NGO projects in the lives of the poor, we have collected data purposively in a way that our respondents have only borrowed credit from the stated organizations and have not taken any other livelihood services such as sanitation or water supply facilities. It is important to mention that these loans are not conditioned to be used in conjunction with the non-financial facilities (such as schooling or social mobilization) of the agencies. For instance, in many remote areas NGOs do not have their schools or medical centres. Thus, poor people, in this regard, are totally dependent on microcredit provided by the NGOs and have no choice other than utilizing public facilities. Credit generates income and poor people can spend their money on either NGO facilities or government ones. Furthermore, this study is not focused on a particular government agency or NGO. This can be justified by the fact that in Bangladesh there is little dispersion of size and activities between GO agencies and between NGOs and only few NGOs (such as Grameen Bank, BRAC, PROSHIKA, ASA, RDRS) and Government agencies (such as Anser VDP Bank, BRDB, BARD, Agricultural bank, etc.) are operating nationally. We aim to develop a model by aggregating information of the existing agencies of both sectors. Although this study aggregates the responses of the beneficiaries of GO agencies and NGOs, the method and result will help rank the effectiveness of various GO agencies and various NGOs with respective to poverty alleviation.

At the time of collecting the primary data, first we have asked the following four questions to the respondents. Only those who have qualified with these questions were asked the remaining livelihood-relevant questions. Thus, households have been chosen randomly by considering four criteria which are: 1) respondents' current income has been generated by the financial support (microcredit) provided by either government or NGO projects and they don't have any other sources of income (such as another family member working in the city areas or abroad); 2) each respondent has only one credit scheme (loan size between US $100-150) from either government or NGO; 3) households with less than half an acre of land were eligible for the study (similar approach was used by Khandkar, 2001) and 4) only those respondents who have borrowed for last 6-8 years have been included in the sample. Previous studies found that it takes approximately 6 years for a poor member to come above the poverty line and it generally takes 8 years before the member is able to function independently from the microcredit institution (Khandker and Chowdhury, 1996). The above mentioned conditions are made to make sure that the present economic and social states of the respondents, to large extent, are the results of the credit-driven project. It is important to mention that our main objective of the study is to compare the effectiveness of credit-driven GO and NGOs, not to compare the living standard of the borrowers and non-borrowers. Thus, we have not collected information about the livelihood status of the non-borrowers[2]. Reviewing all the respondents, it was found that few of them were richer people during their preliminary membership, who had alternative financing ability from sources other than NGO-MFIs including commercial banks and other lending sources. Responses of these respondents were dropped at the time of analysing the data.

The following equation, as suggested by Scheaffer et al. (1996), has been used to determine the number of samples with at least a 95% level of confidence on statistical interference for a given error tolerance.

$$\mathbf{N \geq p\ (1\text{-}p)\ [Z_{\alpha/2}\ /\ e]^2}$$

Where $Z_{\alpha/2}$ = 1.96 for a 95% confidence interval, N is the sample size, p is the proportion for observing a particular trait, e is the error tolerance (given in the units of p, that is, a percentage point). The following sample size can be identified by using the Z-table for 1%, 2% and 5% error tolerance at 95% confidence level.

Confidence interval (CI)	**Error tolerance (% point)**	**Required sample size**
95% ($Z_{\alpha/2} = 1.96$)	1	9604
95% ($Z_{\alpha/2} = 1.96$)	2	2401
95% ($Z_{\alpha/2} = 1.96$)	5	**385**

A 5% error tolerance level has been considered at a 95% level of significance with a prediction that the poverty level of Bangladesh will be between 38% and 34% within next 3 years[3]. In the first set of data (see the discussion on the second set in Section 4.8), a total of 562 questionnaires have been filled in; by 292 male respondents and 270 are female respondents[4]. Of all the respondents, 80% are between the ages of 26-45 years and 100% respondents are microcredit recipients with 85% of these having loans of less than 10,000 Taka.

The areas chosen for the research are different districts and villages of Bangladesh, and the respondents have been selected based on the criteria stated above. Our district and village selection has been a multistage process incorporating different socio-economic measuring variables as shown in Fig-4.1.

Districts have been selected carefully to ensure that they all share many common economic, social and natural features such as degree of poverty, presence of natural calamity (flood and drought), soil type, occupations, agricultural labour size of the households, land-holding patterns, tenancy patterns, percentage of agricultural farms in the areas, literacy rates, crude birth and death rates, per capita expenditure, gender disparity, population density, use of utilities, wage rates, time it takes to travel from capital city, agricultural productivity and so on. We started the process from the Divisional level, and then based on the stated factors; we have selected districts, upazillas[5] and villages for data collection.

Figure 4.1: Sample selection and data collection procedure

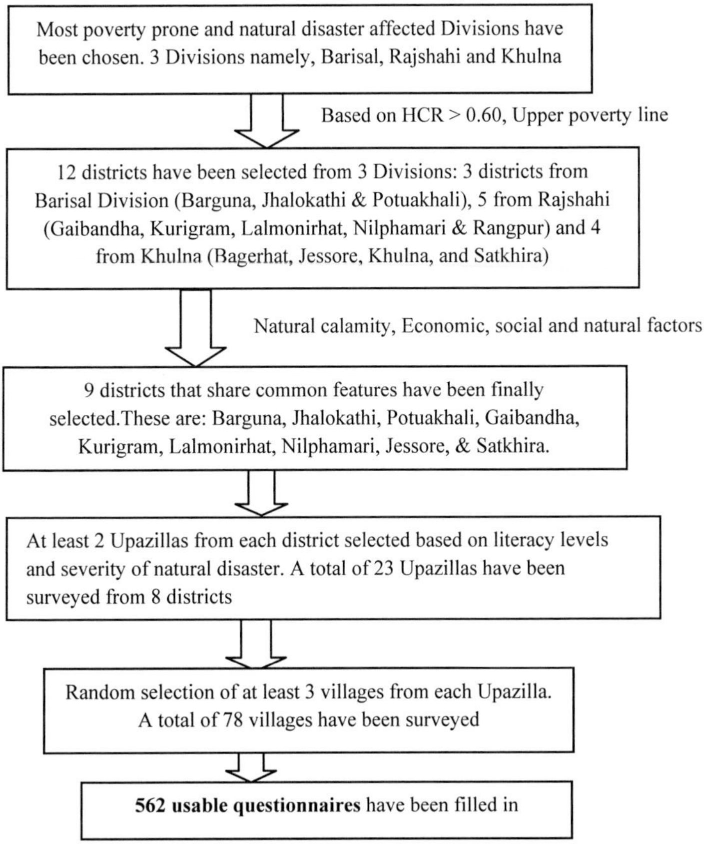

Note: Upazillas are the lowest level of administrative government in Bangladesh; HCR stands for Head Count Ratio.

4.2 Questionnaire preparation

The formal questionnaire **consists of eight sections** (excluding the first section that contains the general and demographic information of the respondents) and 97 questions[6]. It has been developed in English then translated into *Bengali* (the local language) and tested for comparability iteratively before the field survey began.

The second section of the questionnaire is about the health conditions of the respondents which include indicators such as capacity to work normally, average number of sick days of the family members over the last six months, morbidity status of the respondents, health status of other family members, access to public and private health care centres, choice of hospitals or clinics, mental stress status, length of illness of the family members and respondent, frequency of visits to doctors by women who are pregnant, etc.

The third section asks questions regarding education, literacy status, and training received. In this section, the indicators addressed are level of education, level and length of training in job or by the development partner, schooling of child and female family members, type of school chosen, etc.

The fourth section incorporates the items relevant to general wellbeing. Respondents have been asked about their access to electricity, pure water, sanitary latrine, and for different types of information including job, health, education, financial help, natural disaster, political and government activities. In addition, the respondents have been asked about their frequency of contact with beneficial information sources (such as government and NGO offices, the local news agency and library), amount of food intake per day by males, females and children in the family, shock and shortage time food distribution and availability of leisure time per day.

Section 5 is the largest section in the questionnaire consisting of 16 individual asset and income related questions. The questions in this section have been designed to extract information about land-holding size and status, the types of other asset-holding including the approximate market value, type of house and its ownership, occupation, income, savings and expenditure per month, the types of spending on food and non-food items and the relative share of total expenditure, total employment per year, calamity time employment, the contribution by male and female members to the family income, form of savings etc.

Section 6 highlights the issues relevant to empowerment and decision-making which include identifying the major decision makers at home, the extent to which the respondents can make decisions at work, whether they are invited to participate in the local decision-making meetings, whether they are members of any cooperatives, if they can express their opinion in local decision-making committees and cooperative meetings, whether they cast their vote every time, and whether they choose their preferred candidates freely, etc.

Section 7 includes items relevant to security such as experience of violence, robbery and theft by the local majority group, whether or not they can perform their social, cultural and political works freely, how they are treated by government and NGO officials, etc.

Section 8 reflects opinions about support services. This section has been designed to collect information about the support received from the development partners. In this section, respondents have been asked about their choice of GO or NGO, length of membership with the partner, types of help received, the amount of microcredit taken, length of borrowing, loan repayment status, the degree of monitoring and consultation by the partners, etc.

Section 9 of the questionnaire contains questions regarding the perception of the beneficiaries about the performance of the development partners particularly in the services provided. This section is included in order to develop a multidimensional service delivery scale to assess the effectiveness of development partners – the first and second objectives of the study. In this section, 26 questions have been included all with a 5-point Likert scale where 1 denotes highly dissatisfied and 5 stands for highly satisfied. The questions in this section highlight the institutional administration, service delivery mechanism, marketing, skill and knowledge of the workers and managers, decision-making processes, timeliness in service delivery and so on of the development partners (see Section 3.5 for details).

It is important at this stage to mention that the formal questionnaire contains a mixed mode of questions and includes questions with multiple options organized with a Likert-type scale and dichotomous in nature. There is no open-ended qualitative question asked in the questionnaire. However, since the author has conducted the survey face to face, additional relevant qualitative comments and opinions of the beneficiaries have been utilized to strengthen the statistical findings of the study.

4.3 Poverty maps and the choice of Divisions

We have begun the sample selection process with the aid of 'poverty maps' produced by the Bangladesh Bureau of Statistics (BBS) and the World Bank (WB) in collaboration with the World Food Program (WFP)[7]. The earlier poverty map was based on the 2001 HIES which was then upgraded based on HIES-2005. In preparing the poverty map, the BBS and the WB have followed the 'Small Area Estimation' method offered by Elbers (2003)[8] since it incorporates both the population census of 2001 and HIES-2005.

The head count ratio (HCR), which measures poverty as a percentage of the rural population who have fallen below the poverty line, has been used in our analysis for the purpose of district selection. There are two reasons why HCR is used for the selection purpose: First, policy-makers in developing countries are mostly interested in the incidence of poverty. Second, Datta and Ravallion's (1992) finding shows that the signs and magnitudes of parameters in the poverty equation do not change very much; whether poverty is measured by the incidence of poverty or by a poverty gap index. Data show that poverty rates within the upper poverty line in six Divisions of Bangladesh – Barisal, Rajshahi, Khulna, Chittagong, Sylhet and Dhaka – based on head count ratio are 52%, 51.2%, 45.7%, 34%, 33.8% and 32% respectively[9]. This data have been used primarily to identify the most poverty prone Divisions in Bangladesh – Barisal, Rajshahi and Khulna.

When analysing the poverty status at the district level, the researcher found that a few districts of the Divisions of Sylhet and Chittagong are severely poverty prone, especially the Hobiganj and Sunamgonj districts in Sylhet Division, and the Bandarban district of Chittagong Division. All have a poverty head count ratio of more than 0.52 based on the upper poverty line[10]. These districts have not been incorporated into our analysis, however, because of two fundamental reasons. First, these districts have different geographical characteristics of the traditional flat land of Bangladesh. For example, Hobiganj and Sunamgonj are hilly areas and particularly Sunamgonj is a haor[11] area where the population density is low and work opportunity is low, thus creating more poverty. On the other hand, the Bandarban district is one of very high hills (hill tracts) and is considered the most remote area in Bangladesh. Second, the poverty profile of Sylhet and Chittagong Divisions shows that the overall poverty rate is much lower than other districts of the stated Divisions. Based on all these facts, Barisal, Rajshahi and Khulna Divisions have been considered for the sample district selection purpose.

4.4 District selection process

Several economic, social, cultural and natural variables have been considered when selecting districts for data collection.

4.4.1 Head Count Ratio (HCR): the first determinant of district selection

After selecting the Divisions, we have turned to the selection of districts from the respective Divisions. In selecting districts, the severity of poverty with a head count ratio (HCR) based on the upper poverty line has been used as the first criterion. It is found in the literature[12] that the HCR rate of maximum poverty in Bangladesh is above 0.60. Therefore, the most poverty-prone areas have been covered. Those districts where the HCR value is greater than 0.60 have been chosen for the study. Data show that Barguna, Jhalokathi, and Potuakhali districts from the Barisal Division; Gaibandha, Kurigram, Lalmonirhat, Nilphamari and Rangpur districts from Rajshahi Division; and Bagerhat, Jessore, Khulna, and Satkhira districts from Khulna Division all have HCR values greater than 0.60 (BBS, 2008 HIES-2005)[13]. These twelve districts make up the primary selection list.

4.4.2 Natural calamities and poverty

Flood and cyclones frequently cause severe damage to the lives and livelihoods of the rural poor in Bangladesh. There is a clear correlation between poverty and vulnerability to natural disasters[14]. Poor households are to a much extent landless and they are mainly in low-lying regions near rivers and coasts. The Monga[15] and 'char'[16] areas in Bangladesh are closer to rivers and thus they are more vulnerable to flooding. The coastal areas are prone to severe tidal surges and cyclones. Attempts have been made to identify which areas are more vulnerable to the effects of flood, drought, cyclones, and tidal surge and it is found that the southern districts of Barguna, Potuakhali, Bhola, Bagerhat, Satkhira, Khulna are more exposed to severe tidal surges, and cyclones because all are coastal districts (see Fig-A4.2, A4.3 and A4.4 in the Appendix to this chapter). One important clarification required here is that the poverty status of the southern district of Bhola is very high (HCR greater than 0.52. See: BBS-HIES, 2005) yet this district has not been selected in our primary district selection list. Bhola is a 'char' (or island) area with occupation and land patterns being quite different from other plain areas of the country. Thus, to keep the similarity of characteristics of those selected, Bhola has been kept out of our selection list.

The northern districts of Bangladesh, namely Gaibandha, Kurigram, Lalmonirhat, Sirajgonj, Nilphamari, Rangpur, Pabna, and Mymenshing are often severely affected by floods (Monga) and drought[17] (see Fig-A4.1).

The northern region of Bangladesh is situated in the Tista and Jamuna basin, and contains many tributaries of these. Topography and climate make the area ecologically vulnerable to destabilizing variations including floods, river erosion, drought spells, and cold waves; all of which occur more frequently and intensely than in other regions. Amidst these compelling conditions, the local economy shows little diversification and is heavily dependent on agriculture – which yields only one or sometimes two annual harvests, in contrast with three crops per year in more fertile and benign parts of the country. In this setting, local employment is limited from September through December – in average years. As the landless and poorest survive on agricultural wage, their opportunities and ensuing incomes drop in this period, and they become trapped in a condition what is called *Monga*[18].

The monga region is economically weaker than other regions in Bangladesh (Rahman, 1991 and 2005; Zug, 2006a, 2006b). As no comprehensive study with regional comparisons of economies is available, we use GDP as a rough guideline. Table 4.1 shows that of the whole monga-affected areas, five districts in particular are in a weak position, with Gaibandha especially being the lowest in all of Bangladesh (in terms of per capita GDP). Taking GDP components of manufacturing, we selected three districts with the lowest productivity in this sector, namely Lalmonirhat, Nilphamari and Kurigram. In these areas, industrialization is far below the national average.

From the above analysis, it is clear that there is direct correlation between severity of natural calamity and vulnerability to poverty where there is less economic development. Thus, both indicators – HCR and effects of natural calamities – are common in the twelve districts selected.

We then have incorporated the effect of natural calamities (flood and drought) of different years on the selected districts to show that these districts have been the victims of such calamities over many years.

4.4.2A Flood, drought and tidal surge

For the analysis of natural calamities, we have included information on **four different calamities** faced by the selected districts, namely drought, tidal surge, flood and cyclones. Data show that the severity of drought is extreme in the districts of Gaibandha, Kurigram, Lalmonirhat, Nilphamari, and Rangpur, whereas, in other selected districts there is almost no evidence of drought[19].

By analysing the data produced by the Ministry of Food and Disaster Management (MFODM), GoB and BBS, the researcher found that the effects of **tidal surge** in different years (from 2000–2008) are extreme in the districts of Barguna, Potuakhali, Bagerhat, Khulna and Satkhira, whereas it has only moderate effects in Jhalokathi and almost no effect in Gaibandha, Kurigram, Lalmonirhat, Nilphamari, and Rangpur districts[20].

Table 4.1: Per capita GDP and manufacturing productivity in the northern districts

	Per capita GDP		Manufacturing (category of the GDP)	
Districts/Country	**In taka**	**% of national average**	**In Taka**	**% of national average**
Gaibandha	12444	67.2	400	14.7
Kurigram	13757	74.3	341	12.5
Lalmonirhat	13855	74.8	254	9.3
Nilphamari	13292	71.8	263	9.7
Rangpur	14936	80.7	820	30.1
Bangladesh	18511	100	2720	100

Source: BBS, 2004; Statistical Yearbook-2004, p. 495 and p. 506-568.

Attempts have been made to observe the impact of **floods** in the stated districts in different years. It is found in the literature that the highest depth of flood in Bangladesh ranges from 80cm to 90cm (MFODM-GOB, 2008; Banerjee, 2008). Based on this information, the severity of flood in the selected districts for the years 1987, 1995, 1998, 1999, 2005 and 2007 – the years of the most devastating floods has been investigated. Among these years, 1995 is a minor flood year, whereas in other years the flood has been observed to have 'major impact' by the MFODM of GoB.

In 1997, Barguna, Potuakhali, Gaibandha, Kurigram, Rangpur, Bagerhat and Khulna districts were classified as extremely flood damaged, whereas Jhalokathi, Lalmonirhat, Nilphamari, Jessore, and Satkhira were classified as moderately affected districts[21]. In 1995 (a minor flood year), Potuakhali, Jessore and Khulna districts were extremely flood affected and the remaining nine districts had experienced low levels of damage[22]. Potuakhali, Gaibandha, Kurigram, Lalmonirhat, Nilphamari, Rangpur, Bagerhat, and Khulna were severely affected by the flood of 1998, whereas Barguna, Jhalokathi, and Jessore districts had moderate impacts, with Satkhira being less affected still[23]. A major flood year was 1999 when there were devastating impacts on Barguna, Potuakhali, Gaibandha, Kurigram, Lalmonirhat, Nilphamari, Rangpur, Bagerhat, and Khulna districts. In the same year, the effect of flood was moderate in Jhalokathi, Jessore, and Satkhira district (Banerjee, 2008).

In 2005, the extreme flood-prone districts were Barguna, Potuakhali, Gaibandha, Kurigram, Nilphamari, and Rangpur with a moderate impact in the districts such as Jhalokathi, Lalmonirhat, Bagerhat, and Khulna[24]. In the same year, Jessore and Satkhira were declared by MFODM, GoB to be less affected. The year 2007 was a massive destructionyear due to both flood and cyclones that happened in the same year. Data show that Barguna, Potuakhali, Gaibandha, Kurigram, Lalmonirhat, Nilphamari, Rangpur, and Bagerhat suffered severe destruction in the flood of 2007, whereas Jhalokathi, Jessore, and Khulna were moderately affected[25]. The impact of flood in the same year was comparatively less in Satkhira district.

After compiling all the above stated information, we prepared the general view of the impact of flood on the selected districts in different years. Data show that Barguna, Potuakhali, Gaibandha, Kurigram, Lalmonirhat, Nilphamari, Rangpur, and Bagerhat are the severe flood victim districts in different years, while Jhalokathi, Jessore, Khulna, and Satkhira are seen to be moderately affected ones.

4.4.2B Cyclones

In addition to flood, cyclone has devastating impacts on the lives of the vulnerable poor in Bangladesh. Data have been gathered for the years 2007-2009 as Bangladesh experienced most damaging cyclones namely SIDR in 2007, Reshmi and Bijli in 2008 and finally Aila in 2009. Result[26] shows that the districts of northern Bangladesh (Gaibandha, Kurigram, Lalmonirhat, Nilphamari, and Rangpur) were totally free from the effect of any cyclones between 2007 and 2009.

In 2007, cyclone Sidr had an extreme impact on the southern districts of Barguna. Jhalokathi, Potuakhali, Bagerhat, Khulna, and Satkhira with Jessore had been moderately affected[27] (see Fig-A4.2). Reshmi and Bijli were the two major cyclones of the year 2008 (Bijli struck on April 17, and Reshimi on October 27, 2008). Their tracks show that the most affected areas were Barguna, Potuakhali, Bagerhat, Khulna, Jessore, and Satkhira[28] (see Fig-A4.3). The cyclones did not affect the Jhalokathi and northern districts of Bangladesh. Cyclone Aila caused damage to several districts of southern Bangladesh on May 26, 2009 (see Fig-A4.4). Data from MFODM-GoB and USAID show that Potuakhali, Bagerhat, Jessore, and Satkhira were severely affected by Aila, while Barguna and Jhalokathi face moderate damage. One important finding to be noted that whenever there were natural calamities, the mostly affected areas were the northern and southern parts of Bangladesh and thus we have chosen 12 different districts from these two regions.

4.4.3 Economic variables for district selection

In this and later sections, we will continue the district selection process with the aid of several major economic variables such as agricultural labour, land ownership pattern, wage rate, per capita expenditure, etc.

4.4.3A Agricultural labour, tenancy and land ownership

As our targeted samples are from rural Bangladesh, our first set of variables is related to agricultural engagement and land ownership patterns of the households in the selected twelve districts. We have started with the **percentage of households who are agricultural labourers.** Because agriculture is the dominant sector for rural employment in Bangladesh, and around 70% of rural people are directly or indirectly dependent on agriculture for their living. Data show that the proportion of people who are agricultural labourers is 27.62% in Barguna, 21.41% in Jhalokathi, 27.31% in Potuakhali, 49.33% in Gaibandha, 55.95% in Kurigram, 50.99% in Lalmonirhat, 48.72% in Nilphamari, 46.44% in Rangpur, 39.58% in Bagerhat, 42.44% in Jessore, 39.86% in Khulna, and 53.02% in Satkhira. One important finding is that these percentages are higher in the northern districts and in a few southern districts than in other districts. They are even above the national average of 36%. This finding shows a similarity among the selected districts based on percentage of households involved in agricultural labour. The higher percentage of agricultural labourers in the northern districts is due to limited demand for labour in other sectors, especially due to a low level of industrialization (Table 4.1). Unequal land distribution combined with the lack of alternative work sources results in a very high share of agricultural labour households[29] in the region (Zug, 2006a). Moreover, the percentage of agricultural households is comparatively less in Rangpur district (46.44%). The underlying reason is that Rangpur is more industrialized compared to other northern districts as shown in Table 4.1. In Rangpur, tobacco processing industries employ a significant number of people. These positive standings may encourage us to drop Rangpur from the final selection as there are other districts from the same area (or Division) having poorer conditions.

Our next economic variable for comparison is the percentage of total households that are **landless**. This variable has been chosen because in the rural areas the economic condition and status of a person depend largely on land ownership. In addition, for most of the rural Bangladeshi people, land is the only source of income and the preferred collateral for loans. Data show that except for Jhalokathi district (only 3.1%), the percentage of landless people is very high or similar in chosen districts. This strong point could result in dropping Jhalokathi in the final stage of the district selection process. The results show a similar pattern of landless people in the initially selected districts with landless rates being 8.63% in Barguna, 8.58% in Potuakhali, 14.67% in Gaibandha, 14.68% in Kurigram, 16.63% in Lalmonirhat, 15.34% in Nilphamari, 14.76% in Rangpur, 11.64% in Bagerhat, 10.61% in Jessore, 14.15% in Khulna, and 8.75% in Satkhira[30]. The higher percentage of landless people in the rural areas is due to lower wage rates contributing to very low levels of savings. In addition, river erosion makes many people landless and destitute in southern Bangladesh. During economic hardship, poor people sell their lands and migrate to cities. This migration of unlimited labour has profound impact on the wage rates in both rural and urban areas. We will discuss this issue further in later sections.

The next economic variable for the district-wise comparison is the **percentage of households who are tenants**. These households do not have their own land and thus rent the land from the owner for a specific time period (in Bengali called *Barga*). Data show that percentages of rural households who are tenants are 28.13%, 24.99%, 24.34%, 33.07%, 35.76%, 35.84%, 33.56%, 33.49%, 29.4%, 34.65%, 32.79% and 31.23% for Barguna, Jhalokathi, Potuakhali, Gaibandha, Kurigram, Lalmonirhat, Nilphamari, Rangpur, Bagerhat, Jessore, Khulna and Satkhira district respectively (Agricultural Census, 2008; BBS-GoB). One interesting finding is that the Divisional average percentage of tenancy is quite close for Khulna and Rajshahi Divisions (35.69% for Khulna and 35.38% for Rajshahi), giving an impression of similarity between all the districts in these two Divisions. The average tenancy rate for the Barisal Division is somewhat lower (27.83%) than the other two Divisions. However, our next variable-percentage of households having agricultural farms[31] – which shows the percentage of people who are engaged only in agricultural work for their livelihood – is a better way to compare among the districts and Divisions. Results show that the percentages are quite similar among the chosen districts and this justifies our selection of districts based on shared common economic features.

Statistics on **percentage of households operating small agricultural farms** reveal that the rate is 69.96% in Barguna, 74.55% in Jhalokathi, 66.78% in Potuakhali, 56.22% in Gaibandha, 57.57% in Kurigram,

62.14% in Lalmonirhat, 55.35% in Nilphamari, 56.12% in Rangpur, 66.07% in Bagerhat, 64.53% in Jessore, 54.3% in Khulna, and 57.61% in Satkhira (Agriculture Census of Bangladesh, 2008). These data are very relevant to that of the percentage of landless people. For example, in the Barisal Division, the percentage is less than Khulna and Rajshahi Divisions. This explains why the percentage of tenants is greater in the Barisal Division than that of the other two Divisions. This means that the people of Barisal Division let others rent their land for agricultural purposes (not for other purposes such as housing or industrialization). This in turn provides them with an income source.

4.4.3B Wage rates and poverty

For many landless and marginal land holders, agricultural labour is the dominant source of income. In addition, as mentioned above, in our selected districts the level of industrialization is very low and this compels most people to earn a living by selling their labour in the agricultural sector. However, such income is unstable, seasonal, and vulnerable to natural disasters. As almost every year our selected districts suffer either from flood, drought or cyclones, this seasonal pattern of agricultural labour and its corresponding wage rate is a key determinant of rural poverty.

It is found that the northern and southern districts have the lowest wage rate in the country with 39–60 Taka (equals 0.56-0.86 USD) per day[32]. Two major reasons for the lower wage rates are excess labour supply and a lack of agricultural diversification in those areas, especially in the Monga region (northern territory). Agricultural production in the Monga region is mainly paddy, while labour-intensive high-value crops such as vegetables are only rarely cultivated, thus keeping the wage rate well below the national average. Two southern districts – Barguna and Jhalokathi have higher wage rates ranging from 61–77 Taka (0.88 to 1.11 USD) per day. The wage rate in Bagerhat – another southern district – is comparatively much higher at 78–90 Taka (equals 1.13 to 1.30 US dollar) per day. Three reasons can be noted for this higher rate. First, the literacy rate of Bagerhat is quite high (58.7%) which helps more people get jobs in the industrial sectors of other districts, thus creating a shortage of labour in agriculture and this pushes wages up. Second, the population density of Bagerhat is quite low (only 382 per square kilometre) compared to other selected districts. This also creates more demand for agricultural labour. Third, statistics show that the percentage of landless rural people in Bagerhat is only 11.64%, indicating a shortage of agricultural labour which has inflationary impact on wage rates. From the agricultural wage point of view, we can see that two districts – Jhalokathi and Bagerhat – have comparatively higher wage rates than other selected districts and this increases the chance to drop these two districts from the final list. Other than Jhalokathi and Bagerhat, all other districts are similar in wage rate patterns and thus justify the choice of these districts.

4.4.3C Access to markets and poverty

Improved access to markets is an important element of rural development and poverty alleviation (WB and WFP 2009). As most of the businesses are located in the capital city of Dhaka in Bangladesh, it is important to note how long it takes to access the capital city from the primarily selected districts. The reason is that there exists a high correlation between travel time to Dhaka and poverty incidence according to the BBS study (2009). The report claims that from coastal areas it takes more time to get to the capital and those districts have severe presence of poverty and for that reason it would be wise to compare the primarily selected districts based on distance criterion. In addition, the distance factor leads to a comparative disadvantage for the production and marketing of agricultural and non-agricultural products.

Data suggest that other than Rangpur and Khulna (from where it takes slightly more than 8 hours), it takes more than ten hours to reach Dhaka from other ten districts such as Barguna, Jhalokathi, Kurigram, Gaibandha, Lalmonirhat, Nilphamari and so on[33]. From Rangpur, travel time is lower because better roads and highways were built due to the industrial zones of the district. Moreover, Rangpur is a stronghold of former President General Ershad and his party. They built highways connecting this district with the capital at the time of his presidency. On the other hand, Khulna, being the Divisional headquarters, is better integrated with the capital city. However, this whole discussion gives us a positive indication of similarity among the districts chosen based on required time to reach Dhaka.

4.4.3D Per capita expenditure

Per capita expenditure is one vital indicator of the living standards of a community which necessarily explores the purchasing power pattern of that community. Thus, districts have been evaluated based on their per capita expenditure to get a better idea of the economic conditions.

Data show that the lowest per capita expenditure in Bangladesh is in Nilphamari with an amount close to two thousands Taka (1,956) per year.

For Gaibandha, Kurigram, Lalmonirhat, Jessore, and Satkhira per capita expenditure is 2194, 2707, 2404, 2846 and 2088 Taka respectively[34]. Jhalokathi and Barguna have slightly higher per capita expenditure of 4385 and 4214 Taka respectively. Per capita expenditure in the range of 3000 to 4000 Taka was found in the districts such as Potuakhali (3307), Rangpur (3330), and Bagerhat (3250). Only one district – Khulna – was found to have a comparatively high level of per capita expenditure of 6167 Taka. As mentioned earlier, Khulna is the only district in our list which is the Divisional headquarters and therefore has better communications technologies and infrastructure, with a port facility (*Mongla* sea port). Thus, they have better earning and expenditure patterns. However, we will keep this finding in mind in refining our final district list. Other than Khulna, district data show that per capita expenditure ranges from more than two thousand to less than four thousand (acceptably less variation) in all 12 districts of our list.

4.4.4 Social variables in district selection process

4.4.4A Literacy rates and poverty susceptibility

As is widely known, education is critical to upward mobility and allowing access to job and earning opportunities. This is one of the most important determinants of poverty status in the literature[35]. Education levels are often highly correlated with poverty status 'by the heads of households'. However, like other characteristics, educational attainment by itself cannot explain all variations in poverty. For example, some coastal districts of Bangladesh record very high schooling rates (such as Potuakhali, Bhola, Noakhali) while they are also amongst the poorest areas in the country. Data show that the northern part of Bangladesh has lowest literacy rates. For example, the literacy rates in Gaibandha, Kurigram, Lalmonirhat, Nilphamari, and Rangpur districts are 35.7%, 33.4%, 42.3%, 39.8% and 42.9% respectively[36]. Among these, Kurigram has the lowest literacy in the whole country. On the other hand, literacy rates are quite high in Jhalokathi (65.4%), Bagerhat (58.7%), and Khulna (57.8%) districts. This is why, the wage rates of these three districts were found to be comparatively high. Other districts, like Barguna and Satkhira are middle of the road in relation to literacy rates compared to our listed districts. Other than Jhalokathi, Khulna, and Bagerhat, literacy rate patterns are similar in other selected districts and all of them have a lower rate compared to the national literacy rate of 56.1%[37]. The results of this important dimension of poverty will be utilized to refine our list further.

4.4.4B Crude birth and death rate and population density

Crude birth and death rates, population density and gender disparity data have been analysed to compare among the listed districts. Statistics on crude birth rate (CBR) show that in most of the districts, rates range between 21 and 26 per thousand for Potuakhali, Gaibandha, Nilphamari, Lalmonirhat, Rangpur, Bagerhat, Khulna, and Satkhira. Kurigram has a high CBR of 31.31 and only two districts, namely Barguna and Jessore have a CBR less than 20. However, an important finding is that the CBR of most of the listed districts is more than that of the national CBR of 20.9 (Economic Review by MOF-GoB, 2008, p. xix) which shows their similarity in social factor.

Crude death rates (CDR) are comparatively lower in the districts of Khulna Divisions with 5.79 per thousand for Bagerhat, 5.22 per thousand for Jessore, 4.34 per thousand for Khulna, and 5.77 per thousand for Satkhira (BBS, 2008). That these rates are even lower than the national CDR of 6.2 (Ministry of Finance, 2008, p. xix), especially that of Khulna (4.34 per thousand), is worth noting. On the other hand, districts such as Kurigram, Lalmonirhat, and Nilpahamari are all in an alarming position with rates as high as 9.52, 8.61 and 8.17 respectively. The remaining districts (Barguna, Jhalokathi and Potuakhali) have higher CDR compared to the national average.

Even though population density per square kilometre among the listed districts is somewhat diverse, they are all below the national average of 979/square km. Data show that all the listed districts of Rajshahi Division have a population density within the range of 800 to 1000 persons per square km. The values are 971, 810, 877, 945 and 990 person/square km for the Gaibandha, Kurigram, Lalmonirhat, Nilphamari and Rangpur districts respectively. On the other hand, density statistics for the districts of Khulna Division are diverse[38] and range from 350 to 1000 persons/square km. This statistic is similar in the case of the districts of Barisal Division. That means there is a Division-wise disparity in population density. However, it is important to note that all the listed districts have rates below the national average. In the population density data of Bagerhat district, it is especially important to note that there are only 382 persons/square km. This doesn't match other districts in the list in this regard. This shows a diverse character of Bagerhat district which differs from others, and this is a point that we will consider at the time of final district refinement.

4.4.4C Gender disparity

With gender equality being the central theme of policy-making in developing countries, the integration of women into the development process, and therefore women's participation in economic activities alongside men, has been gaining importance in many national plans (Lewina, 1999). It is now widely recognized mainly because of global awareness and NGO movements that women's contribution to development is essential for the success of national development as well as for poverty alleviation, and thus this variable too is important for the purpose of comparison.

The Centre for Policy Dialogue (CPD), Bangladesh, in collaboration with UNFPA has conducted a survey on gender issues in several districts of Bangladesh. Different dimensions such as disparity in education, wage rates, nutrition, earnings and occupations have been analysed in the report. Considering all these factors, a district-wise summary profile for gender disparity has been constructed. Surprisingly, the report shows that nine out of twelve selected districts reveal a low level of gender disparity, whereas only two districts (Nilphamari and Khulna) show moderate gender disparity (CPD-UNFPA, 2008). Only in Satkhira district the gender disparity is reported to be high. One major reason for low gender disparity is of course the massive NGO movement in the stated districts where women are preferred as microcredit recipients. Findings from this final social factor further strengthen the argument that the selected districts are of a similar pattern from both economic and social view points.

4.4.5 Natural factors

At this point an explanation of the characteristics of natural factors (especially soil pattern) is important. As mentioned earlier, we mainly selected districts from the plain lands and avoided special areas such as haors, islands, hills, etc. Table 4.2 shows the type of soil of the primarily selected districts.

Data from Table 4.2 show that the annual rainfall, temperature, humidity and soil structure are quite similar in the districts listed above. However, due to a few changes in soil types, agricultural products are slightly different in the southern and northern regions.

Table 4.2: Soil pattern, humidity and annual rainfall of the selected districts

District	Soil characteristics	Annual rainfall and (temperature)
Gaibandha	Silty clay with gray silty	2727 mm (32.9 – 11.7 degree) 86% humidity
Kurigram	Barind trackt silty clay, alluvium	2727 mm (32.7 – 11.5 degree) 83% humidity
Nilphamari	Brown loamy soil, gray silty, alluvium	2605 mm (31.8 – 11.7 degree) 85% humidity
Lalmonirhat	Non calcareous gray silty alluvium	2728 mm (32.6 – 11.8 degree) 84% humidity
Rangpur	Gray silty clay	2576 mm (33.4 – 12 degree) 85% humidity
Potuakhali	Silty clay, tidal flood plain, alluvium	2678 mm (35.9 – 13.4 degree) 51-81% humidity
Jhalokathi	Non calcareous gray silty alluvium	2997 mm (34.5 – 12.4 degree) 60-84% humidity
Barguna	Silty clay, tidal flood plain, alluvium	2987 mm (33 – 11.7 degree) 71-82% humidity
Satkhira	Silty lands with clay from tidal flood	2230 mm (36 – 12.8 degree) 64-84% humidity
Jessore	Gray clay, silty clay and flood alluvium	2299 mm (37.5 – 11.8 degree) 68-87% humidity
Khulna	Silty lands with clay from tidal flood	2877 mm (33.2 – 11.4 degree) 84% humidity
Bagerhat	Gray silty, non calcareous alluvium	2877 mm (34 – 11.5 degree) 83% humidity

Source: Community Series data, BBS-2007.

4.5 Finalizing the district list

Our primarily listed districts have been Barguna, Jhalokathi and Potuakhali from the Barisal Division; Gaibandha, Kurigram, Lalmonirhat, Nilphamari and Rangpur from Rajshahi Division; and finally Bagerhat, Jessore, Khulna and Satkhira from the Khulna Division. Each and every district has been evaluated individually against each of the other districts on the list based on the socio-economic variables discussed earlier.

- **Rangpur** district can be dropped from the final selection because, as mentioned earlier, Rangpur is famous for its tobacco industries, and thus creates a lot of industrial employment. Per capita expenditure of Rangpur is 3330 Taka which is much higher than the other districts of the northern territory. Moreover, Rangpur has the lowest CDR (5.86 per thousand) in the list. Rangpur district is also privileged because of its improved communication (especially road ways) with other parts of the country and in particular, its relatively easy access to the capital city market, given that it takes less than 8 hours to travel to the capital. Last but not least is that we want to have participating districts from all three poverty-prone Divisions. From Rajshahi Division, we have four more disadvantaged districts other than Rangpur. From that priority point of view, and considering other socio-economic factors, we can exclude Rangpur from our final set of districts.

- **Bagerhat district** has been found to be in a good socio-economic position and is a candidate to be dropped from the final list. The fundamental factors behind this decision are wage rates, population density, literacy rates and percentage of landless rural people in the district. Data show that the wage rates of Bagerhat are too high to compare (78–90 Taka per day) with other districts, and this is due to its very high literacy rate of 59% (even higher than the national average of 56.1%). Particularly the population density of the district is worth mentioning at only 382 person/square km which is much lower than other districts (the average is 800 persons/square km). Moreover, the percentage of rural landless people in Bagerhat is only 11.64%. Even though the effect of natural calamities (particularly tidal surge and flood) has been severe here, based on its positive standing in economic and social factors, it has been decided to drop Bagerhat from the final list.
- Finally, **Khulna** has been disqualified because of many economic and social factors. Khulna is the Divisional headquarters and a port city, and thus has improved communication and market access. Employment generation in the district is high due to the export/import activities at the port. Statistics show that Khulna has the highest per capita expenditure of 6167 Taka with a very high literacy rate (57.8%) compared to other primarily selected districts. The crude death rate of the district is the lowest (4.34 person per thousand) on the list and even much below than the national average of 6.2. The district has been dropped from tyhe list due to such positive standings.

Nine districts namely, Barguna, Jhalokathi, and Potuakhali from Barisal Division; Gaibandha, Kurigram, Lalmonirhat and Nilphamari from Rajshahi Division and Jessore and Satkhira from Khulna Division have been selected for study purpose, after dropping three districts, namely Bagerhat, Rangpur and Khulna. It can now be seen that we have chosen the maximum number of districts from Rajshahi Division and that decision requires clarification. As the earlier discussion shows, the northern districts are the most disadvantaged in relation to all the socio-economic variables, and are more vulnerable to extreme effects of natural calamities. Therefore, it has been decided to select more districts from the northern part of the country, and chosen four of them from Rajshahi Division. For example, the average values of the percentages of agricultural labour (43.98%), landless rural people (13.99%) and the percentage of tenancy (35.38%) are higher in Rajsahhi Division than those of Barisal and Khulna. If we look to the individual districts, we can see that wage rates, per capita expenditure, and literacy rates of the northern districts are lowest compared to other districts. Moreover, these districts are of high population density, higher poverty, high CBR and CDR. Their access time to the capital city is comparatively higher than other districts. Most importantly, the impact of natural calamity, especially floods and drought, is maximum in these districts. All these factors influenced us to select more districts from the more poverty- and natural calamity-prone Rajshahi Division.

Surveyed districts: With a tentative plan to survey nine districts, finally data have been collected from eight districts excluding Satkhira. Two reasons behind that are: (1) time and resource constraints; and (2) it was convenient to survey Jhalokathi district which was on the way between Potuakhali and Barguna district.

4.6 Upazilla selection process

Upazilla from each district has been selected once the task of district selection has been done. It is important to note that data on each and every socio-economic variable at upazilla level is unavailable. For this reason, it has benn decided to choose upazillas from each districts based on two major criteria, namely literacy rates and the severity of natural calamity based on the availability of required information (although not for all districts). For simplicity and similarity in the selection process, upazillas in the selected districts with lower literacy rates have been selected. Table A4.2 shows the literacy rates of the upazillas in the selected districts.

4.6.1 Literacy and educational attainment

Data from Table A4.2 in the Appendix shows that the lowest literacy rate is noticed in Amtali (45.9%), Barguna Sadar (55.2%) and Betagi

(59.7%) upazilla in the Barguna district. In Potuakhali, the lowest literacy rates are found in Dashmina (41.8%), Galachipa (42.9%), Bauphal (52.7%) and Kalapara (53.3%) upazilla. Fulchari (27.7%), Sundarganj (31.1%) and Sadullapur (35.7%) upazillas have been found to have the lowest literacy rates in Gaibandha district. In Kurigram, Raumari (24.7%), Bhurungapur (29.6%), Chilmari (33.6%) and Ulipur (34.9%) have the lowest literacy rates among all the upazillas. Hatibandha (39.3%), Aditmari (39.8%) and Kaligonj (41.1%) upazilla in Lalmonirhat district have been found to experience lower literacy rates. In Nilphamari district, Jaldhaka (33.0%), Dimla (36.2%) and Domar (44.7%) upazilla have low literacy rates. Sharsha (42.7%), Chougacha (43.9%) and Keshabpur (47.2%) have been found to be lowest literacy rate upazillas in Jessore district. And finally, Satkhira, Shyamnagar (39.7%), Assasuni (40.9%) and Kolaroa (45.5%) indicate less literacy rates compared to other upazillas. In Jhalokathi the literacy rate is comparatively higher than other districts. We have chosen the least literate upazillas of Jhalokathi, namely Nolchiti (61.2%), Rajapur (64%), Sadar (64.2) and Konabali (59.6). Even though our plan is to select two upazillas per district, we have considered more upazillas on the list to keep the options open for increasing sample size.

4.6.2 Natural calamity and poverty

Researcher has also attempted to explore the impact of natural calamities in the upazillas of the selected districts. However, reports on post flood and drought situations for every district are not available and statistics are only found for the selected districts of Rajshahi Division. Table 4.3 demonstrates the effect of flood in selected upazillas in the northern territory of Bangladesh.

Table 4.3 shows that Fulchari, Shaghata, Sadullapur and Sundarganj are the most calamity-affected upazillas in Gaibandha district. In Nilpahamari, the most affected upazillas are Jaldhaka, Dimla and Domar. In Kurigram, flood has had the most devastating effect in Bhurungamari, Nageshwari, Ulipur, Chilmari and Roumari upazilla. And finally, Lalmonirhat Sadar, Aditmari, Kaligonj and Hatibandha are the most devastated areas in Lalmonirhat districts. These findings match our primarily selected upazillas (based on literacy rates) from the same districts which mean natural calamity-affected areas also have lower literacy rates. Based on these discussions, 30 upazillas have been selected for data collection procedure.

Table 4.3: List of Monga-affected areas in selected northern districts

Upazilla	Total number of villages	Number of affected villages	Number of affected families	Affected population
Gaibandha district				
Fulchari	82	82	30691	150386
Shaghata	135	135	59031	271544
Sadar	140	96	47679	228858
Sundarganj	186	186	86950	395623
Palashbari	110	107	36386	167376
Gobindaganj	375	243	76725	350320
Sadullapur	168	157	57199	257396
Nilpahamari District				
Jaldhaka	69	58	712	Not available
Dimla	53	50	4350	
Domar	47	43	3200	
Saidpur	40	21	211	
Kurigram district				
Bhurungamari	112	110	2092	Not available
Nageshwari	369	201	1860	
Sadar	264	133	1100	
Ulipur	358	315	43000	
Chilmari	144	123	NA	
Roumari	197	158	6500	
Rajarhat	180	98	4500	
Lalmonirhat district				
Sadar	148	101	21474	NA
Aditmari	102	98	6215	27138
Kaligonj	80	70	13127	62486
Hatibandh	65	54	11877	51855

Source: MOFDM-GOB data base. Report on 2007 flood.

Upazillas surveyed: A total of **23 upazillas** have been surveyed from eight districts. Among 23 upazillas, three are from Nilphamari district (Dimla, Jaldhaka and Kishoreganj), two from Barguna district (Betagi and

Barguna sadar), four from Lalmonirhat (Kaligonj, Aditmari, Hatibandha and Sadar), three from Kurigram (Nageshwari, Vurungamari and Fulbari), two from Jessore (Keshabpur and Sharsha), four upazillas (Nolchiti, Rajapur, Konabali and Sadar) from Jhalokathi, three from Gaibandha (Sadullapur, Sadar and Sundarganj), and finally, two of the largest upazillas of Potuakhali namely Golachipa and Kolapara have been surveyed. One upazilla (Raumari) from Kurigram district has been dropped from the list as it is found to be too remote.

4.7 Village selection technique

Villages have been selected at random from the chosen upazillas with a single criterion that they are more distant from the district headquarters such that the grass-roots level and most disadvantaged people could be surveyed. It could be argued that these people are deprived of many social facilities due to remoteness and the undeveloped infrastructure of the areas in which they live. Data have been collected randomly from local *Bazars* (small markets), individual homes, and while walking in the muddy streets of villages. A total of 78 villages have been surveyed from the listed 23 upazillas and in most cases three villages per upazilla were covered. Table 4.4 is a summary of the villages surveyed along with the total number of respondents.

Table 4.4: Summary of the districts, upazillas and villages surveyed with number of respondents

Districts (8)	Upazillas (23)	Villages (78)	Number of respondents
Nilphamari	Dimla, Jaldhaka, Kishoregonj	Jhunagach Chapani, Magura, Paikar para, Bogla Gari	83
Lalmonirhat	Kaligonj, Aditmari, Hatibandha, Lalmonirhat sadar	Komlabari, Kumrir Hat, Shalmar, Durakuthhi, Fulgach, Mishon Mor, Vatapora, Velabari, Boro Kamola Bari, Gobordhon, Sarpukur, Gila bari, sapti bari, Hari vanga, Jamuk tari, Nayek Gor Tadi	86

Districts (8)	Upazillas (23)	Villages (78)	Number of respondents
Kurigram[39]	Nageshwari, Vurungamari, Fulbari	Sukhati, Baidyabari, Bagdanga, Sontaspur Dewani Kahamar, Nolaya, Kamar Danga, Angaria, Nagar Banda, Chandra Khana, Taluk Simul Bari, Joar Hat, Fulmati, Paikarchara	45
Gaibandha	Sadulla Pur, Sadar, Sundarganj	South Kola Bari, Rogunath Pur, Robilat Pur, Chander Hat, Chapa Khamar, Kuptola, Khucra Para, Sundar Ganj, Vuruvaga, Mokhrom Pur, Jormo Nodi, Huramaya	64
Jessore	Keshabpur, Sharsha	Gopalmoti, Mirza Nagaar, Suborno Khali, Shib chandra pur, Horina pota	47
Jhalokathi	Nolchiti, Konabali, Rajapur, Sadar	Monohor Pur, Fulhal, Pargopal Pur, Sener Taluk, Mohadeb Pur, Chadkathi, Baroi Karan, Jagannath Pur, Fulkathi, Nurulla Pur	72
Potuakhali	Golachipa, Kolapara	Badurtoli, Rahamat Pur, Etim Khana, Notun Para, Nachna Para, Shanti pur Chaka Maiya, Daroga Pur, Chunga Bashar, Noiapara, Chingubia, Manik Chad, Kamar Howla, Cader Howla	120
Barguna	Betagi, Barguna Sadar	Baraitola, Dalvanga, Morkhali	45

4.8 Second set of data

Responses on 26 questions related to service delivery (Section 9 of the questionnaire) have further been collected from new groups of samples in order to validate the findings of the earlier samples (562 questionnaires, as discussed in Fig-4.1). Thus a new set of data have been collected. Four new districts of Bangladesh have been chosen on this issue, namely Barisal, Lakshmipur, Brahmanbaria, and Feni. These districts have been chosen randomly based on few criteria. For example, districts have been chosen which are neither in the southern nor in the northern side of Bangladesh. They are rather somewhere near the middle of the country and close to the capital city. Thus, Brahmanbaria and Feni have been chosen. Barisal district has been chosen because this is a more poverty-prone Divisional headquarters in Bangladesh. Lakshmipur has been chosen due to convenience of data collection and travelling. A total of 12 upazillas[40] and 29 villages[41] have been surveyed from these four districts. A total of 441 questionnaires were filled in from the stated areas. Eight questionnaires were found faulty due to missing information and threfore removed from the study. A total of 433 usable questionnaires have been obtained. However, due to the filtering of data, **finally 368 questionnaires** have been found to be appropriate for the analysis.

A total of 930 questionnaires (first set of 562 + second set of 368) were usable for this study and a summary of the samples can be found in Table 4.5.

Table 4.5: Summary of the samples of the study

	Number of sample	Percentage
Based on gender		
Male	467	50.2
Female	463	49.8
Type of beneficiary		
Government	413	44.4
NGOs	517	55.6
Age of the respondents		
21-25 years	40	4.3
26-30	210	22.6
31-35	196	21.3
36-40	191	20.5
41-45	141	15.2
46-50	143	15.4
51-55	7	0.8
Microcredit recipient	930	100

4.9 Pilot study and modification of the questionnaire

Before conducting the main survey, author organized a pilot study on a small sample (40 samples) in Patalkandi village of Bhuapur upazilla in Tangail district of Bangladesh. This district and village have been chosen as they have many similar characteristics[42] shared by other districts selected for final data collection. In addition, as can be seen in Table A4.1, the HPI index for Tangail increased in all the years under consideration. Moreover, the average annual change of HPI in this district is also very high. There were no significant problems found with the language or wording of the questionnaire at the time of pilot study. However, a few unexplored answers have been found in several questions with this face-to-face interview session. These are discussed below:

a) One of our questions is found related to the reasons for choosing a particular health care facility with four alternative answers: (1) prompt service (2) less expensive (3) better facility (4) close to home. At the time of the pilot study, a few respondents also mentioned that they choose a particular health care service (especially those who visit the village doctors) since such services can be taken on credit.
b) A second refinement was in the question about who in the family goes to school, which included options like (1) boys (2) girls (3) both (4) none. In few cases it was noticed that none of their children go to school because they are under-aged, which has not been initially mentioned in our answer options. We then asked people which school they prefer for their children with options: (1) government school, (2) private school and (3) NGO schools. However, many reported that their children go to *Madrasa*[43] (government and private) instead of formal school.
c) We had a question asking respondents the ownership status of lands with answering options: (1) bought new land (2) inherited land (3) sold out the owned one. While asking the question to the people living on the banks of the rivers, many replied that their land is lost in the sea.
d) Our next question was regarding listing of other assets (other than land) owned by the respondents. We found a few new answers in addition to those that are listed in the earlier questionnaire. Two new answers are: (1) bedding and (2) have nothing at all. In continuation of this question we have further asked them to report the value of other assets. As in the earlier question we introduced a

new answer: 'have nothing at all', and one new option has been added for the total value of the asset as 'zero Taka'.

e) We had three answers (owned house, rented house, buying with loan) in the question asking the respondents about their home-ownership status. In such circumstances, a few mentioned that they are living in government's free land (in Bengali called *Khas Land*) at no cost.
f) A final modification has been made in the question where they were asked about the source of their credit with options such as: (1) government (2) NGO and (3) informal rural lenders (also called *Mohajon*). Some mentioned that they got credit from the local co-operatives.

All of these above stated modifications have been made to the questionnaire and this refined version (see Appendix) has then been used for final survey in the selected districts.

Appendix B

Final questionnaire (English) after pilot study

Please circle your answer(s)

Section-1: General information:

Location: 1) Gender: a) M b) F
2) Age: a) 21-25 Yr b) 26-30 c) 31-35 d) 36-40
e) 41-45 f) 46-50 g) 51-55 h) 56-60 i) 60+
3) Marital status: a) Single b) Married c) Divorced d) Widowed
4) Household type: a) Single family (single earner)
b) Single family (multiple earners) c) Joint family (single earner)
d) Joint family (multiple earners)
5) Household size: ____________ Male kid ( ) Female kid ( )

Section-2: Health status

6) Do you have capacity to work normally (For example, can you work continuously 5 hours in a day)
a) Yes (always) b) Yes (Mostly) c) No
7) Who fell sick more often in the family
a) Male (adult) b) Male (Kid) c) Female (Adult) d) Female (Kid)
8) Average sick days/ month in last six months (For working people of the family):
a) Male _________ b) Female ___________
9) How often do you suffer from any health problem:
a) Always b) Very often c) Sometimes d) Rarely e) No
10) Do you have access to public health care (close to home)
a) Yes b) No
11) Do you have capacity to get access to private health care
a) Yes b) No
12) Where do you usually go for treatment:
a) Government hospital b) Private clinics c) NGO clinics/hospitals
d) Village doctor
13) Why do you choose that specific health care center (answer may be more):
a) Prompt service b) Less expensive c) Better treatment
d) Close to home e) I can get facilities on credit
14) How often do you feel mental stress
a) Always b) Very often c) Never
15) Suffering from illness: a) Short term (1 week- 15 days)
b) Mid-term (16 days-1 month) c) Long time (More than 1 month)
16) The pregnant woman in your family visited the health clinic:
a) Once a week b) Once a fortnight c) Once a month
d) Once in the whole period (or until there is any problem)
17) Food intake/day by woman:
a) One meal b) Two meal c) Three meal d) 3 meal +

Section-3: Education/literacy and training:

18) Education level: a) No education b) Some literacy
c) Primary passed d) Secondary e) Higher secondary f) Others

19) Did you get any training related to work: a) Yes b) No

20) If Yes, length of training a) Less than a week b) More than week but less than fortnight c) Less than a Month d) One month
e) More than a month

21) Who does your family go to school:
a) Boys b) Girls c) Both d) None e) None (as under-aged)

22) (If any one goes to school) Where do you send your child for schooling:
a) GO institute b) Private school c) NGO operated schools
d) Government Madrasa e) Private Madrasa

23) Food intake/day by kids: a) One meal b) Two meal
c) Three meal d) 3 meal +

Section-4: Wellbeing:

24) Do you have the access to electricity a) Yes b) No

25) Do you have the access to safe water a) Yes b) No

26) Do you use sanitary latrine a) Yes b) No

27) In what extent you have the access to following public information?
a) Job related information 1) Full 2) Partial 3) Nominal 4) No
b) Health related information 1) Full 2) Partial 3) Nominal 4) No
c) Education information 1) Full 2) Partial 3) Nominal 4) No
d) Financial help (loan) info 1) Full 2) Partial 3) Nominal 4) No
e) Natural disaster information 1) Full 2) Partial 3) Nominal 4) No
f) Political information 1) Full 2) Partial 3) Nominal 4) No
g) Government information 1) Full 2) Partial 3) Nominal 4) No

28) Frequency of contact with beneficial info sources (Like, government agency, NGO office, local news agency, library, etc)
a) Regularly b) Fairly often c) Seldom d) Never

29) Food intake/day for adults male: a) One meal b) Two meal
c) Three meal d) 3 meal +

30) At the time of shortage, who in the family get more share of food:
a) Male (adult) b) Male (Kid) c) Female (Adult)
d) Female (Kid) e) Equal share

31) Do you get time available for leisure:
a) Regularly b) Fairly often c) Seldom d) Never

Section-5: Asset/liability side:

32) Land holding size: a) No land b) Less than acre c) More than one acre

33) Land holding status:
a) Bought new b) Same inheritance land c) Sold out
d) Lost in river

34) Other assets holding (answer can be more than one):
a) Poultry & livestock b) Fishing net c) Boat d) Radio e) TV
f) Cassette player g) Wood furniture h) Chair i) Table

j) Almirah k) Fan l) Bedding m) Nothing
35) Value of other assets: a) < 1000 Tk b) 1000-2000 c) 2001-3000
d) 3001-4000 e) 4001-5000 f) 5001-10,000 g) 10000+ h) Nothing
36) Type of Ownership of house:
a) Owner b) Rented c) Owning with loan
d) Living in other's land (Free)
37) Type of house: a) Brick build b) Mud build c) Tin build
d) Straw build
38) Occupation: a) Agriculture based b) Off-farm c) Business
d) Services e) Others
39) Income/month: a) Nothing b) <500 c) 500-1000
d) 1001-2000 e) 2001-3000 f) 3001-4000 g) 4001-5000 h) 5001-10000
40) Who contributes more in the family income: a) Male b) Female
41) Total employment/year a) < a month b) < 3 month c) < 6 month
d) < 9 month e) Full year
42) What you do at the time of natural calamity:
a) Do the same b) Work off-farm c) Work for others d) Migrate to city
e) Doing socially wrong works f) Do nothing
43) Monthly expenditure: a) < 500 b) 500-1000 c) 1001-1500
d) 1501-2000 e) 2001-3000 f) 3001-4000 g) 4001-5000 h) 5000 +
44) Food expenditure (% of total expenditure)
a) Below 20% b) 20-Below 40% c) 40-below 60% d) 60-below 80%
45) Non-food expenditure:
a) For cloth ________% b) Loan Payment ________%
c) Transportation ________% d) Social cost __________%
e) Medical cost ___%
46) How much do you save/ month: a) Nothing b) < 500 c) 500-1000
d) 1001-2000 e) 2001-3000 f) 3001-4000 g) 4001-5000 h) 5000+
47) Form of saving a) Cash b) Crop c) Jewelry d) Cattle
e) Other

Section-6: Empowerment/ decision making:

48) Who makes the major decisions at household level:
a) Male b) Female c) Collectively
49) In what extent you can make decision in your job:
a) Always b) Very often c) Sometimes d) Rarely e) Never
50) Do you actively participate in the local decision making meetings to express your opinion?
a) Always b) Very often c) Sometimes d) Rarely e) Never
51) Are you the member of any local cooperative? a) Yes b) No
52) If yes, can you express your voice in the decision making of the cooperative?
a) Always b) Very often c) Sometimes d) Rarely e) Never
53) Do you cast your vote every time (Male)?
a) Always b) Mostly not always c) Sometimes d) Never
54) Do you cast your vote every time (Female)?
a) Always b) Mostly not always c) Sometimes d) Never

55) Can you cast your vote for your preferred candidate?
a) Always b) Mostly not always c) Sometimes d) Never

Section-7: Insecurity:

56) Do you feel unsecured anytime:
a) Always b) Very often c) Sometimes d) Rarely e) Never
57) Do you have the experience of theft/robbery:
a) Always b) Very often c) Sometimes d) Rarely e) Never
58) As a common citizen can you act/do following freely?
a) Religious works: a) Always b) Very often c) Sometimes d) Rarely e) Never
b) Cultural works: a) Always b) Very often c) Sometimes d) Rarely e) Never
c) Political works: a) Always b) Very often c) Sometimes d) Rarely e) Never
59) How do the government officials treat you?
a) Best b) Good c) Bad d) Worst

Section-8: Support services:

60) From where did you take help for income generation?
a) Govt. b) NGO c) Both d) None (Self help)
61) Length of membership in NGO or/and Government works: a) Less than year
b) 1-< 5 Years c) 5-<10 Years d) 10-<15 Years e) More than 15 years
62) What sort of help did you receive? (**Answer may be more**)
a) Financial b) Non-financial (like schooling) c) Training d) Family planning
e) Advocacy f) Health care g) Sanitation h) Other
63) Where did you get the information about these services:
a) Neighbor b) Relatives c) Friends d) Colleagues e) Field workers
f) TV g) Local administration h) News paper
64) Did you ever take loan: a) Yes b) No
65) If yes, from whom:
a) Government b) NGO c) Local lenders d) Cooperatives
66) Whose interest rate on loan is higher: a) b) c)
67) If yes, amount of loan taken:
a) < 5000 b) 5000-10000 c) 10001-15000 d) 15001-20000
e) 20001-50000
68) For how long you are borrowing money:
a) < year b) 1-<2 c) 2-<3 d) 3-<4 e) 4-<5 f) 5-<6
g) 6-<8 h) 8-<10 i) 10 year +
69) Your loan amount was not repaid in time:
a) Always b) Very often c) Sometimes d) Rarely e) Never
70) How frequently the loan provider monitors your activities:
a) Always b) Very often c) Sometimes d) Rarely e) Never
71) Source of job creation
a) Government b) NGO c) Own d) Alternative

Section-9: Performance analysis (For Government and NGO-driven projects)
Circle one:
(Performance indicators: 5– Best, 4= Good, 3= Medium, 2– Bad, 1= Worst)

Effectiveness Indicator	**Worst**	**Bad**	**Medium**	**Good**	**Best**
72. Timeliness in loan disbursement/providing other services	1	2	3	4	5
73. If you had a problem, how sincerely the service provider resolved it	1	2	3	4	5
74. Speed of decision making by the organization	1	2	3	4	5
75. Regularity of information sharing through field workers	1	2	3	4	5
76. Fairness in decision making by the organization	1	2	3	4	5
77. How sincerely the service provider keeps their promise	1	2	3	4	5
78. Quality maintenance of the service by the provider	1	2	3	4	5
79. How good are the workers in answering your queries quickly	1	2	3	4	5
Did you ever have interaction with managers of the service provider?	1) Yes (Go to question no. 80)			2) No (Go to question no. 81)	
80. Responsiveness of the officers of service provider	1	2	3	4	5
81. How good the organization is in listening to any of your suggestions	1	2	3	4	5
82. Quality in additional technical support (Like, how to use a machine, fertilizer, seeds, watering)	1	2	3	4	5
83. Willingness of the workers to help you	1	2	3	4	5
84. Frequency of visits by the workers is enough for you	1	2	3	4	5
85. Transparency in transaction process of the service provider	1	2	3	4	5
86. Attitude of the workers while interacting with beneficiaries	1	2	3	4	5
87. Service knowledge of the workers	1	2	3	4	5
88. How helpful the service provider been in dealing with other organizations	1	2	3	4	5
89. Attention of the service provider towards your welfare	1	2	3	4	5
90. Attention of the workers towards you	1	2	3	4	5
91. Worker's understanding of the individual beneficiary's need	1	2	3	4	5

Effectiveness Indicator	Worst	Bad	Medium	Good	Best
92. Formal participation (Like in monthly meeting) of beneficiaries in the supportive decision making process of the service provider	1	2	3	4	5
93. Service provider's location is convenient	1	2	3	4	5
94. Service provider's business hours are convenient	1	2	3	4	5
95. Equipment the service provider propose is convenient to get	1	2	3	4	5
96. Timing of the visit by the workers	1	2	3	4	5
97. Availability of the workers	1	2	3	4	5

Table A4.1: Human poverty index for 64 districts in Bangladesh

District name	HPI 1995	HPI 2000	HPI 2003	Average annual change in HPI during 1995-2003
Bandarban	51.6	39.77	35.40	-3.92
Rangamati	46.24	35.74	31.98	-3.85
Jhalokathi	31.54	25.4	28.50	-3.74
Jamalpur	51.06	41.87	33.26	-3.63
Nilphamari	46.86	38.5	31.40	-3.55
Tangail	39.33	32.48	36.73	-3.51
Pirojpur	31.16	25.82	22.98	-3.39
Comilla	31.88	26.72	27.50	-3.39
Barguna	33.79	28.43	28.75	-3.36
Potuakhali	35.76	30.56	28.90	-3.26
Khagrachari	43.86	37.58	27.36	-3.23
Khulna	32.51	27.95	31.51	-3.19
Mymenshing	40.3	34.7	31.77	-3.17
Moulovibazar	37.77	32.69	30.11	-3.16
Bogra	37.72	32.75	27.65	-3.13
Rajbari	43.75	38.03	32.44	-3.10
Shariatpur	42.28	36.76	29.39	-3.09
Naogaon	36.91	32.32	33.04	-3.06
Lalmonirhat	40.67	35.63	29.40	-3.06
Gaibandha	39.95	35.08	30.22	-3.05
Thakurgaon	40.32	35.87	28.35	-2.98
Satkhira	35.53	31.74	27.33	-2.94
Chandpur	33.28	29.76	30.85	-2.94
Pabna	40.36	36.11	28.23	-2.91
Sylhet	39.11	35.08	29.64	-2.90
Madaripur	38.59	34.64	29.76	-2.89
Narayangonj	31.58	28.45	29.20	-2.88

District name	HPI 1995	HPI 2000	HPI 2003	Average annual change in HPI during 1995-2003
Kishoregonj	39.35	35.59	27.51	-2.82
Chittagong	32.29	29.21	35.05	-2.80
Panchagar	38.71	35.03	32.40	-2.79
Jhenidaha	35.74	32.37	28.33	-2.73
Magura	36.34	33.04	28.23	-2.69
Noakhali	36.33	33.05	24.19	-2.69
Manikganj	38.93	35.44	25.73	-2.61
Sirajgonj	42.59	38.83	25.25	-2.60
Bagerhat	32.58	29.72	28.34	-2.59
Barisal	31.8	29.03	26.38	-2.59
Feni	30.83	28.15	24.46	-2.56
Kurigram	43.14	39.42	32.25	2.51
Gopalgonj	32.51	29.77	27.21	-2.50
Jessore	30.77	28.2	25.48	-2.48
Sunamgonj	43.01	39.44	28.92	-2.46
Rangpur	41.7	38.26	28.33	-2.46
Dinajpur	36.24	33.31	25.08	-2.44
Hobiganj	37.23	34.45	26.37	-2.36
Narshingdi	37.93	35.25	33.81	-2.36
Gazipur	34.93	32.49	26.46	-2.30
Lakshmipur	34.8	32.39	28.60	-2.26
Rajshahi	35.98	33.57	29.84	-2.24
Chuadanga	34.02	32.11	24.38	-2.23
Netrokona	39.04	37.06	32.45	-2.19
Nwabgonj	41.68	39.66	26.67	-2.18
Sherpur	45.15	42.98	30.32	-2.07
Natore	36.02	34.42	36.16	-1.99
Joypurhat	37.23	35.7	26.61	-1.97
Brahmanbaria	39.26	37.65	28.51	-1.95
Narail	32.41	31.26	27.92	-1.79
Bhola	37.48	36.32	33.81	-1.73
Kushtia	36.79	35.78	32.20	-1.69
Meherpur	36.91	36.01	23.42	-1.60
Munshiganj	29.68	29.07	33.84	-1.30
Faridpur	35.26	34.59	33.90	-1.19
Dhaka	26.87	26.51	32.28	-.91
Cox's Bazar	38.68	38.44	37.91	-.25

Source: Adapted from Ali and Begum, 2006, p. 19.

Technical notes for Table A4.1:

- HPI index is calculated as follows: $HPI = [1/3\ (P_1^{\ 3} + P_2^{\ 3} + P_3^{\ 3})]^{1/3}$
- P1 is deprivation in longevity depends on probability of dying before age 40
- P2 is deprivation of knowledge depends on adult literacy and child aged 6-10 yr attednign school
- P3 is Deprivation of economic provisioning depends on access to health services by children, access to proper sanitation, percentage of people not living in a house with electricity, and malnutrition among children under 5 years.

Table A4.2: Upazilla level literacy rate in the selected districts of Bangladesh

District	Upazilla	Literacy rate (In percent)
Barguna		55.3
	Amtali	45.9
	Bamna	64.2
	Barguna Sadar	55.2
	Betagi	59.7
	Patharghata	63.2
Potuakhali		51.5
	Bauphal	52.6
	Dashmina	41.8
	Dumki	66.0
	Galachipa	42.9
	Kalapara	56.9
	Mirzaganj	60.4
	Potuakhali Sadar	53.3
Gaibandha		35.7
	Fulchari	27.7
	Gaibandha Sadar	39.7
	Gobindaganj	37.8
	Palashbari	38.9
	Sadullapur	35.7
	Saghatta	34.3
	Sundarganj	31.1

District	Upazilla	Literacy rate (In percent)
Kurigram		33.4
	Bhurungamari	29.6
	Charrajibpur	25.6
	Chilmari	33.8
	Phulbari	38.1
	Kurigram Sadar	38.3
	Nageswari	29.9
	Rajarhat	40.7
	Raumari	24.7
	Ulipur	34.9
Lalmonirhat		42.3
	Aditmari	39.8
	Hatibandha	39.3
	Kali Ganj	41.1
	Lalmonirhat Sadar	45.5
	Patgram	44.7
Nilphamari		38.8
	Dimla	36.2
	Domar	44.7
	Jaldhaka	33.0
	Kishoreganj	32.7
	Nilphamari Sadar	39.2
	Saidpur	48.5
Jessore		51.2
	Abhaynagar	53.5
	Bagherpara	50.6
	Chaugacha	43.9
	Jhikargacha	52.0
	Keshabpur	47.2
	Jessore Sadar	58.7
	Manirampur	50.8
	Sharsha	42.7

District	Upazilla	Literacy rate (In percent)
Satkhira		45.5
	Assasuni	40.3
	Debhata	49.9
	Kalaroa	45.5
	Kaliganj	46.8
	Satkhira Sadar	50.7
	Shyamnagar	39.7
	Tala	45.7

Source: BBS (2008); Ministry of Finance (2008).

Figure A4.1: Monga Areas in Bangladesh

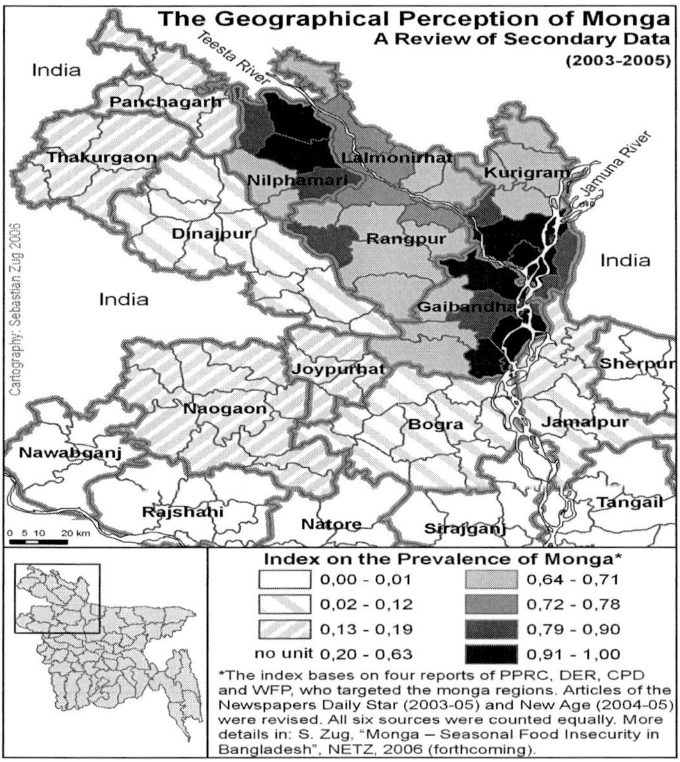

Adapted from: Sebastian Zug, 'Monga – Seasonal Food Insecurity in Bangladesh – Bringing the Information Together' in *The Journal of Social Studies*, No. 111, July-Sept. 2006, Centre for Social Studies, Dhaka.

Figure A4.2: Sidr, 2007 – affected districts

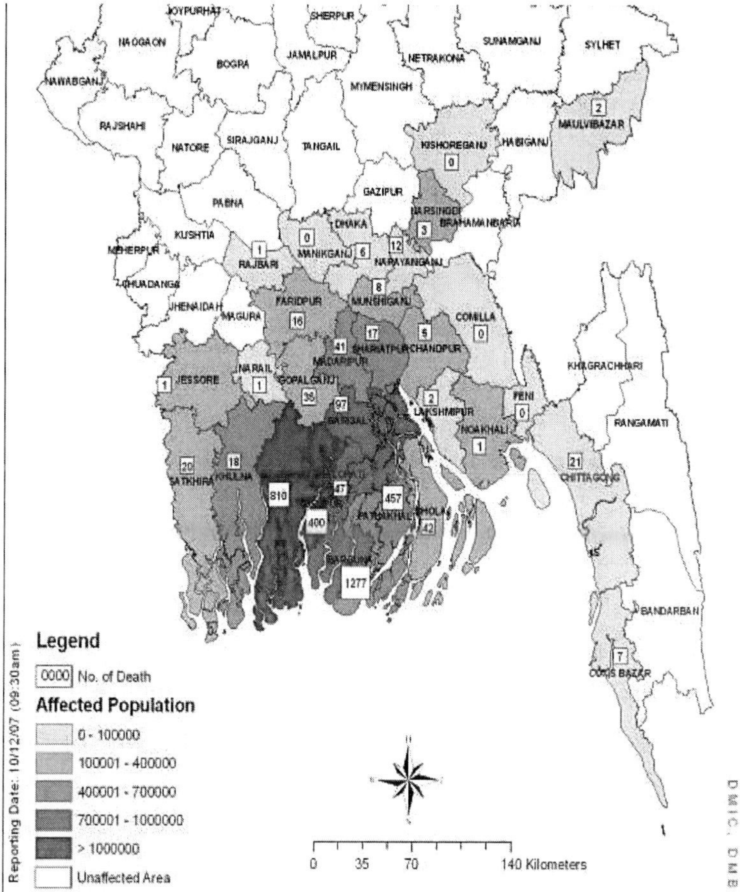

Source: Ministry of Food and Disasters Management, Government of Bangladesh.

Figure A4.3: Track of cyclone Reshmi

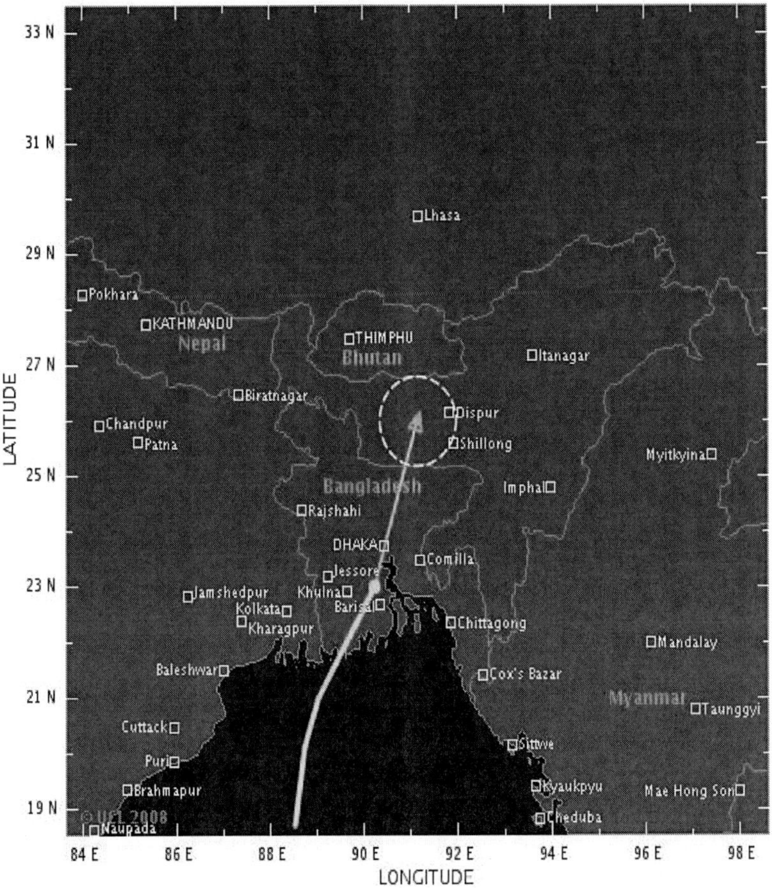

Source: NASA (2008).

Figure A4.4: Cyclone Aila – affected areas in Bangladesh

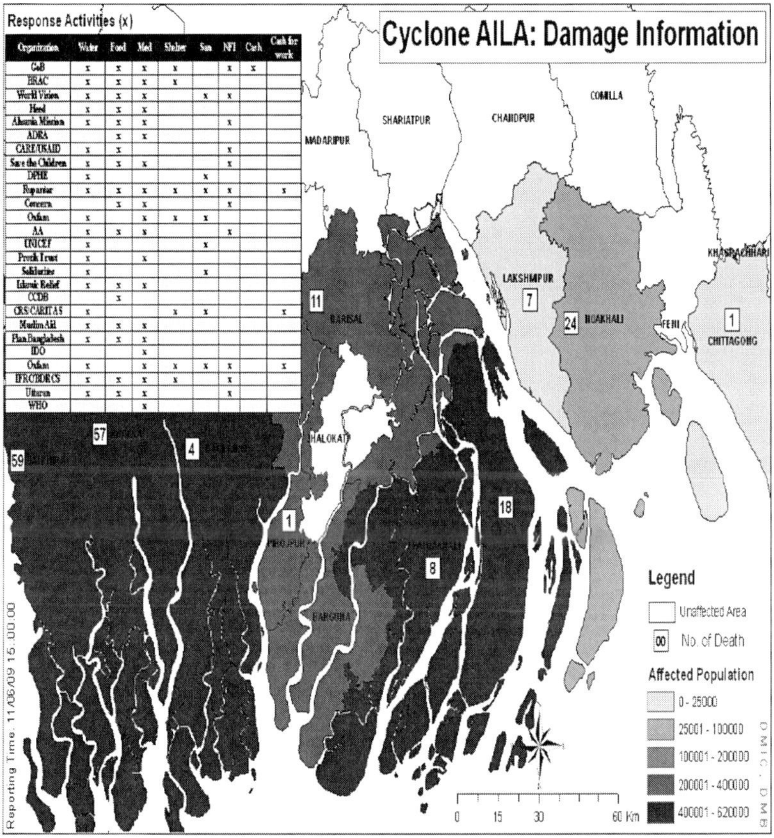

Organization	Water	Food	Med	Shelter	San	NFI	Cash	Cash for work
GoB	x	x	x	x		x	x	
BRAC	x	x	x	x				
World Vision	x	x	x		x	x		
Heed	x	x	x					
Ahsania Mission	x	x	x			x		
ADRA		x	x					
CARE/USAID	x	x				x		
Save the Children	x	x	x			x		
DPHE	x				x			
Rupantar	x	x	x	x	x	x		x
Concern		x	x			x		
Oxfam	x		x	x	x			
AA	x	x	x			x		
UNICEF	x				x			
Protik Trust	x		x					
Solidarites	x				x			
Islamic Relief	x	x	x					
CCDB		x						
CRS/CARITAS	x			x	x			x
Muslim Aid	x	x	x					
Plan Bangladesh	x	x	x					
IDO			x					
Oxfam	x		x	x	x	x		x
IFRC/BDRCS	x	x	x	x		x		
Uttaran	x	x	x			x		
WHO			x					

Source: MFODM-GOB; DFID; UNDP; CDMP and UN (2009).

Notes

[1] Questionnaires are given in full in the appendix

[2] An alternative way to do this analysis is by using a control group study. However, because of our focus towards the comparison between GO and NGO borrowers, we didn't collect data from non-borrowers. In addition, at the time of field survey, it was observed that it is hard to find rural people without at least one credit scheme.

[3] A similar rate of poverty reduction has been found in recent statistics (unpublished) from the BBS. See The Daily Prothom Alo, 18th April, 2011 web edition.

[4] Even though female credit borrowers are large in number (around 92%), we have collected similar sizes of responses from male and female beneficiaries. We have followed disproportionate stratified random sampling in collecting the primary data. Our initial plan was to collect data from 500 respondents. If we follow the proportional random sampling, the number of male respondents would be to be 40 (8% of 500). We believe that where hundreds and thousands of men are poor in rural Bangladesh, 40 is not a representative sample size. Any opinion derived from the comments of 40 respondents would not be statistically significant. Thus by considering the large population of poor in rural areas, we have decided to collect data of similar sample sizes. This methodology has been suggested by Judy, Keysik and Jerry Finn (2010, p. 174) by arguing that especially in social research we can collect equal size of samples in case of disproportionate population size to make the policy more representative to each group. We also planned to collect a second set of data of 300 samples. Had we followed the disproportionate random sampling, the total sample for male in this set would be 28 (8% of 300). In that case our total sample size (from two sets) for male beneficiaries would be 64 (40 + 24). But according to the sample size determination equation (see page 66), we need 385 samples to confirm 95% confidence level. That's why we have collected similar sizes of samples (which is 463 for female and 467 for male) that is representative and that satisfies the required sample size criteria (both greater than 385).

[5] Districts are sub-divided into upazillas. The upazillas are the lowest level of administrative government in Bangladesh. In 1983, the Local Government Ordinance of 1982 was amended to re-designate and upgrade the existing thanas as upazillas.

[6] Out of these 97 questions, a few have several sub-questions and so the total number of questions asked is 107. However, out of these same 97 questions, 59 are relevant to wellbeing issues, 12 are regarding support services and 26 were asked so as to collect relevant data for the development of effective service delivery scale.

[7] See, Updating Poverty Maps of Bangladesh, BBS, WB and WFP-2009.

[8] For further discussion see, Elbers, Lanjouw and Lanjouw (2003).

[9] See, BBS, WB, WFP-2009 (p. 8); HIES-2005; Ministry of Finance (2008.p. 180).

[10] See, Ministry of Finance (2008).

[11] The word *haor* is corrupted form of the Bengali word *sagor* (meaning sea) in the regional dialect. A **haor** is a wetland ecosystem in the north eastern part of Bangladesh which physically is a bowl or saucer shaped shallow depression, also known as a backswamp.
[12] See: BBS, WB, WFP-2009; Ministry of Finance (2008).
[13] Table A4.1 in the Appendix to this chapter shows the rate at which these districts are improving in their Human Poverty Index and those rates are quite similar for the stated dirstricts.
[14] See, Upgrading Poverty Maps of Bangladesh, 2009.
[15] Monga is a seasonal food insecurity in ecologically vulnerable and economically weak parts of north-western Bangladesh, primarily caused by an employment and income deficit before Aman (rice grown in monsoon) is harvested. It mainly affects those rural poor who have an undiversified income that is directly or indirectly based on agriculture.
[16] Chars are unstable islands in the river formed from alluvial sediments.
[17] BBS, WB, MFDM-GOB, 2009.
[18] Report on "Monga" in Northern Bangladesh, CARE, November 2005, p. 1.
[19] See: BBS, WB, WFP, 2009, p. 6.
[20] See: MFODM-GOB, 2008; BBS and WB, 2009, p. 10.
[21] See: UN Humanitarian Affairs, Different years.
[22] See: UN Humanitarian Affairs, Different years; MFODM-GoB, 2008; WFP, 2009.
[23] See: Banerjee, 2008.
[24] See: Red Cross and Red Crescent, various years.
[25] See: UNICEF, 2007.
[26] MFODM-GOB, 2010
[27] See: Red Cross and Red Crescent; USAID, 2008.
[28] See: MFODM-GOB, 2008; NASA, 2008; UNISYS and SWERA, 2008.
[29] Between 40.2% and 50.5% of all holdings in the Northern districts were agricultural labour households in 2003. The national average is 35.9%, which is substantially lower. See, The Bangladesh Census of Agriculture, 2004; BBS Statistical Yearbook, 2004.
[30] Agricultural Census, 2008 by GoB.
[31] Households operating 0.05 acres of cultivable land.
[32] See: BBS, 2008; Agriculture Census of Bangladesh, 2008.
[33] BBS, WB and WFP, 2009, p. 12. Note that travel time was estimated from the road network information using GIS software.
[34] See BBS HIES (2005); BBS (2008).
[35] See: Sen (2000), Bossert, D'Ambrosio and Paragine (2007); Chakravarty and D'Ambrosio (2006); Whelan et al. (2002); Tsakloglou and Papadopoulos, (2002b); Poggi (2007a and 2007b).
[36] Note, literacy rate is for the year 2006 (BBS, 2008).
[37] Ministry of Finance, GoB (2008, p. xix) .
[38] For Bagerhat 382, for Jessore 946, for Khulna 680 and for Satkhira 510 person/square km.

[39] Kurigram is the only surveyed district which has been detached from other northern districts by two giant rivers namely Jamuna (or Brahmaputra) and Tista. There are few 'chars' in Kurigram as well which were not covered in this study. Due to the remoteness of the villages in Kurigram, it was hard to travel and collect more samples and thus the number of respondents of Kurigram district is comparatively low.

[40] Two upazillas from Lakshmipur, namely Lakshmipur Sadar and Raipur; six from Feni district, namely Panchgachia, Sonagaji, Pathan bari, Fozilpur, Fotehpur, Chagalnaiya; Sarail and Ashuganj are the upazillas from Brahmanbaria and finally two upazillas from Barisal, namely Kaderabad and Mehendigonj.

[41] Sahapur, Bancha nagar, Somserabad, Khilbaicha , Rakhalia of Lakshmipur district; Mohipal, Madhyam Charipur, Chowdhury Bari Bosti, Fotehpur, Dholia, Dorga bari, Barahipur, Birinchi bosti, Jabbar para, Kochua, Sundar pur, Miabari, Shantir bazar, Shanua and Lakshmipur of Feni; Bertola, Durgapur, Tazpur, Bijoynagar, Mirzabari of Brahmanbaria and; Fultola, Karapara, Noyapara, Gobindoganj from Barisal.

[42] For example, high poverty rate and surrounded by many rivers thus the victims of river erosion and other natural calamities.

[43] *Madrasa* (also known as Moktob) is a special kind of educational institution where religious education is provided along with some formal education. The main concentration is given on religious education of course.

CHAPTER FIVE

GOVERNMENT AND NGO PROJECTS COMPARED USING A MULTIDIMENSIONAL SERVICE DELIVERY EFFECTIVENESS SCALE

5.1 Introduction

The debate on government-NGO effectiveness is not new and there is a common myth[1] in the existing literature that NGOs are more effective than government in poverty reduction projects in the developing countries. However, as discussed in Chapter-1, this claim is inconclusive. Development literature suggests that government and NGO credit-driven poverty reduction projects were compared based on cost effectiveness (Mahmud and Ahmed, 2003), rapid response rate (McGhee, 1999), number of beneficiaries covered (Chao, 2003) and the rate of loan recovery (Morshed, 2000). In this chapter we will compare the effectiveness of credit-driven GO and NGO projects from a different yet important dimension – with respect to their service delivery effectiveness. At the foundation of the study the question may arise: why is this perspective important?

Our argument is that large scale credit disbursement cannot make a sea-change in the poverty reduction rate unless the borrowed money is utilized effectively. As the majority of the credit borrowers are illiterate, they require customized services to better utilize the borrowed money. Thus, customized and effective service delivery can be the potential strength of credit-driven GO and NGO projects. Fig-3.3 in Chapter-3 described how effective service delivery can be important to accelerate poverty reduction rate in developing countries. As we are focusing on credit-driven projects, it would be significant contributions in addressing the effectiveness debate if GO and NGO projects are evaluated from a new perspective – service delivery effectiveness. We call this a '*process-based*' effectiveness comparison. Chapter 3 also justified the need for effective service delivery for poverty reduction with the aid of the Capability Approach (Sen, 1984, 1993) and the Sustainable Livelihoods Model

(Chambers and Conway, 1992) (see Section 3.4). However, even though both the models stress the need for effective service delivery, they don't offer any guidelines on the major dimensions and fields of service delivery that need to be prioritized to make the service delivery process more pro-poor, sustainable and effective (as mentioned in Chapter 3, see gaps 3 and 4 in Fig-3.4).

The multidimensional service delivery scale which will be developed in this chapter can be used to compare the effectiveness of Government and NGOs in delivering services (*process-based* comparison) to the beneficiaries. Performance assessment of the non-profits through a developed and validated multidimensional scale is new to the development literature. This scale is authentic as it is based on the opinions of the credit borrowers and the results are statistically significant too. We believe this scale development methodology can be of use to any social project in customizing service requirements and evaluating the performance of the development partners in delivering effective services to the beneficiaries. It is also expected that the derivation and appropriate use of the scale will help the policy-makers in both GOs and NGOs better realize the degree of ineffectiveness in the service delivery process.

5.2 Conceptualizing effectiveness

Buchanan (1987) indicated that the service provider (in our case GO or NGO) is seen as effective if it can make a situation in which people receive the services they need in the way they require them. In our case, we are conceptualizing effectiveness from a service delivery perspective, unlike the more traditional way of looking at profits or number of consumers covered (in our case beneficiaries). In analysing the effectiveness of GOs and NGOs in poverty alleviation programs, it is more important to examine to what extent they reach the beneficiaries, reduce the *ill-beings* of the poor, support them with income generation, build the *capability* of the people, and mobilize them in social activities, other than measuring the quantity of profit they make by disbursing microfinance to the poor. Thus, the effectiveness of the stated participants can be compared based on service delivery mechanisms and support services. Therefore, for our case, effectiveness (or efficacy) is defined[2] as:

> "a comparison of what is expected by the beneficiaries (poor people) and what is actually performed by the participating organizations (GO and NGO) in the poverty alleviation projects with respect to management and administrative credibility, service delivery process, skills of the workers,

problem solving capacity, interaction procedure, social mobilization skills, etc." (definition used in Section 3.5).

5.3 Scale development

We have developed an instrument that we term the 'Effectiveness Scale' which can be used to measure the service delivery efficacy of the participating organizations in the poverty alleviation programs. Construction of a unique scale for participants' efficacy analysis is important for many reasons.

First, as mentioned (Section 5.1), both the Capability Approach (Sen, 1982, 1985) and the Department for International Development's (DFID) 'Sustainable Livelihoods Model'[3] fail to identify the required fields of effective service delivery and the method for strengthening the service delivery process. Our scale addresses these issues.

Second, a scale is developed because this process, unlike simple descriptive statistics, detects and eliminates a number of redundant or insignificant variables, the presence of which may generate an erroneous result and consequently wrong policy prescriptions.

Third, in using multidimensional scaling (MDS), the overall goal is to identify the dimensions that affect perception or behaviour which may not have been readily evident in the data and cannot be explored through traditional descriptive methods. This then provides the analyst with a global overview of the relationships between variables. As such, variables that are closer together on the data set represent similar objects while those that are further apart represent dissimilar ones (Mugavin, 2008).

Finally, available scales such as those found in marketing and management (often termed 'Performance Scales') are quite different from the scale we have developed in this study (discussed in Section 3.5).

5.3.1 Dimension selection and item generation

This section has been developed following the lead provided by literature in psychology, education, marketing, and management. By considering the non-profit nature of poverty reduction projects and welfare issues related to poverty, at the initial stage 38 items have been generated (refer to Section 3.5); they were then grouped under five dimensions based on the item's underlying nature and the definition of the individual dimensions as given in Table 5.1:

Table 5.1: Preliminary dimensions and items of the scale

Dimensions	Explanation/definition	Corresponding items
Credibility	The degree to which people can rely on the activities of the service provider	Items reflecting issues such as timeliness, sincerity in operation, speed in the process, fairness in decision making, information sharing, etc.
Reactive	The way the service provider responds to the queries or problems of the beneficiaries	Includes items like responsiveness of field workers and managers, workers' attitudes with beneficiaries, feedback approach, technical support activities, etc.
Confidence	The service recipients' level of trust in the organization	Issues related to transparency in the transactions, professionalism, consultation and guiding ability, knowledge of the workers, problem solving capacity and sincerity, keeping promises, etc.
Empowering	The extent to which the service organizations value suggestions from the beneficiaries	Provider's attention towards individual's welfare, worker's focus towards beneficiaries, sincerity of the providers in the participatory process of the beneficiaries, caring attitudes, etc.
Accessibility	The degree to which communication is facilitated between beneficiaries and the service provider	Locational advantage, area covered, office hours, availability of the technology suggested by the providers, etc.

5.3.2 Scale purification

A five-person judging panel has been utilized (following the methodology used by Shimp and Sharma, 1987) to purify the suggested 38 items and five dimensions. A decision criterion that follows the agreement of four judges out of five (all are PhDs in the fields of Economics, Marketing and Management) in a specific issue was used to refine the scale items and dimensions. After the modifications, 26 items and five dimensions were approved by the experts and these 26 items were used as individual questions in the final questionnaire. A five-point Likert scale was incorporated asking for responses ranging from 1 ('worst') to 5 ('best') in the scale items.

5.3.3 First-stage purification

A total of 562 questionnaires have been completed from 78 villages of eight northern and southern districts of Bangladesh (refer to Fig-4.1 and Section 4.7). However, due to the filtering process, the total sample size in this first set was reduced to 366. Among the usable questionnaires, 186 (50.8%) were from male respondents and 180 (49.2%) from female respondents. The multi-stage sample selection procedure is described in Chapter 4.

Before beginning the further statistical purification, we conducted a measure of sample adequacy[4] (MSA) test through *Kaiser-Mayer-Olkin* (KMO)[5] statistics to see the data appropriateness. Sampling adequacy predicts if data are likely to factor well, based on correlation and partial correlation[6]. The KMO for 26 items was found to be 0.963 with the individual MSA for scale items ranging from 0.842 to 0.988, which satisfies the requirement[7]. Moreover, principal component analysis (PCA) requires that the probability associated with Bartlett's Test of Sphericity be less than the level of significance. The probability associated with the Bartlett test is <0.001 which satisfies this requirement.

5.3.4 Second-stage purification

To test the hypothesis that a relationship exists among the selected 26 items and five underlying latent dimensions, an exploratory factor analysis (EFA) has been conducted. As our main intention was to reduce several variables to a more tractable number, we used a *moderately strict* decision rule of deleting items having cross loading (having loading greater than 0.50 in two factors) or a loading of less than 0.50 on any factor[8] (loading value is similar to regression weight and show explanatory power of the item). At this stage of purification, four items (as shown in Table 5.2) have been dropped and the results suggest that the *eigenvalue* dropped below 1 (*Kaiser Criterion*[9]) after incorporating three dimensions instead of the hypothesized five dimensions, thus the remaining 22 items can be grouped into three dimensions. Table 5.2 explains the justifications of dropping four items at this stage of purification.

Table 5.2: Items dropped in second stage scale purification

Item	Statistical justification (see Table 5.4)	Economic justification
1. Attitude of the workers while interacting with beneficiaries	Cross loading and communality of only 0.42	
2. Service knowledge of the workers	Cross loading (0.51 and 0.52)	Beneficiaries mostly do not consult on additional issues with workers as workers only meet for instalment collection
3. Responsiveness of the officers of service provider	Low loading (0.44) and communality (0.35)	There is almost no interaction with the officers of service providers. Everything is done through field workers
4. Equipment the service provider proposes is convenient to get	Low loading (0.48) and communality (0.34)	Illiterate beneficiaries are reluctant to use new technologies or are unable to purchase equipment due to low level of savings

At this stage, value of total variance explained is 65% (see Table 5.3) which is above the standard value of accepting the results. As the communality and loading values (see Table 5.4) of the 22 items were both high and significant, we accepted them as scale items.

Table 5.3: Total variance explained in 26-item study

Component	Initial Eigenvalues			Extraction sums of squared loadings		
	Total	% of variance	Cumulative %	Total	% of variance	Cumulative %
1	13.706	52.716	52.716	13.706	52.716	52.716
2	1.893	7.281	59.996	1.893	7.281	59.996
3	1.223	4.702	64.699	1.223	4.702	64.699
4	.892	3.431	68.130			
5	.818	3.145	71.274			
6	.759	2.920	74.194			
7	.678	2.608	76.802			
8	.630	2.423	79.225			
9	.513	1.974	81.199			
10	.467	1.797	82.996			
11	.449	1.725	84.722			
12	.419	1.610	86.331			
13	.384	1.477	87.809			
14	.350	1.347	89.155			
15	.322	1.237	90.392			
16	.313	1.205	91.598			
17	.308	1.184	92.782			
18	.277	1.065	93.846			
19	.263	1.012	94.858			
20	.247	.951	95.809			
21	.226	.871	96.680			
22	.201	.774	97.454			
23	.197	.757	98.211			
24	.177	.682	98.893			
25	.167	.644	99.537			
26	.120	.463	100.000			

Table 5.4: Rotated component matrix for 26 items with the loading values

Name of the item	Component/Factor		
	1	2	3
If you had a problem, how sincerely the service provider resolved it	.848		
Speed of decision making by the organization	.807		
Regularity of information sharing through field workers	.807		
Timeliness in loan disbursement/providing other services	.802		
Fairness in decision making by the organization	.788		
Willingness of the workers to help you	.757		
How sincerely the service provider keeps their promise	.742		
Frequency of visits by the workers is enough for you	.707		
How good are the workers in answering your queries quickly	.685		
Quality maintenance of the service by the provider	.665		
Transparency in transaction process of the service provider	.663		
Attitude of the workers while interacting with beneficiaries	.633	.506	
Availability of the workers	.578		
Quality in additional technical support (like, how to use a machine, fertilizer, seeds)	.574		
Timing of the visit by the workers	.536		
How helpful the service provider been in dealing with other organizations		.773	
Attention of the service provider towards your welfare		.696	
How good the organization is in listening to any of your suggestions		.642	
Attention of the workers towards you		.622	
Worker's understanding of the individual beneficiary's need		.620	
Service knowledge of the workers	.526	.512	
Equipment the service provider propose is convenient to get		**.480**	
Responsiveness of the officers of service provider		**.442**	
Service provider's location is convenient			.866
Service provider's business hours are convenient			.827
Formal participation (like in monthly meetings) of beneficiaries in the supportive decision-making process of the service provider			.516

5.3.5 Third-stage purification

After dropping the four above-mentioned items, the **remaining 22 items** were put under factor analysis again. The results show that the value of total variance explained by the variables increased to 66.235 from 64.699 from the previous study (3-factor) (see Table A5.1 in the Appendix to this chapter). In addition and most importantly, the communality values of 21 items have increased and are in very good numbers with a minimum value of 0.532 (see Table A5.2 in Appendix). However, the communality value of the item, 'Formal participation in the decision-making process' is low with a value of 0.369. This necessarily shows that this stage of factor analysis has become more explanatory for these 22 items. In the rotated factor loading table (see Table A5.3 in Appendix), it was found that 17 variables now have a higher loading, and five have slightly lower loadings compared to the previous study with all 22 loadings having more than the cut-off value of 0.50. However, only one variable ('Quality in additional technical support') was found to report cross loading and comparatively low loadings of 0.506 and 0.577 (Table A5.3 in Appendix). After dropping the item 'Quality in additional technical support' due to cross loading and low communality, analysis on the remaining 21 items shows that there is no item remaining with loading less than 0.50 or cross loading (Table A5.4 in Appendix). In addition, the results show that the value of total variance as explained in the scale has increased from 66.235 to 67.883 due to this refinement (Table A5.5 in Appendix).

Most of the variables (17 out of 21) are now experiencing a bigger loading compared to earlier tests (compare Table A5.3 and A5.4 in Appendix). Only three variables have a slight reduction in loading value and one has an almost unchanged factor loading. At this point there are 13 items under factor-1, five items under factor-2, and three items under factor-3. The *Cronbach's Alpha* of 0.955 emphasizes the scale's reliability and internal consistency[10]. A comparative study of this refinement process is shown in Table 5.5.

Table 5.5: Comparison between the earlier and refined study based on 3-factor analysis

Items	Loading value		Communality value	
	With 26 items	With 21 items	With 26 items	With 21 items
If you had a problem, how sincerely the service provider resolved it	0.848	0.854	0.788	0.792
Timeliness in providing other services (e, g; loan disbursement)	0.802	0.815	0.737	0.747
Speed of decision making by the organization	0.807 0.807	0.815 0.811	0.744 0.722	0.749 0.720
Regularity of information sharing through field workers	0.742	0.758	0.726	0.731
How sincerely the service provider keeps their promise	0.788	0.798	0.701	0.705
Fairness in decision making by the organization	0.665	0.680	0.698	0.698
Quality maintenance of service by the provider	0.685	0.705	0.633	0.632
How good are the workers in answering your queries quickly	0.757	0.759	0.693	0.673
Willingness of the workers to help you	0.707	0.727	0.632	0.633
Frequency of the visit by the workers is enough for you	0.696	0.734	0.691	0.730
Attention of the service provider towards your welfare	0.773	0.787	0.685	0.708
How helpful the service provider been in dealing with other org.	0.620	0.636	0.665	0.687
Worker's understanding of the individual beneficiary's need	0.622	0.649	0.689	0.718
Attention of the workers towards you (beneficiary)	0.578	0.591	0.622	0.625
Availability of the workers	0,663	0.673	0.604	0.611
Transparency in transaction process of the service provider	0.536	0.560	0.651	0.645
Timing of the visit by the workers	0.866	0.871	0.783	0.797
Service provider's location is convenient	0.827	0.839	0.757	0.784
Service provider's business hours are convenient	0.642	0.610	0.518	0.495
How good the organization is in listening to any of your suggestion	0.516	0.543	0.331	0.376
Formal participation of beneficiaries in decision making process of the service provider				

Note: Column-1 reflects 21 questions from the questionnaire employed for this study. Column-1 of Table 5.2 reflects other remaining questions from the questionnaire. For the details of the questionnaire, see the Appendix to Chapter 4.

5.3.6 Fourth-stage purification with confirmatory factor analysis (CFA)

The 21 items refined in the last stage were subject to confirmatory factor analysis designed to (1) substantiate the dimensionality of the 3-factor structure obtained from the last purification study; (2) eliminate additional unreliable items; and (3) validate the remaining items for the final scale. For this purpose the same questionnaire has been utilized on a new sample group. Four new districts from central areas of Bangladesh were chosen for this (refer to Section 4.8 in). A total of 12 upazillas and 29 villages[11] have been surveyed in this region and a total of 368 questionnaires were appropriate for CFA. Of these respondents, 47.6% and 52.4% were male and female respectively; 42.9% and 57.1% of the respondents were the beneficiaries of government and NGOs respectively.

In the first stage CFA, we have three factors/dimensions[12] (shown by ellipses in Fig-5.1) that are inter-correlated by two headed arrows; 21 observed variables shown by rectangles and are associated with their respective factors; and 21 error terms shown by circles. Each measured variable is loaded in only one factor which satisfies the uni-dimensionality constraint of CFA. Each of the factors or dimensions is measured by at least three variables that satisfy the minimum criteria[13] (Hair et al., 2010, p. 702). A summary of the parameters of the first stage CFA model are given in Table 5.6, and shows that the model is estimated[14] to be over-identified[15]. In addition, the critical ratios for each variable is found to be more than 1.96, thus the first stage CFA model is statistically significant.

Figure 5.1: First stage CFA model with 21 scale items

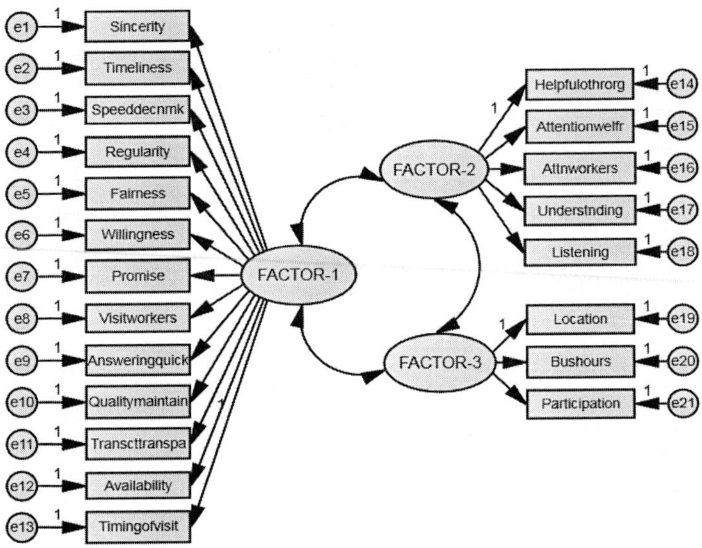

Table 5.6: Parameter summary

	Weights	Cov	Variances	Means	Intercepts	Total
Fixed	24	0	0	0	0	24
Labelled	0	0	0	0	0	0
Unlabelled	18	3	24	0	0	45
Total	42	3	24	0	0	69

Computation of degrees of freedom (effectiveness model)

Number of distinct sample moments: 231

Number of distinct parameters to be estimated: 45

Degrees of freedom (231 – 45): 186

Regression Weights

Items and factors			Estimate	S.E.	C.R.	P
Sincerity	<---	Factor-1	1.000			
Timeliness	<---	Factor-1	.731	.079	9.282	***

Items and factors			Estimate	S.E.	C.R.	P
Speeddecnmk	<---	Factor-1	1.033	.088	11.796	***
Regularity	<---	Factor-1	1.115	.093	11.984	***
Fairness	<---	Factor-1	1.280	.098	13.043	***
Willingness	<---	Factor-1	1.086	.103	10.516	***
Promise	<---	Factor-1	1.159	.092	12.568	***
Visitworkers	<---	Factor-1	1.016	.087	11.685	***
Answeringquick	<---	Factor-1	1.082	.084	12.837	***
Qualitymaintain	<---	Factor-1	1.253	.095	13.165	***
Transcttranspa	<---	Factor-1	1.138	.093	12.173	***
Availability	<---	Factor-1	.927	.108	8.582	***
Timingofvisit	<---	Factor-1	.558	.078	7.122	***
Helpfulothrorg	<---	Factor-2	1.000			
Attentionwelfr	<---	Factor-2	1.443	.178	8.118	***
Attnworkers	<---	Factor-2	1.428	.178	8.015	***
Understnding	<---	Factor-2	1.166	.158	7.395	***
Listening	<---	Factor-2	1.112	.149	7.447	***
Location	<---	Factor-3	1.000			
Bushours	<---	Factor-3	.521	.079	6.591	***
Participation	<---	Factor-3	.402	.068	5.867	***

In deciding whether the CFA model is of good fit or not, the goodness-of-fit index (see Table 5.7) was reviewed to check the model fit of the scale.

The first part of Table 5.7 entails the chi-square statistics (χ^2) value of 772.286 with 186 df and a probability less than 0.0001, thereby suggesting that the fit of the model is not adequate for the study[16].

The next group of statistics are suggested (Byrne, 2009) to better represent the fit analysis of a model which includes the values of Root Mean Squared Residual (RMR), Goodness of fit index (GFI), Adjusted GFI (AGFI) and Parsimony goodness of fit index (PGFI) (the technical explanation of these values are given in the Appendix to this chapter). A rule of thumb is that a RMR value of less than 0.05 is a presentation of good fit. Our RMR value for the model is 0.064 which shows that the model explains the correlation to within an average error of 0.064 (See: Hu and Bentlar, 1995).

Table 5.7: Model goodness-of-fit summary in the first stage of CFA

Model	NPAR	CMIN	DF	P	CMIN/DF
Our model	45	772.286	186	.000	4.152
Saturated model	231	.000	0		
Independence model	21	3267.522	210	.000	15.560

Model	RMR	GFI	AGFI	PGFI
Our model	.064	.801	.753	.645
Saturated model	.000	1.000		
Independence model	.248	.295	.224	.268

Model	NFI Delta1	RFI rho1	IFI Delta2	TLI rho2	CFI
Our model	.764	.733	.810	.784	.808
Saturated model	1.000		1.000		1.000
Independence model	.000	.000	.000	.000	.000

Model	RMSEA	LO 90	HI 90	PCLOSE
Our model	.093	.086	.100	.000
Independence model	.199	.193	.205	.000

Model	AIC	BCC	BIC	CAIC
Our model	862.286	868.025	1038.150	1083.150
Saturated model	462.000	491.461	1364.767	1595.767
Independence model	3309.522	3312.200	3391.592	3412.592

Model	ECVI	LO 90	HI 90	MECVI
Our model	2.350	2.126	2.594	2.365
Saturated model	1.259	1.259	1.259	1.339
Independence model	9.018	8.523	9.532	9.025

Model	HOELTER .05	HOELTER .01
Our model	104	112
Independence model	28	30

Both GFI and AGFI indices range from a value of zero to 1.00, with values close to 1.00 being indicative of good fit[17]. Our results show that the GFI and AGFI values for our model are 0.801 and 0.753 respectively which show a bad fit at this stage.

Typically a parsimony-based index (PGFI) has lower values than the threshold level generally perceived as acceptable[18]. Our finding of PGFI = 0.645 (see Table 5.7) is quite acceptable based on our previous findings.

Bentlar (1990) revised the NFI to take sample size into account and offered comparative fit index[19] (CFI; see the last column). Although a CFI value >0.90 was originally considered representative for a good model (Bentlar, 1990), a revised cut-off value close to 0.95 has since been advised (Hu and Bentlar, 1999). From that point of view, our CFI value of 0.808 necessarily shows a bad fit of the model (see technical note in Appendix).

In our model, incremental fit index (IFI) value of 0.810 is consistent with other fit indices and shows a bad fit of the model. The Tucker-Lewis index (TLI) ranges from 0 to 1 and a value close to 1 shows better fit[20]. Our TLI value is 0.784 is an indication of bad fit[21].

Values less than 0.05 for RMSEA (see technical note in Appendix) indicate good fit, and values as high as 0.08 represent reasonable errors of approximation[22] in the population (Browne and Cudeck, 1993). Our RMSEA value of 0.093 shows a bad fit of the model. In addition, our finding of PCLOSE = 0.000 also shows a poor fit of the model.

In our proposed model, the AIC and CAIC (AIC = 862.286 and CAIC = 1083.150, see Table 5.7) values are greater when compared to other models, thus showing a poor fit.

The expected cross-validation index (ECVI) for our model is 2.350 (See Table 5.7) which is higher than the ECVI of the saturated model (1.259) and lower than the ECVI of the independence model (9.018) and therefore shows that the model at this stage is not better than other models.

As shown in Table 5.7, the Hoelter's CN values for our model are 104 and 112 which are less than 200, showing a poor fit of the proposed model.

Based on our above stated identifications, especially the values related to RMR, CFI, GFI, AGFI, RMSEA, PCLOSE, AIC, ECVI, and Hoelter's CN, it is quite evident that the estimated values are not acceptable when compared to the proposed or cut-off values. It can therefore be concluded that the model needs further modification. An administrative decision rule[23] was specified that item loadings less than 0.50 were unreliable and should be eliminated from the scale to make it more reliable, and the modification index was reviewed to find problem variables in the scale.

Results of the loading values show that the items titled, 'Timing of the visit by the workers', 'Formal participation of beneficiaries in the supportive decision-making process of the service provider', 'Availability of the workers' and 'Service provider's business hours are convenient' have loadings of 0.39, 0.39, 0.48 and 0.39 respectively and are subject to elimination. However, the item entitled, 'Service provider's business hours are convenient' was found to be important to the respondents at the time of face-to-face interview and therefore we have decided not to delete this item at this stage. In addition to these values, the modification index for the 21-item model was also checked (see Table A5.6 in Appendix to this chapter). As shown in Table A5.6, the most problematic item with the highest MI value is 'Willingness of the workers to help you' (MI value is 55.181) with the next one being 'Availability of the workers', which has a MI value of 40.784. The MI value between 'Availability of the workers' and 'Timing of the visit by the workers' is high which is 32.372. Moreover, it was found that the MI value between 'Willingness of the workers to help you' and 'Service provider's location is convenient' is 38.416. On the other hand, in no way have we found higher MI value for the item, 'Service provider's business hours are convenient', thus decided to keep the item. For further assurance, we analysed the MI values of error terms (see the second part of Table A5.6) and we have ended up with similar findings to those mentioned above. Results show that the MI for error term e-6 (of the item 'Willingness of the workers to help you') has highest values like 62.427, 50.716 and 32.568 with few other error terms. This necessarily shows that this item ('Willingness of the workers to help you') is problematic for the model fit. In addition, the error term e-12 (item 'Availability of the workers') has higher MI values of 44.311, 38.856, and 30.378 with other error terms showing the item as problematic.

Based on the loading values and modification index, it was decided at this stage to drop 4 more items from the scale as listed in Table 5.8.

Table 5.8: Items dropped in CFA stages

Item	Justification for deletion
6. Willingness of the workers to help you	Highest modification index (55.18) with high error modification index of 62.42

Item	Justification for deletion
7. Formal participation of beneficiaries in the supportive decision making process of the service provider	Low loading (0.39)
8. Availability of the workers	High MI value (40.784) and error MI value (44.311) plus higher '*par change*' value (0.284)
9. Timing of visit by the workers	Low loading (0.39) and highest '*par change*' value of 0.367

5.3.7 Fifth-stage purification

The scale at this stage has 17 items and three dimensions and is subject to a further check of model fit through CFA. Results showed significant improvement in fit statistics. However, in some areas the model was still a 'bad fit' compared to the saturated model[24]. GOF results show (refer to Table A5.7) that there is significant decline in the chi-square value in this new 17-item model to 342.766 from 772.286 which shows a tendency towards a better fit model. The RMR value of this refined model is 0.044 which is below the previous RMR value of 0.064 and even lower than the suggested value of 0.050. The GFI value of the current model has increased from 0.801 to 0.892. While the AGFI value increased from 0.753 to 0.858. Still the GFI and AGFI values are less than the proposed value for a good fit. Most interestingly, the CFI value showed a drastic positive change to 0.906 from the earlier value of 0.808. However, the CFI value is still less than the 0.95 suggested value. The IFI has a very good value of 0.906 which was 0.810 in the earlier model. The NFI also increased to 0.865 from 0.764. The RMSEA value dropped to 0.073 from 0.093 with this modification. This shows that the new RMSEA value is less than 0.08 which is an indication of moderate fit of the model from an earlier bad fit. The AIC and ECVI values (see Table A5.7) of the proposed model are still higher than the saturated model, and this shows a moderately bad fit as well. Finally, the Hoelter's statistics are 153 and 166 (which were initially 105 and 112) which are still below the suggested value of 200. A further modification was therefore required.

Table 5.9: Items dropped in the fifth stage of scale purification

Item	Statistical reason	Economic justification
10. Frequency of visits by the workers is enough for you	High MI values (All >20.00) with many items with largest '*par change*' value of 0.474 plus high error MI value of 27.555	High standardized residual covariance (3.60 and 3.19)
11. Speed of decision making by the organization	High MI (>15) with high standardized residual covariance (3.19) with above item	Beneficiaries are less eager to get speedy services; rather they prefer to have 'timely services'
12. Business hours of the service provider	Low loading value (0.47)	Beneficiaries have less to do with the office hours due to their major interaction with the workers only

Modification and error indices of the scale items (refer to Table A5.8 in appendix) show that there are a few significantly large MI values. Both parts of Table A5.8 show that the items titled, 'Speed of decision-making' and 'Frequency of visits by the workers' have large modification (16.88 and 21.47 respectively) and error index values (27.55 and 18.32 respectively). Moreover, two error terms, namely e1 (for sincerity) and e2 (timeliness) were found to be highly correlated (37.88) which means timeliness in solving problems is considered by the beneficiaries as a sign of sincerity. Based on loading values and the modification index it was decided to drop three more items (see Table 5.9).

5.3.8 Final refinement of the effectiveness scale

With the above modifications, CFA was run on 14 items and three dimensions. It was found that the third dimension contained only a single item which may be problematic due to the fact that running CFA requires at least three items per dimension (or factor). However, by conducting a discriminant validity analysis we found that the goodness-of-fit (GOF) values were almost unchanged if we re-grouped the single item of factor-3 into factor-2. Consequently, a final decision was made to drop the third dimension and re-run CFA with the remaining two dimensions and 14 items. The results of this final stage are shown in Table 5.10 (last column) and indicate a good fit of the effectiveness scale.

Table 5.10: Comparative study of GOF values in different stages of scale refinement

GOF index	Preferred value	21-item scale	17-item scale (first stage refined)	15-item scale with new correlates	Finalized scale items (14 items & 2 dimension)
RMR	< 0.05	0.064	0.044	0.034	0.033
GFI	> 0.90	0.801	0.892	0.946	0.950
AGFI	> 0.90	0.753	0.858	0.925	0.931
PGFI	> 0.50	0.645	0.677	0.678	0.670
CFI	Close to 0.95	0.808	0.906	0.964	0.970
NFI	> 0.90	0.764	0.865	0.924	0.933
IFI	> 0.90	0.810	0.906	0.965	0.969
TLI	> 0.80	0.784	0.889	0.956	0.962
RMSEA	< or equal 0.05	0.093	0.073	0.047	0.044
PCLOSE	> 0.50	0.000	0.000	0.664	0.712
AIC	Lower than saturated model	862.286 Bigger than saturated	416.766 Bigger than saturated	222.86 Lower than saturated	194.117 Lower than saturated
ECVI	Lower than saturated model	2.350 Bigger than saturated	1.136 Bigger than saturated	0.607 Lower than saturated	0.529 Lower than saturated
HOELTER	> 200	105 & 112	153 & 166	258 & 283	272 & 301
Chi-square	Smaller the better	772.286	342.766	154.865	132.117
Total fit		Bad fit	Improved but bad fit	Major improvement	**Best fit**

5.3.9 Aggregate test and finalized scale

An aggregate test was performed by incorporating all data of the two different sets. We found the goodness-of-fit index to be satisfactory (*RMR* = 0.031, *GFI* = 0.964, *AGFI* = 0.949, *CFI* = 0.978, *RMSEA* = 0.049, *PCLOSE* = 0.610, and *Hoelters* are 373 and 413). There is no significantly large modification index value. This necessarily shows that the developed scale is robust in nature. The finalized 14-item effectiveness scale is shown in Table 5.11 with the scale items' respective loadings.

Table 5.11: 14-item effectiveness scale

Item no.	Scale Item	Loading in factor-1	Loading in factor-2
I1	Timeliness in loan disbursement/providing other services	0.70	
I2	If you had a problem, how sincerely the service provider resolved it	0.64	
I3	Regularity of information sharing through field workers	0.68	
I4	Fairness in decision making by the organization	0.78	
I5	How sincerely the service provider keeps their promise	0.75	
I6	Quality maintenance of the service by the provider	0.77	
I7	How good are the workers in answering your queries quickly	0.76	
I8	Transparency in transaction process of the service provider	0.65	
I9	How good the organization is in listening to any of your suggestion		0.67
I10	How helpful the service provider has been in dealing with other org.		0.62
I11	Attention of the service provider towards your welfare		0.70
I12	Attention of the workers towards beneficiaries		0.68
I13	Workers' understanding of the individual beneficiary's need		0.77
I14	Service provider's location is convenient		0.68

As can be seen from only a brief review of the items in the first dimension (see Table 5.11), they are all related in some way to the functioning of the service provider and its trustworthiness and reliability, thus we named this dimension the 'credibility dimension'. The second factor gives the impression that all corresponding items represent the service provider's attention to the individual beneficiaries or the welfare consciousness of the providers. Thus, we named this factor the 'beneficiary focus dimension' of the effectiveness scale (see Fig-5.2).

Figure 5.2: 14-Item finalized Effectiveness Scale

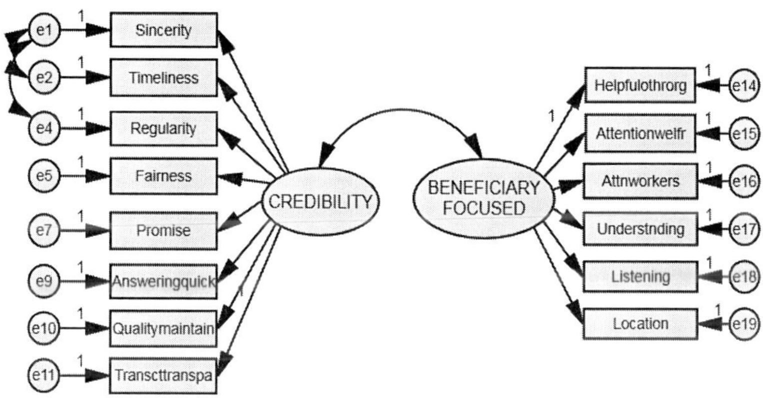

5.4 Validation of the scale with the three areas study and the implications

After developing the effectiveness scale, the researcher conducted three separate studies to assess reliability and construct validity of the 14-item scale. These studies are identified as, 'Northern Study', 'Southern Study' and 'Central Areas Study'. Since the northern and southern parts of Bangladesh are the most poverty prone, albeit due to different reasons, we sought to find whether or not the same scale items are equally applicable to both areas. Furthermore, a few districts were chosen from the central part of the country where the prevalence of poverty is lower when compared to the northern and southern areas. Comparison with this area will further validate the strength of the effectiveness scale. Sample characteristics of each study are shown in Table 5.12.

Table 5.12: Sample characteristics for three studies

	Northern Study	**Southern Study**	**Central Areas Study**
Number of district covered	**4**	**4**	**4**
Characteristics	Lengthy drought in every year, absence of industries, backward infrastructure, low literacy, high unemployment	Very vulnerable to natural shocks like cyclone, tidal surge that creates more destitute	More poverty prone compared to other districts of the area and this is our hold out sample and chosen purposively
Sex			
Male	134 (48.2%)	158 (55.6%)	175 (47.6%)
Female	144 (51.8%)	126 (44.4%)	193 (52.4%)
Member of			
GO	126 (45.3%)	143 (50.4%)	158 (42.9%)
NGO	152 (54.7%))	141 (49.6%)	210 (57.1)
Age (Years)			
21-25	2 (0.7%)	0 (0%)	38 (10.3%)
26-30	67 (24.1%)	45 (15.8%)	98 (26.6%)
31-35	63 (22.7%)	71 (25%)	64 (17.4%)
36-40	44 (15.8%)	69 (24.3%)	78 (21.2%)
41-45	43 (15.5%)	44 (15.5%)	54 (14.7%)
46-50	55 (19.8%)	55 (19.4%)	33 (9%)
51-55	4 (1.4%)	0 (0%)	3 (0.8%)
56-60	0 (0%)	0 (0%)	0 (0%)
Total Sample	**278**	**284**	**368**

The effectiveness scale's reliability and internal consistency is very high. Coefficient alpha for Northern, Southern and Central areas are 0.918, 0.949 and 0.90 respectively. For more assurance, a split-half method of reliability test was conducted and values were found to be ranging from 0.876 to 0.900. Both sets of results indicate that the effectiveness scale is a reliable measure for judging organizational efficacy in poverty related projects.

5.4.1 Convergent validity and discriminant validity

The author performed the validity analysis of the effectiveness scale which confirmed that items in a single dimension are all correlated to each other and their corresponding dimension (also called *convergent validity)* in all three areas based on correlation values. The convergent validity was found in favour of the effectiveness scale in all areas. Strong evidence was found that the two dimensions are in fact different from each other and that each one of them contains certain phenomena that are not found in the other (also called *discriminant validity*) in all three areas. As the results did not vary much within the regions, to avoid repetition we present the findings from Central Areas Study only. The results (Table 5.13) support the existence of convergent and discriminant validity in the Central Areas Study.

Table 5.13: Evidence of convergent and discriminant validity in Central Areas Study

	I1	I2	I3	I4	I5	I6	I7	I8	I9	I10	I11	I12	I13	I14
I1	1.00								0.28	0.16	0.17	0.14	0.11	0.12
I2	0.56	1.00							0.36	0.19	0.27	0.24	0.24	0.23
I3	0.57	0.56	1.00						0.33	0.19	0.22	0.22	0.19	0.26
I4	0.62	0.54	0.59	1.00					0.39	0.23	0.27	0.31	0.17	0.25
I5	0.63	0.64	0.61	0.58	1.00				0.32	0.21	0.26	0.23	0.18	0.27
I6	0.68	0.67	0.59	0.60	0.58	1.00			0.34	0.28	0.28	0.30	0.26	0.32
I7	0.68	0.56	0.59	0.57	0.68	0.60	1.00		0.34	0.32	0.32	0.24	0.30	0.33
I8	0.66	0.65	0.52	0.68	0.67	0.60	0.64	1.00	0.35	0.25	0.24	0.27	0.28	0.26
I9									1.00					
I10									0.56	1.00				
I11									0.55	0.53	1.00			
I12									0.61	0.33	0.50	1.00		
I13									0.42	0.66	0.46	0.57	1.00	
I14									0.54	0.57	0.46	0.52	0.63	1.00

Note: *Pearson Correlations* are significant at 0.01 level. I1, I2, I3 are the items as labelled in Table 5.11.

In Table 5.13 correlation values are shown for the 14 scale items that were developed and discussed in the previous section. Values below the diagonal show the correlation among the items of the individual dimensions (I1-I8 for the first dimensions and I9-I14 for the second dimensions). Higher and significant values (most are above 0.52) of the correlation coefficient (*r*) between the scale items and the dimensions show that there is convergent validity in the scale items in the effectiveness scale in the case of both dimensions. This implies that our developed scale is appropriate to express the message of each individual item without any redundancy between dimensions. On the other hand, values above the diagonal show the inter-dimension items' correlation. Note that these values are very low compared to the correlation values of convergent validity which support the evidence of discriminant validity in the 14-item effectiveness scale for the Central Areas Study, and are a strong point in favour of the effectiveness scale's construct validity – the combined outcome of convergent and discriminant validity.

5.4.2 Nomological validity

To find out whether the dimensions and their items behave as they should within a system of related coordinates with another sample characteristic[25], we used age as the demographic variable for several reasons. First, different age groups have different work capabilities. For instance, while young beneficiaries may apply for microcredit for any purpose they choose, including farming or other laborious businesses, older people apply only for less-laborious businesses due to the fact that their age would not permit them to go for farming or other such labour-intensive work. Thus, the choice preference of occupation varies with age and this age-factor is considered at the time of approval and disbursement of loans to the beneficiaries. Second, the need preference of different age groups varies and this factor is also incorporated in the study. For example, young female beneficiaries are in need of family planning counselling services or informal schooling, whereas older female beneficiaries are more likely to be concerned about health issues. It is therefore important to examine whether or not the opinions of the beneficiaries vary within age groups to test the nomological validity of the scale items. Multi-group discriminant analysis was performed to test the following hypothesis in three areas to support nomological validity of the scale items:

H_1: Score of the effectiveness scale shows no significant differences among the opinions/items and beliefs of different age groups.
H_2: Score on the effectiveness scale should be positively and highly correlated with the beneficiaries of different ages.

5.4.2A Northern Area Study

Results of the discriminant analysis on the Northern Area Study are presented in Table 5.14.

Table 5.14: Discriminant analysis on Northern Area Study

Items	Mean value for different Age groups[26] 26-30 yrs	31-35 yrs	36-40 yrs	41-45 yrs	46-50 yrs	Mean difference Hi-Lo	Wilks' lambda	F value	sig.
I1	3.76	3.71	3.95	3.77	3.78	0.24	0.995	0.368	0.73
I2	3.84	3.83	3.86	3.72	3.71	0.15	0.996	0.277	0.78
I3	3.78	3.94	4.00	3.77	3.64	0.36	0.982	1.21	0.30
I4	3.76	4.00	3.91	3.84	3.55	0.45	0.975	1.72	0.15
I5	3.84	4.00	3.86	3.95	3.87	0.14	0.994	0.42	0.79
I6	3.81	3.84	3.91	3.91	3.93	0.12	0.997	0.187	0.84
I7	3.93	4.08	3.95	4.09	3.93	0.16	0.993	0.483	0.74
I8	3.87	4.11	4.25	3.88	3.87	0.38	0.980	1.33	0.25
I9	3.37	3.17	3.18	3.00	3.36	0.36	0.976	1.60	0.17
I10	3.60	3.54	3.61	3.35	3.65	0.30	0.986	0.940	0.44
I11	3.81	3.81	4.07	3.88	3.95	0.26	0.986	0.920	0.44
I12	3.93	3.89	3.93	3.84	3.89	0.09	0.999	0.083	0.78
I13	3.85	3.75	3.86	3.81	3.71	0.15	0.996	0.243	0.71
I14	3.88	3.95	4.00	3.84	3.73	0.27	0.992	0.520	0.72

Note: I1, I2, I3 and I14 are the items as labelled in Table 5.11.

Table 5.14 shows no significant differences in the mean values of scale scores for different age groups even when the highest and lowest mean values are considered. It can be seen that pair-wise differences in the groups' mean values are much smaller. High *Wilks' lambda* values with small but significant *F* values dictate that there is no item with significant univariate differences among different groups. All these findings are in favour of accepting H_1.

Table 5.15 presents coefficients and respective factor loading results for each individual item in the scale. It can be observed that the function coefficients for each item are strongly positively correlated with different age groups. This means that every age group is responding in a similar way with respect to the scale items. In addition, the absolute values of factor loadings for all individual items are less than 0.40. This confirms that there is no identification of substantive discriminant variables in the scale based on group preferences. In four cases (see in bold) the absolute loading value is above 0.40; however, this variation is negligible.

The canonical correlation value of the study has also been calculated as 0.888 which means 78.85% (square of 0.888) of the total variation is explained by these variables. This higher explanatory power of the items, positive coefficients and better loading values demonstrate that H_2 is true indeed for the Northern Area Study. We conducted the same analysis for other areas of the study (refer to Table A5.9). The combined results of two areas on initial study show that the mean differences for the Southern and Central Area studies are small enough to prove that there is no significant discriminating item in terms of age groups. In addition, factor loadings for both the areas were found to be mostly less than 0.40 which verifies that there are no significant discriminant items in the scale.

Table 5.15: Coefficient and factor loading for different items based on different groups in the Northern Area Study

	Discriminant function coefficient					Factor loading			
Items	**26-30 yrs**	**31-35 yrs**	**36-40 yrs**	**41-45 yrs**	**46-50 yrs**	**1**	**2**	**3**	**4**
I1	.250	.561	.037	.046	.152	**-.484***	-.058	.324	.068
I2	.731	.586	.408	.164	.280	-.251*	-.117	-.116	.108
I3	.638	.729	.819	.495	.437	.357	**.444***	.071	.072
I4	.007	.352	.033	.175	.442	.205	-.335*	.238	.101
I5	1.376	1.779	1.030	1.793	1.664	.078	-.173*	-.040	.111
I6	.719	.756	.514	.369	.241	-.164	-.181	**.499***	.398
I7	1.925	2.184	1.758	2.237	1.910	-.279	-.082	**.464***	.120
I8	.142	.299	.488	.070	.262	-.185	-.008	.312*	-.023
I9	1.656	1.321	1.103	1.021	1.462	-.074	.090	.250*	-.057
I10	2.035	2.043	2.117	1.563	2.206	.103	-.163	.236*	-.079
I11	1.299	1.356	2.165	1.854	1,732	.044	.067	.126*	-.013
I12	.494	.435	.045	.177	.353	-.024	-.013	.153	-.342*
I13	.613	.893	.620	.568	.972	.271	.214	.238	.308*
I14	1.847	1.738	1.836	1.689	1.708	-.213	-.068	-.104	.270*

Note: Fisher's linear discriminant functions. I1-I14 are the items listed in Table 5.11.

5.5 Perceptions of the beneficiaries on the efficacy of GO and NGO projects

Our main purpose in this section is to compare the effectiveness between GOs and NGOs based on variations in opinions between GO and

NGO beneficiaries in rural Bangladesh. It is expected that any variation in opinion will help the policy-makers of GOs and NGOs find their respective gaps in service delivery efficacy. Thus, we have proceeded with the following null hypothesis:

> H_3: There is no significant difference between the opinions of GO and NGO beneficiaries on effectiveness scale items

To test our hypothesis, we combined data from all areas used in the scale development process. Thus, our sample size is 734 of which 49.4% (362 samples) and 50.6% (372 samples) are beneficiaries of GOs and NGOs respectively.

We begin with the results of two group discriminant analyses and these results show that there are five variables with large mean differences (I1, I2, I6, I7 and I13 are the items and their mean differences are 0.68, 0.74, 0.57, 0.57 and 0.53 respectively). It was also found that that *F values* for these five variables are quite high with lower *Wilks' lambda* value. For example, item (I2) with the highest mean value has the largest *F* (128.13) and lowest *Wilks' lambda* (0.879) with a significance of 0.000. These tests indicate that the five aforesaid scale items are also the variables that have significant univariate differences between the opinions of GO and NGO beneficiaries. As we followed a step-wise estimation procedure, we first decided to add item I2 in the discriminant model because of its significant group differences. We re-ran the discriminant analysis after incorporating I2 and continued the process until there was no significant discriminant item left based on *F* values, *Wilks' lambda* and tolerance levels. A summary of the final stage discriminant analysis is provided in Table 5.16.

Table 5.16: Summary of discriminant analysis between GO and NGO beneficiaries

	Discriminant coefficient	Classification function coefficient		Loadings	Rank	Canonical correlation	Eigenvalue
Items		GO	NGO				
I1	Nil	Nil	Nil	0.650	3		
I2	0.672	1.88	2.52	0.784	1		
I3	Nil	Nil	Nil	0.535	8		
I4	-0.330	0.31	0.091	0.434	12		
I5	Nil	Nil	Nil	0.548	6		
I6	Nil	Nil	Nil	0.554	5		
I7	0.423	1.01	1.41	0.672	2	0.759	0.625
I8		Nil		0.453	10		
I9	-0.316	3.39	3.18	0.171	14		
I10	Nil	Nil	Nil	0.385	13		
I11	Nil	Nil	Nil	0.444	11		
I12	Nil	Nil	Nil	0.542	7		

	Discriminant coefficient	Classification function coefficient		Loadings	Rank	Canonical correlation	Eigenvalue
Items		GO	NGO				
I13	0.307	1.26	1.55	0.608	4		
I14	0.345	1.94	1.64	0.489	9		

Note: Discriminant items are: 'if you had a problem, how sincerely the service provider resolved it' (I2); 'fairness in decision making by the service provider' (I4); 'how good are the workers in answering your questions quickly' (I7); how good the organization is in listening to any of your suggestions' (I9); 'worker's understanding of the individual beneficiary's need' (I13); and 'service provider's locations are convenient' (I14)'.

The canonical correlation value for the analysis is 0.759 which shows that around 58% (square of 0.759) of the variance in dependent variable can be accounted for by this model.

5.5.1 Discriminant equations of the model for combined study

It was found in the above analysis that the opinions of the beneficiaries measured using our effectiveness scale vary in six items. Thus, the combined discriminant equation can be written as:

$$DF_{GO\ \&\ NGO} = -4.685 + 0.67\, I_2 - 0.33\, I_4 + 0.42\, I_7 - 0.32\, I_9 + 0.31\, I_{13}\ 0.34\, I_{14} \quad (1)$$

In our scale items, lower absolute coefficient values for the independent variables (or items) are desired as these indicate fewer requirements for improvement, in other words, the existence of more effective service delivery from the providers. Equation-1 shows that the value of the coefficient of item-2 (Question: 'If you had a problem, how sincerely the service provider resolved it') is maximum which means beneficiaries are very concerned about the sincerity of the providers in solving their problems. A one percent increase in this particular item causes 67% improvement in the satisfaction of the beneficiaries in the service delivery process. The second important item for the beneficiaries is the service knowledge of the field workers with prompt reply (item-7), the improvement of which rewards a 42% increase in satisfaction among the beneficiaries.

Another aspect of interest is found when checking the individual discriminant functions of GOs and NGOs independently as given below:

$$DF_{GO} = -16.172 + 1.88\, I_2 + 0.31\, I_4 + 1.01\, I_7 + 3.39\, I_9 + 1.26\, I_{13} + 1.94\, I_{14} \quad (2)$$
$$DF_{NGO} = -20.620 + 2.52\, I_2 + 0.091\, I_4 + 1.41\, I_7 + 3.18\, I_9 + 1.56\, I_{13} + 1.64\, I_{14} \quad (3)$$

A relatively higher negative intercept value in equation-3 (compared to equation-2) indicates that other factors remaining constant, an equal improvement made by both GOs and NGOs in the stated discriminant items will have an enhanced positive impact on the lives of the beneficiaries of the GOs. **This observation necessarily emphasizes that GOs are able to contribute more to the lives of the poor beneficiaries compared to NGOs if proper policy packages are implemented.**

These validated[27] findings demonstrate a significant difference between the opinions of the beneficiaries of GOs and NGOs in poverty alleviation programs in Bangladesh, thus our H_3 is rejected.

It is clear from our findings (see equation-2) that government agencies need to concentrate particularly on the issue of 'listening and incorporating suggestions from the beneficiaries' (I9) in their decision-making processes since this item has the highest coefficient value of 3.39, and the largest coefficient value gap (0.30) between GOs and NGOs. As can be seen from equation-2, a one percent increase in effort in this item by GOs will increase their efficacy by more than three times that of their present performance. Our survey results show that only 26% of GO beneficiaries agree that the option of formal meetings with officials on a regular basis would improve services, while this rate is around 49% for the NGO beneficiaries. We believe that ideas for new and customized strategies can only come from the service recipients, thus incorporation of the justified (or experience oriented) opinions of the beneficiaries will certainly increase the level of effectiveness of service delivery by the GO officials and workers.

Another key item that requires considerable attention by GOs is the 'location issue' (I14) which has a higher coefficient value for GOs (1.94) compared to NGOs (1.64). The same result is found in the Northern and Southern Area Studies (see further below). We collected data from many of the most remote areas where the coverage by government agencies was found to be nominal. At the time of the survey, it was found that government agencies have branches only at *upazilla* level and not at village level. As roads and other infrastructure in rural areas are to a great extent underdeveloped, it is quite difficult for the beneficiaries of GOs to travel long distances to reach GO offices for any assistance. Monitoring and visiting by the GO field workers is also minimal due to non-availability of branches in most remote areas. Another important result expected from our study is that in order to provide better and more accessible services to their rural beneficiaries, GO managers need to increase coverage through, for example, setting up new branches with more field workers in remote areas. And, therefore, a large scale investment is required to achieve this.

A further important discriminating issue between GOs and NGOs is with respect to 'fairness in decision making' (I4), especially considering that government agencies are often accused (coefficient of GOs and NGOs are 0.31 and 0.091 respectively) of unfair decision-making due to perceptions of corruption, favouritism, and too much red tape. Many beneficiaries report that government officials ask for bribes through a class of broker before approving a loan. It was also reported that there is an unofficial rule which states that beneficiaries must pay 10% of the approved fund as a gift to the GO officials. In addition, many believe that GOs prefer to provide loans to males and they do so often without any pre-assessment of the project to be funded[28]. According to our survey results, for 70% of the respondents there is almost no monitoring or visit to the beneficiaries from government officials after providing microfinance. This finding necessarily indicates a lack of efficacy in service delivery by GO agencies. Monitoring of the activities of the beneficiaries by the field workers is important primarily to ensure the utilization of the approved fund by the person under whom the credit was sanctioned. As many female respondents reported, their husbands or male family members used the sanctioned loan and this practice defies the purpose of self-dependency and empowerment of women. Secondly, it is important for the government agencies to check whether the credit recipients require any extra help in utilizing the loan to ensure a better return from the project, and thirdly, it is necessary to ensure that the funding is utilized in the project as proposed because many recipients reported during our field survey that the loan amount had instead been utilized for personal consumption (for example, to buy daily consumer goods or even to pay dowry) rather than for the approved venture. Equations-2 and 3 show that the NGOs are four times better than the GO agencies at monitoring the spending patterns (including who is utilizing the loan) of the approved funds. It is therefore important for GO policy-makers to maintain fairness by reducing the level of corruption through elimination of the 'middle man' which creates leakage of funds.

Some problems have been noticed regarding NGOs (see equation-3) as well. It is observed that NGOs need to pay more attention to the issue of sincerity in solving any problems (I2) the beneficiaries may have because in this item NGOs are far behind (largest coefficient gap of 0.64) than GO agencies (coefficient for GOs and NGOs are 1.88 and 2.52 respectively). As coverage by the NGOs has widened, it has become increasingly difficult for them to handle beneficiaries' problems with their existing workforce, and thus beneficiaries observe a lack of sincerity. At the time of the survey many respondents reported that the field workers are prompt and serious in sanctioning loans, however, their sincerity declines soon after the loan disbursement which highlights the workers' negligence in the provision of additional services. The financial sustainability requirement of cutting costs to a minimum has led many programs to seriously cut complementary services (Mayoux, 2000). A possible long-run consequence of all these would be the loss of beneficiaries due to a high degree of dissatisfaction. As a result, dissatisfied beneficiaries may move to another service provider (such as other GO agencies or another NGO) who provides more complementary services in time. Concerned NGOs thus need to increase the number of field workers with a second option being to create a special group of mobile field workers who will deal only with the problems of the beneficiaries.

NGOs also need to invest heavily in staff training to make their workers more skilled in promptly solving any technical problems the beneficiaries may have (I7) (coefficient value is 1.41). It is important to note that as most of the beneficiaries are illiterate, they need more meticulous advice regarding the utilization of their funds. Moreover, beneficiaries who receive other special services (like family planning, immunization, sanitation) require further assistance from the workers. Periodic training of officials and workers based on findings from nationwide (and area specific) reviews may help the NGO policy makers in this issue.

Beneficiaries of NGOs tend to believe that NGOs and their workers are not considerate enough of their individual needs (I13) rather, the NGOs evaluate all the beneficiaries in the same way (coefficient value is 1.56 for NGOs). For instance, interest charged by NGOs is comparatively higher than that charged by GO agencies; however, a high rate of interest is charged by all. This needs to be overhauled and should be customized in such a way that the interest charged would be based on expected earnings from each particular project in which the funds are being invested. For instance, service providers could consider conducting studies to identify possible rates of return from different on-farm and off-farm activities[29] and then the interest on credit may be fixed based on those findings. In this way, interest charged for different purposes can be customized instead of charging identical rate of interest to all. In addition, it is essential that workers and managers consider special cases at the time of approving the loan. For instance, a lower rate of interest could be charged for those who are living in disadvantaged locations such as the islands of Bhola, Hatia, Sandwip, etc., or on land that is surrounded by bodies of water (like Sunamgonj district), or in extremely hilly areas (like Bandarban, Khagrachori, etc.). A lower rate of interest should be offered to physically challenged, widowed and divorced (especially women) beneficiaries. A one-to-one consultation approach should be implemented before approving the loan instead of following the traditional way of disbursing loans to everyone. It is important to note that understanding the individual needs of the beneficiaries, and advising them accordingly will enhance the capability of the beneficiaries in the better utilization of the loan resulting in regular repayments and, in turn, breaking the poverty trap. For instance, the service requirements of the less capable people such as the illiterate and physically challenged poor are greater than those of the semi-literate and physically able poor. In such circumstances, better and more adequately customized training would help the less capable poor bring in better returns from the projects. This would generate both larger surpluses for re-investment and increased consumption which, in turn, will help break the vicious cycle of poverty. In addition, as indicated earlier, location (plain land or hilly areas or islands) and age-related issues need to be considered when dealing with the service requirements of the beneficiaries.

5.5.2 Estimating variations in discriminant items in different areas of Bangladesh

To examine whether there exists any variation in the opinions of the beneficiaries of different areas, we conducted discriminant analysis separately in three areas: Northern, Southern and Central (see Table 5.17 for details). A summary of the discriminant functions for these three areas are presented below:

$$DF_{North} = -3.33 + 0.79\, I_2 + 0.53\, I_7 - 0.46\, I_{14} \quad (4)$$
$$DF_{GONorth} = -14.21 + 1.83\, I_2 + 3.12\, I_7 + 2.41\, I_{14} \quad (5)$$
$$DF_{NGONorth} = -16.61 + 2.43\, I_2 + 3.52\, I_7 + 2.04\, I_{14} \quad (6)$$
$$DF_{South} = -4.57 + 0.88\, I_6 + 0.40\, I_{14} \quad (7)$$
$$DF_{GOSouth} = -9.28 + 3.25\, I_6 + 2.60\, I_{14} \quad (8)$$
$$DF_{NGOSouth} = -13.65 + 4.09\, I_6 + 2.21\, I_{14} \quad (9)$$
$$DF_{Central} = -5.09 + 0.62\, I_5 + 0.65\, I_8 + 0.24\, I_{14} \quad (10)$$
$$DF_{GOCentral} = -11.23 + 3.01\, I_5 + 2.54\, I_8 + 1.43\, I_{14} \quad (11)$$
$$DF_{NGOCentral} = -15.88 + 3.59\, I_5 + 3.14\, I_8 + 1.65\, I_{14} \quad (12)$$

In all areas surveyed I14, 'Service provider's location is convenient', stood out as the item perceived by most as requiring further improvement. Other discriminant items (based on individual discriminant equation of 5, 6, 7, 8, 9, 11, and 12) are listed in Table 5.17.

Table 5.17: Area-wise discriminating scale items for GOs and NGOs

Area	Service provider	Item of the effectiveness scale chosen for improvement	Coefficient value
North	GO	Location of the service provider is convenient (I14)	2.41
	NGO	If you had a problem, how sincerely the service provider resolved it (I2)	2.43
		How good are the workers in answering your queries quickly (I7)	3.52
South	GO	Location of the service provider is convenient (I14)	2.60
	NGO	Quality maintenance of the service by the provider (I6)	4.09
Central	GO	None	
	NGO	How sincerely the service provider keeps their promise (I5)	3.59
		Transparency in transaction process of the service provider (I8)	3.14
		Location of the service provider is convenient (I14)	1.65

The findings shown in Table 5.17 further confirm that there are significant differences amongst the opinions of the beneficiaries regarding GOs and NGOs, thus H_3 is rejected.

Moreover, as can be observed from Table 5.17, there are considerable differences in opinions among beneficiaries in different areas. For the NGOs, effectiveness items vary among regions, whereas for GO agencies location or coverage shows as the only issue that requires improvement. Beneficiaries from the Southern region put more emphasis on 'quality maintenance' (with the highest coefficient value of 4.09), whereas in the Northern region the preferences are for 'sincerity' (value is 2.43) and 'skill of the workers' (3.52) (see equations 5, 6, 8 and 9). One fundamental reason behind these variations is that in the Southern region, NGOs have been operating for many years (since 1972) and thus they are more skilled in solving problems which explains why beneficiaries in the South scored service quality maintenance[30] highly. Presumably, the priority for these beneficiaries is speedier, effective, and informed solutions to their problems.

On the other hand, in the Northern region, the presence of NGOs is comparatively new. Thus, beneficiaries in that region seem to focus more on the sincerity and skill of the officials and workers.

It is observed that in the Central region, NGOs are covering the more remote areas but have created a vacuum in the areas (location has coefficient value of 1.65) that are closer to the district headquarters or capitals. GO agencies may consider filling this space in the future, however, at present, due to the low coverage by GO agencies, beneficiaries are deprived of the services of both GOs and NGOs.

Levels of expected improvement in GO and NGO services are relatively less in the Central areas. So these beneficiaries put more emphasis on the issue of the service providers keeping their promises (I4) (coefficient value is 3.59 and highest for this region). This is seemingly due to the negligence of the service providers in making available other value added (family planning, sanitation, pure water supply) services to the beneficiaries. Less coverage, fewer workers, and less concentration by the service providers in the Central areas seem to have resulted in the beneficiaries being more suspicious about transparency in transaction processes by the NGOs (coefficient value is 3.14). This is a very important message for the NGOs; they have to break away from the perceived negative image of microfinance institutions (MFI) by re-establishing themselves as non-profit service providers. Several past cases of bankruptcy of NGOs and MFIs (for instance, Jubo Karmasangsthan Society (Jubok) and Islamic Trade and Commerce Ltd (ITCL)) or cancellation of registration[31] can be seen as reasons behind such an image. In addition, charging higher rates of interest along with a reduction in the provision for additional services (like sanitation, pure water supply, immunization, etc.) characterizes NGOs as the new form of traditional money lenders (Muhammad, 2006). Our study recommends that both GOs and NGOs improve their coverage and concentration, particularly in the Central areas.

The findings as shown in Table 5.17 emphasize that in the Northern region, two out of three discriminant items ('sincerity in problem solving' and 'how good the workers are in responding quickly') show that further improvement is required by NGO beneficiaries, while in the Central area this claim is true for all three discriminant items ('promise keeping', 'transparency in transaction process' and 'location of the provider'). In the Southern area, both government agencies and NGOs have one item each that requires improvement. For GOs, it is location, and for NGOs it's quality maintenance. However, the coefficient value of the discriminant item for NGOs (4.09) is much larger than that for government agencies

(2.60). Most importantly, as can be seen from Table 5.17, GOs have only one common item appearing in all areas that needs further improvement; ‘location of the service provider’. Furthermore, NGOs need to improve in multiple diversified items (6 items listed above) across three regions. *This finding provides evidence that government agencies are more effective in delivering services to the rural poor in Bangladesh than are the NGOs.*

5.6 Proposed modified Sustainable Livelihoods Model

Figure 5.3: Suggested modifications to DFID’s sustainable livelihood framework

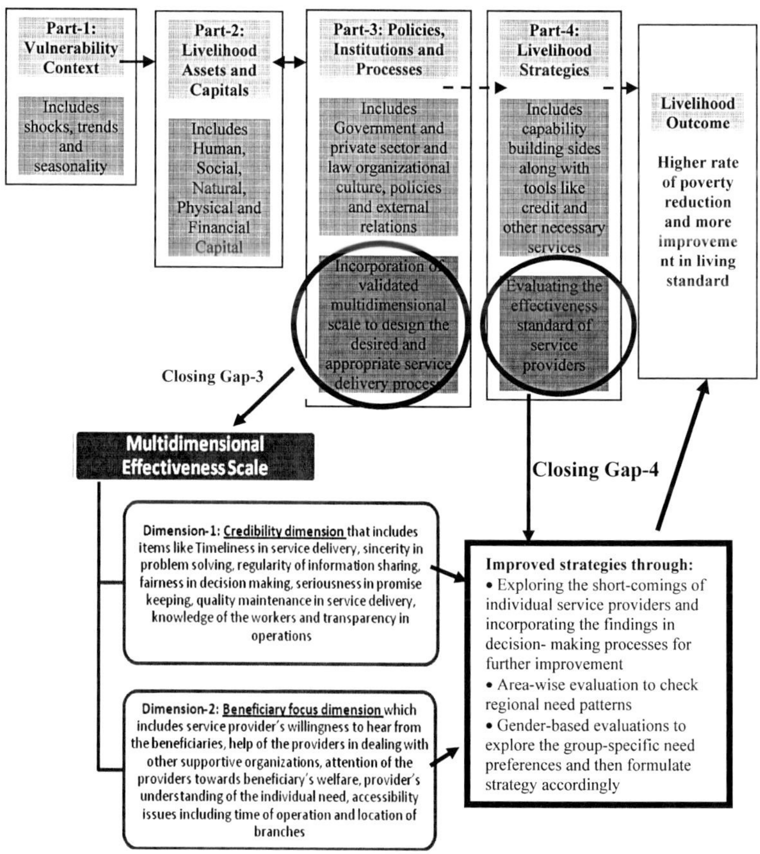

In order to improve the institutional policies and processes (gap 3 and 4 in Fig-3.4 in Chapter 3) in poverty reduction programs, a revised

livelihood model is proposed in Fig-5.3. The modified model suggests that to be more pro-poor and effective in delivery processes, service providers must be judged through a multidimensional service delivery effectiveness scale (following the solid arrows not the broken ones). In addition, this scale and the livelihood strategies (gap 4) should be evaluated on the basis of gender and regional issues in order to formulate more customized strategies. It is recommended that the proposed multidimensional scale along with the livelihood model should be finetuned by considering country of origin and time of study issues before applying it to a specific region.

5.7 Conclusion

In this chapter a two-dimensional multi-item scale has been developed and validated through construct, convergent, discriminant, and nomological validity by using three different sets of data which capture distinct aspects of 'credibility dimensions' and 'focus towards beneficiaries dimensions' of the service providers in poverty alleviation programs in Bangladesh. A scale development process was chosen which, unlike simple descriptive statistics, can detect and eliminate a number of redundant or insignificant variables, the presence of which (insignificant variables) may generate an erroneous result and consequently wrong policy prescriptions. This scale can be utilized to assess the efficacy in the service delivery processes of GOs and NGOs in Bangladesh and other parts of the world. Minor regional adjustments may be required due to the fact that this scale is validated through discriminant validity, nomological validity, and convergent validity.

Significant differences in opinions of the beneficiaries were found with respect to the effectiveness of GOs and NGOs, and these can be listed as follows:

- GOs require more improvement in the items related to the beneficiary focus dimension, namely listening to the suggestions of beneficiaries, and expanding coverage along with increased fairness in operation. On the other hand, NGOs need to concentrate more on issues related to credibility dimensions such as sincerity of the providers in solving problems, and increasing workers' skills in dealing with individual problems.
- In the case of regional analysis for GO agencies, improvement is required with respect to their locations or coverage; for NGOs the results vary. For instance, in the Northern region, NGOs need to

concentrate on issues related to skills of the workers, whereas in the Southern region more attention should be paid to service quality maintenance; in the Central areas, NGOs need to pay more attention to credibility-related issues, particularly with regard to keeping their promises in service delivery by establishing transparency in transaction processes.

- Finally, our study demonstrates that the beneficiaries of poverty reduction programs strongly believe that GOs are more effective than NGOs in delivering the services.

This study recommends the necessity of a cultural change in the service providers in rural Bangladesh by ameliorating the GO corruption through the elimination of middlemen and by speeding up lending processes. Beneficiaries of government agencies require more support by providing monitoring and liaison before and after loan approval. Furthermore, GOs need to invest more in infrastructure and coverage through employing more field workers and by setting up more branch offices.

NGOs need to distance themselves from the notion that they are MFIs through re-scheduling rates of interest and repayment processes. They need to change the perception of 'workers as money collection agents' by investing more in human resource practices, and training, and by keeping in close and regular contact with the beneficiaries.

All these findings are definitely based on the beneficiaries' opinions of GOs and NGOs. It is equally important to explore differences in the opinions of male and female beneficiaries on the service delivery scale items such that any evidence of gender discrimination in delivering services can be explored. This gender-based study is explained in Chapter 6.

Appendix C

Technical notes

'CMIN represents the discrepancy between the unrestricted sample covariance matrix and the restricted covariance matrix and commonly expressed as **chi-square statistics (χ^2)**. Researchers[32] have addressed the limitations of χ^2 in deciding goodness of fit of the model and have suggested CMIN/df as a better statistic for fit analysis' (Byrne, 2005).

'The root mean squared residual (RMR) represents the average residual value. This standard value of RMR is useful in comparing fit across models although it is widely used for the fit analysis of single models. Lower RMR values represent better fit and higher values represent worse fit; and sometimes known as badness-of-fit measures' (Hair et al., 2010).

'Goodness-of-fit index (GFI) is a measure of the relative amount of variance and covariance in the model. GFI was produced only for a goodness test which is less sensitive to sample size'.

'Adjusted GFI (AGFI) differs from GFI only in the fact that it adjusts for the number of degrees of freedom in the specified model' (Byrne, 2005).

'The parsimony goodness-of-fit index (PGFI) introduced by James, Mulaik and Brett (1982) to address the issue of parsimony in structural equation modelling. PGFI takes into account the complexity of the hypothesized model in the assessment of overall model fit and thus provides a more realistic evaluation of the model' (Mulaik et al., 1989).

The incremental index of fit (IFI) was proposed by Bollen (1990) to address the issue of parsimony and sample size.

'Tucker-Lewis index (TLI; Tucker and Lewis, 1973) is conceptually similar to the NFI, but it varies in that it is actually a comparison of the normed chi-square values for the null and specified model which to some degree takes into account model complexity' (Hair et al., 2010).

One of the most widely used measures attempting to correct for the tendency of the χ^2 GOF test statistics to reject models with a large sample or large number of observed variables is **the root mean square error of approximation (RMSEA)**. It better represents how well a model fits a population, not just a sample used for estimation. Joreskog and Sorebom (1996a) suggest that the ***p value*** for this test is better if it is >0.50.

'Akaike's (1987) information criterion (AIC) with Bozdogan's (1987) consistent version of AIC[33] (CAIC) is related to the issues of parsimony in the assessment of model fit. The AIC and CAIC are used in the comparison of two or more models with smaller values representing a better fit of the hypothesized model' (Hu and Bentlar, 1999).

The expected cross-validation index (ECVI) compares among all competitive models, and the model with the smallest ECVI value is potentially the one with a better fit.

The last GOF statistics are **Hoelter's** (1983a) critical N (CN) (labelled as Hoelter's 0.05 and 0.01 indices). Development of Hoelter's index arose from an attempt to find a fit index that is independent of sample size. Hoelter (1983) proposed that a value in excess of 200 is desirable for a model to have good fit with the sample data.

Table A5.1: Total variance explained with 22 items using Principal Component Analysis

	Initial Eigenvalues			Extraction Sums of Squared Loadings		
Component	**Total**	**% of Variance**	**Cumulative %**	**Total**	**% of Variance**	**Cumulative %**
1	11.802	53.647	53.647	11.802	53.647	53.647
2	1.809	8.222	61.869	1.809	8.222	61.869
3	1.181	5.366	67.235	1.181	5.366	**66.235**
4	.851	3.867	71.102			
5	.716	3.253	74.355			
6	.683	3.104	77.459			
7	.559	2.541	80.000			
8	.519	2.358	82.358			
9	.438	1.990	84.349			
10	.406	1.846	86.194			
11	.389	1.766	87.961			
12	.328	1.491	89.451			
13	.315	1.431	90.882			
14	.288	1.310	92.192			
15	.286	1.301	93.492			
16	.263	1.193	94.686			
17	.257	1.170	95.856			
18	.225	1.023	96.879			
19	.205	.932	97.811			
20	.190	.862	98.672			
21	.170	.774	99.446			
22	.122	.554	100.000			

Table A5.2: Communalities with 3-factor analysis and 22 items

Item	Initial	Extraction
Timeliness in loan disbursement/providing other services	1.000	.742
If you had a problem, how sincerely the service provider resolved it	1.000	.790
Speed of decision making by the organization	1.000	.746
Regularity of information sharing through field workers	1.000	.720
Fairness in decision making by the organization	1.000	.704
How sincerely the service provider keeps their promise	1.000	.727
Quality maintenance of the service by the provider	1.000	.688
How good are the workers in answering your queries quickly	1.000	.629
How good the organization is in listening to any of your suggestions	1.000	.532
Quality in additional technical support (Like, how to use a machine)	1.000	.612
Willingness of the workers to help you	1.000	.695
Frequency of visits by the workers is enough for you	1.000	.633
Transparency in transaction process of the service provider	1.000	.606
How helpful the service provider been in dealing with other org.	1.000	.697
Attention of the service provider towards your welfare	1.000	.708
Attention of the workers towards you	1.000	.711
Worker's understanding of the individual beneficiary's need	1.000	.679
Formal participation (Like in monthly meeting) of beneficiaries in the supportive decision making process of the service provider	1.000	.369
Service provider's location is convenient	1.000	.780
Service provider's business hours are convenient	1.000	.755
Timing of the visit by the workers	1.000	.644
Availability of the workers	1.000	.625

Extraction Method: Principal Component Analysis.

Table A5.3: Rotated component matrix[a] for 22 items

Item	Component		
	1	2	3
If you had a problem, how sincerely the service provider resolved it	.854		
Speed of decision making by the organization	.812		
Timeliness in loan disbursement/providing other services	.812		
Regularity of information sharing through field workers	.809		
Fairness in decision making by the organization	.796		
Willingness of the workers to help you	.755		
How sincerely the service provider keeps their promise	.754		
Frequency of visits by the workers is enough for you	.720		
How good are the workers in answering your queries quickly	.701		
Quality maintenance of the service by the provider	.674		
Transparency in transaction process of the service provider	.668		
Availability of the workers	.587		
Quality in additional technical support (Like, how to use a machine)	.577	.506	
Timing of the visit by the workers	.554		
How helpful the service provider been in dealing with other org.		.768	
Attention of the service provider towards your welfare		.687	
How good the organization is in listening to any of your suggestions		.645	
Attention of the workers towards you		.625	
Worker's understanding of the individual beneficiary's need		.616	
Service provider's location is convenient			.862
Service provider's business hours are convenient			.824
Formal participation (Like in monthly meeting) of beneficiaries in the supportive decision making process of the service provider			.540

Extraction Method: Principal Component Analysis.
Rotation Method: Varimax with Kaiser Normalization.
[a]Rotation converged in 6 iterations.

Table A5.4: Rotated component matrix[a] for 21 items in exploratory factor analysis

Name of the item	Component		
	1	2	3
If you had a problem, how sincerely the service provider resolved it	.854		
Timeliness in loan disbursement/providing other services	.815		
Speed of decision making by the organization	.815		
Regularity of information sharing through field workers	.811		
Fairness in decision making by the organization	.798		
Willingness of the workers to help you	.759		
How sincerely the service provider keeps their promise	.758		
Frequency of visits by the workers is enough for you	.727		
How good are the workers in answering your queries quickly	.705		
Quality maintenance of the service by the provider	.680		
Transparency in transaction process of the service provider	.673		
Availability of the workers	.591		
Timing of the visit by the workers	.560		
How helpful the service provider been in dealing with other org.		.787	
Attention of the service provider towards your welfare		.734	
Attention of the workers towards you		.645	
Worker's understanding of the individual beneficiary's need		.636	
How good the organization is in listening to any of your suggestions		.610	
Service provider's location is convenient			.871
Service provider's business hours are convenient			.839
Formal participation (Like in monthly meeting) of beneficiaries in the supportive decision making process of the service provider			.543

[a]Extraction Method: Principal Component Analysis.
Rotation Method: Varimax with Kaiser Normalization.

Table A5.5: Total variance explained with 21 items

Component	Initial Eigenvalues			Extraction Sums of Squared Loadings		
	Total	% of Variance	Cumulative %	Total	% of Variance	Cumulative %
1	11.386	54.218	54.218	11.386	54.218	54.218
2	1.729	8.235	62.453	1.729	8.235	62.453
3	1.140	5.430	67.883	1.140	5.430	**67.883**
4	.828	3.945	71.828			
5	.707	3.366	75.194			
6	.645	3.074	78.267			
7	.556	2.649	80.916			
8	.443	2.110	83.026			
9	.430	2.048	85.074			
10	.389	1.851	86.925			
11	.360	1.714	88.640			
12	.322	1.534	90.174			
13	.302	1.437	91.611			
14	.287	1.369	92.979			
15	.266	1.265	94.245			
16	.261	1.245	95.490			
17	.243	1.159	96.648			
18	.220	1.048	97.696			
19	.190	.906	98.603			
20	.171	.812	99.415			
21	.123	.585	100.000			

Table A5.6: Modification index for items and error terms in 21-item CFA

Item			M.I.	Par Change
Bushours	<---	Timingofvisit	18.644	.219
Location	<---	Timingofvisit	11.237	.215
Location	<---	Availability	33.030	.269
Location	<---	Willingness	38.416	.306
Listening	<---	Speeddecnmk	15.734	.152
Attentionwelfr	<---	Speeddecnmk	11.884	-.134

Item			M.I.	Par Change
Timingofvisit	<---	Bushours	25.464	.232
Timingofvisit	<---	Location	18.202	.144
Timingofvisit	<---	Understnding	11.569	.166
Timingofvisit	<---	Availability	29.321	.191
Availability	<---	Factor-3	10.435	.266
Availability	<---	Location	40.784	.284
Availability	<---	Attentionwelfr	10.112	.199
Availability	<---	Timingofvisit	32.372	.362
Availability	<---	Timeliness	22.384	-.303
Transcttranspa	<---	Willingness	15.399	.138
Visitworkers	<---	Attnworkers	14.138	.160
Visitworkers	<---	Willingness	31.729	.191
Willingness	<---	Factor-3	12.614	.256
Willingness	<---	Factor-2	13.180	.468
Willingness	<---	Location	55.181	.290
Willingness	<---	Understnding	10.414	.182
Willingness	<---	Attnworkers	14.060	.202
Willingness	<---	Timingofvisit	10.219	.179
Willingness	<---	Transcttranspa	11.976	.166
Willingness	<---	Visitworkers	26.896	.267
Fairness	<---	Willingness	12.452	-.121
Speeddecnmk	<---	Attnworkers	18.777	-.184
Speeddecnmk	<---	Attentionwelfr	17.503	-.181
Speeddecnmk	<---	Timeliness	19.390	.194
Timeliness	<---	Availability	23.758	-.161
Timeliness	<---	Speeddecnmk	14.159	.156
Timeliness	<---	Sincerity	22.804	.209
Sincerity	<---	Timeliness	32.817	.234

Item			M.I.	Par Change
e18	<-->	Factor-2	14.132	-.039
e18	<-->	Factor-1	18.249	.059
e13	<-->	Factor-3	30.841	.165
e13	<-->	Factor-1	21.277	-.074
e13	<-->	e20	20.016	.124
e13	<-->	e19	13.724	.130
e12	<-->	Factor-3	30.378	.215
e12	<-->	Factor-2	10.215	.053
e12	<-->	Factor-1	23.966	-.103

Item			M.I.	Par Change
e12	<-->	e19	44.311	.308
e12	<-->	e13	38.856	.217
e8	<-->	Factor-2	20.782	.052
e8	<-->	Factor-1	14.583	-.055
e6	<-->	Factor-3	32.568	.195
e6	<-->	Factor-2	16.738	.059
e6	<-->	Factor-1	30.739	-.102
e6	<-->	e19	62.427	.321
e6	<-->	e13	12.262	.107
e6	<-->	e12	11.146	.135
e6	<-->	e11	24.600	.143
e6	<-->	e8	50.716	.198
e6	<-->	e7	13.457	-.101
e5	<-->	e19	10.354	-.104
e5	<-->	e8	10.513	-.072
e5	<-->	e6	19.862	-.126
e4	<-->	e5	12.220	.081
e3	<-->	Factor-2	22.202	-.054
e3	<-->	Factor-1	10.755	.047
e3	<-->	e16	13.795	-.081
e3	<-->	e15	12.535	-.075
e3	<-->	e6	13.714	-.103
e2	<-->	e12	31.472	-.183
e2	<-->	e6	11.924	-.099
e2	<-->	e3	27.224	.117
e1	<-->	e4	11.992	.073
e1	<-->	e3	12.198	.071
e1	<-->	e2	46.066	.141

Table A5.7: Goodness-of-fit statistics for 17-item scale model

Model	NPAR	CMIN	DF	P	CMIN/DF
Our model	37	342.766	116	.000	2.955
Saturated model	153	.000	0		
Independence model	17	2538.296	136	.000	18.664

Model	RMR	GFI	AGFI	PGFI
Our model	.044	.892	.858	.677
Saturated model	.000	1.000		
Independence model	.250	.316	.231	.281

Model	NFI Delta1	RFI rho1	IFI Delta2	TLI rho2	CFI
Our model	.865	.842	.906	.889	.906
Saturated model	1.000		1.000		1.000
Independence model	.000	.000	.000	.000	.000

Model	RMSEA	LO 90	HI 90	PCLOSE
Our model	.073	.064	.082	.000
Independence model	.219	.212	.227	.000

Model	AIC	BCC	BIC	CAIC
Our model	416.766	420.583	561.365	598.365
Saturated model	306.000	321.782	903.937	1056.937
Independence model	2572.296	2574.050	2638.734	2655.734

Model	ECVI	LO 90	HI 90	MECVI
Our model	1.136	.995	1.297	1.146
Saturated model	.834	.834	.834	.877
Independence model	7.009	6.573	7.465	7.014

Model	HOELTER .05	HOELTER .01
Our model	153	166
Independence model	24	26

Table A5.8: Modification index for the items in 17-item scale model

Item		Factor	M.I.	Par Change
Listening	<---	Factor-1	10.989	.202
Listening	<---	Answeringquick	10.602	.131
Listening	<---	Fairness	10.333	.111
Listening	<---	Speeddecnmk	17.127	.159
Attentionwelfr	<---	Speeddecnmk	10.699	-.128
Transcttranspa	<---	Visitworkers	10.133	.138
Visitworkers	<---	Factor-3	11.214	.218
Visitworkers	<---	Factor-2	20.066	.474
Visitworkers	<---	Location	20.369	.144
Visitworkers	<---	Attnworkers	21.477	.204
Visitworkers	<---	Attentionwelfr	14.556	.171
Speeddecnmk	<---	Attnworkers	16.887	-.170
Speeddecnmk	<---	Attentionwelfr	15.042	-.163

Item		Factor	M.I.	Par Change
Speeddecnmk	<---	Timeliness	13.098	.156
Timeliness	<---	Sincerity	17.843	.182
Sincerity	<---	Timeliness	25.597	.204

			M.I.	Par Change
e18	<-->	Factor-2	14.260	-.041
e18	<-->	Factor-1	19.027	.066
e8	<-->	Factor-2	27.555	.064
e8	<-->	Factor-1	20.790	-.075
e8	<-->	e19	13.992	.127
e8	<-->	e11	17.358	.101
e3	<-->	Factor-2	18.320	-.049
e3	<-->	e16	12.694	-.076
e3	<-->	e15	10.665	-.068
e2	<-->	e3	19.389	.095
e1	<-->	e2	37.886	.124

Table A5.9: Discriminant analysis on South and Central Area study shows mean, *Wilks' lambda* and *F* values

Items	Mean value for different age groups					Mean Differ. Hi-Lo	Wilks' lambda	F- value	Sig.
	26-30 yrs	31-35 yrs	36-40 yrs	41-45 yrs	46-50 yrs				
I1	3.71	3.77	3.91	3.68	3.69	0.23	0.993	0.46	0.76
	(3.46)	(3.45)	(3.67)	(3.52)	(3.55)	(0.21)	(0.988)	(0.94)	(0.43)
I2	4.13	3.99	4.14	3.91	3.95	0.13	0.992	0.55	0.69
	(3.32)	(3.45)	(3.68)	(3.44)	(3.33)	(0.36)	(0.970)	(2.13)	(0.04)
I3	4.16	3.89	4.00	3.86	3.80	0.20	0.987	0.94	0.44
	(3.32)	(3.33)	(3.51)	(3.41)	(3.48)	(0.19)	(0.991)	(0.70)	(0.59)
I4	3.87	3.97	4.04	3.80	3.98	0.24	0.993	0.48	0.74
	(3.33)	(3.50)	(3.54)	(3.37)	(3.18)	(0.35)	(0.986)	(1.17)	(0.32)
I5	3.98	3.96	4.00	3.91	3.69	0.31	0.989	0.76	0.54
	(3.34)	(3.53)	(3.50)	(3.41)	(3.33)	(020)	(0.992)	(0.66)	(0.61)
I6	4.11	3.80	3.86	3.73	3.62	0.47	0.979	1.50	0.20
	(3.28)	(3.53)	(3.50)	(3.28)	(3.36)	(0.25)	(0.985)	(1.26)	(0.28)
I7	4.11	3.83	3.93	3.95	3.67	0.44	0.983	1.23	0.29
	(3.37)	(3.44)	(3.53)	(3.43)	(3.30)	(0.23)	(0.993)	(0.60)	(0.66)
I8	3.89	3.99	4.14	3.98	3.95	0.16	0.991	0.60	0.65
	(3.28)	(3.30)	(3.69)	(3.35)	(3.39)	(0.42)	(0.967)	(1.72)	(0.03)
I9	3.36	3.31	3.51	3.30	3.16	0.34	0.978	1.54	0.19
	(3.31)	(3.39)	(3.50)	(3.46)	(3.15)	(0.30)	(0.978)	(1.81)	(0.12)
I10	3.36	3.17	3.55	3.25	3.16	0.20	0.966	2.49	0.04
	(3.27)	(3.06)	(3.21)	(3.17)	(3.15)	(0.21)	(0.973)	(2.23)	(0.06)
I11	3.49	3.45	3.64	3.52	3.42	0.22	0.991	0.62	0.64
	(3.39)	(3.28)	(3.35)	(3.20)	(3.03)	(0.36)	(0.981)	(1.58)	(0.17)
I12	3.76	3.77	3.88	3.57	3.58	0.29	0.984	1.10	0.35
	(3.16)	(3.13)	(3.31)	(3.17)	(3.27)	(0.14)	(0.986)	(1.14)	(0.33)
I13	3.73	3.58	3.68	3.57	3.33	0.40	0.982	1.29	0.27
	(3.19)	(3.16)	(3.40)	(3.13)	(3.14)	(0.27)	(0.971)	(1.42)	(0.04)

Items	Mean value for different age groups					Mean Differ. Hi-Lo	Wilks' lambda	F- value	Sig.
	26-30 yrs	31-35 yrs	36-40 yrs	41-45 yrs	46-50 yrs				
I14	2.98 (2.98)	2.92 (3.16)	2.94 (3.56)	2.91 (3.41)	3.07 (3.27)	0.16 (0.58)	0.974 (0.957)	1.84 (1.63)	0.12 (0.00)

Note: Values in parentheses are for Central area study. I1-I14 are the items as labelled in Table 5.11 in main text.

Notes

[1] Jelinek (2006, pp. 2) stated that, 'NGOs clearly feel frustrated with the government's lack of trust in them and more significantly, the lack of skilled and trained staff within the government. A national NGO director in Herat stated: 'If NGOs don't take over service provision and project implementation, who will do it? The government simply does not have the capacity'.
Sundaram (1986) saw, 'the human touch and dedication as the real assets of NGOs in Asia. Unlike government agencies, NGOs were highly motivated and tended to accept hardships as a challenge rather than punishment. Unlike business organisations, their smaller sizes, selective tasks, and personal leadership allowed them to innovate and adapt themselves to new circumstances, experiment and face risks'.

[2] Similar definitions are available in literature. 'Effectiveness is a relationship between ends and means. When we call a situation ineffective, we are claiming that we could achieve the desired ends with less means, or that the means employed could produce more of the ends desired. 'Less' and 'more' in this context necessarily refer to less and more value. Thus, economic effectiveness is measured not by the relationship between the physical quantities of ends and means, but by the relationship between the value of the ends and the value of the means' (Heyne, 2007, pp. 3).

[3] For details see,
http://www.eldis.org/vfile/upload/1/document/0901/section4_2.pdf

[4] 'The measure of sampling adequacy (MSA) is used to quantify the degree of inter-correlations among the variables and the appropriateness of the factor analysis. Its value ranges from 0 to 1; the closer the value to 1 the more appropriate is the factor analysis. Measure guidelines are: 0.80 or above is meritorious; 0.70 or above is middling; 0.60 or above is mediocre and 0.50 or above is miserable' (see Hair et al. p. 104).

[5] There is a KMO statistic for each individual variable, and the sum of the variables is the KMO overall statistic. KMO varies from 0 to 1.0 and overall should be 0.60 or higher to proceed with factor analysis. If it is not, the indicator variables with the lowest individual KMO statistic values need to be dropped until the KMO overall rises above 0.60 (some researchers use a more lenient 0.50 cut-off).

[6] 'In the old days of manual factor analysis, this was extremely useful. KMO is still the most reliable one to assess which variables to drop from the model because they are too multicollinear' (Hair et al, 2009, p. 130).

[7] 'Acceptable range of MSA is above 0.50' (Hair et al, 2009, p.132).

[8] Similar rules were followed in marketing studies, for example, Shimp and Sharma (1987); Bawa (2004); in psychology studies, for example, MacCallum and Austin (2000); in research methodology by Black et al., (2009).

[9] Kaiser criterion – a common rule of thumb for dropping the least important factors from the analysis is the K1 rule. Though originated earlier by Guttman in 1954, the criterion is usually referenced in relation to Kaiser's 1960 work that relied upon it. The Kaiser rule is to drop all components with *eigenvalues* under 1.0. It may overestimate or underestimate the true number of factors; the preponderance of simulation study evidence suggests it usually overestimates the true number of factors, sometimes severely (Lance et al., 2006).

[10] Cronbach's alpha reliability coefficient normally ranges between 0 and 1. However, there is actually no lower limit to the coefficient. The closer Cronbach's alpha coefficient is to 1.0 the greater the internal consistency of the items in the scale. George and Mallery (2003) provide the following rules of thumb: '_ > .9 – Excellent, _ > .8 – Good, _ > .7 – Acceptable, _ > .6 – Questionable, _ > .5 – Poor, and _ < .5 – Unacceptable' (p. 231). It should also be noted that while a high value for Cronbach's alpha indicates good internal consistency of the items in the scale, it does not mean that the scale is unidimensional (Gliem and Gliem, 2003).

[11] Refer to Section 4.8 for details.

[12] These factors are also called *constructs* in CFA analysis

[13] It is proposed that if the number of factors is five or less, the number in the sample should be 100-150 (Byrne, 2009). On the other hand, if the number of factors is 6 or more, the appropriate sample size is up to 500. In our case, a three-factor model with a sample size of 368 is adequate to satisfy the sampling requirement.

[14] The model has 231 pieces of information with 45 parameters to be estimated, leaving us with 186 degrees of freedom. The model has 21 observed variables. Based on the formula p (p + 1)/2, computation of the sample covariance matrix for these data therefore yields {21(21+1)/2} = 231 sample moments. As the model has more unique covariance and variance terms (231) than parameters (45) to be estimated, it is an over-identified model.

[15] Over-identification is the desired state for CFA and structural equation modelling in general (Hair et al., 2009, p. 704).

[16] 'Although the chi-square test provides a test of statistical significance, its mathematical properties are a trade-off for the researchers. Although large sample sizes are often desirable, just the increase in sample size itself will make it more difficult for those models to achieve a statistically insignificant goodness of fit. Moreover as more indicators are added to the model, this will make it more difficult in using chi-square to assess model fit' (Hair et. al, 2009 p. 666)

[17] 'GFI and AGFI values of 0.90 are always considered as a good fit. However, few prefer them to be more than 0.95' (Hair et. al, 2009)

[18] Mulaik suggested that non-significant chi-square statistics and GOF in the 0.90s, accompanied by parsimonious fit index in the 0.50s are not unexpected (Byrne, 2009)

[19] 'As CFI has many desirable properties, including its relative, but not complete, insensitivity to model complexity, it is among the most widely used indices' (Hair et. al, 2009 p. 669)
[20] 'The TLI is not normed, and thus its value can fall below 0 or above 1' (Hair et. al, 2009 p. 668)
[21] According to Hu and Bentlar (1999), TLI value close to 0.95 is a very good fit.
[22] MacCallum et al. (1996) recently elaborated on these cut points and noted that, 'RMSEA values ranging from 0.80 to 0.10 indicate mediocre fit, and those greater than 0.10 indicate poor fit'. Although Hu and Bentlar (1999) suggested a value of 0.06 to be indicative of good fit between the hypothesized model and the observed data.
[23] According to Hair et al., (2009), 0.30 is a suggested factor loading if the sample size is 350 or above. However, considering 0.50 as the minimum loading value for item acceptance would be an indication of better fit.
[24] *CFI* = 0.906, *RMSEA* = 0.073, *Hoelters* are 153 and 166, *AIC* and *ECVI* values are still larger than the saturated model.
[25] Also called *nomological validity*, see Cronbach and Meehi (1955).
[26] Age groups 21-25 and 51-60+ have been dropped because of insignificant size
[27] This validation is based on a holdout sample that comes from the original data. Results show that 67% of the original group cases are correctly classified in the combined study and the results for other areas are 66%, 68% and 69% for the Northern, Southern and Central Area Studies respectively, which necessarily signifies the internal and external validity with these classification accuracy and hit ratios.
[28] We found cases where beneficiaries had managed to get a loan for cultivation by presenting other people's land as their own.
[29] Our study suggests that, in general, microcredit is used in certain common activities such as, crop production, poultry, livestocks production, fisheries, starting a corner shop, buying non-automotive transport and selling raw materials for agriculture. Thus it would not be unmanageable for the service providers to identify the expected returns from these few activities.
[30] By 'service quality maintenance' we mean continuous up-grading of the existing services based on the changes in the environment where the services are provided.
[31] According to the Microcredit Regulatory Authority, there are 4200 NGOs working with microcredit among which only 453 have a licence to operate (*The Daily Janakantha*, May 16, 2010),
[32] According to many, chi square is a pragmatic approach of evaluation. For reviews, see: Gerbing and Anderson (1993); Hu and Bentlar (1995); Marsh and Balla (1988).
[33] Bozdogen (1987) noted that, 'the AIC carried a penalty only as it related to degrees of freedom and not to sample size'. Presented with factor analytic findings that revealed the AIC to yield asymptotically inconsistent estimates, he proposed the CAIC, which takes sample size into account (Bandalos, 1993).

CHAPTER SIX

GENDER VARIATION IN THE PERCEPTION OF THE BENEFICIARIES TOWARDS SERVICE DELIVERY EFFECTIVENESS OF CREDIT-DRIVEN GOVERNMENT AND NGO PROJECTS

6.1 Introduction

There is evidence to suggest that gender discrimination is widespread in the developing countries, and this reduces empowerment and increases poverty among women in rural areas. Therefore, to better combat poverty, women require improved service delivery with personal and customized services from both Government and Non-government organizations. Existing literature[1] suggest that 'women's empowerment has five major components: women's sense of self-worth; their right to have and to determine choices; their right to have access to opportunities and resources; their right to have the power to control their own lives, both within and outside the home; and their ability to influence the direction of social change to create a more just social and economic order, nationally and internationally'. These findings are in line with the suggestions offered by Sen (1985, 1999) who advocated that the basic purpose of development is to enlarge people's own choices for leading their life. The choices and the functionings in Sen's approach can create 'capabilities' and the actual levels of achievement which may accelerate poverty reduction rate. The 'capabilities' and 'functionings' can be achieved by empowering women more and more. To eliminate gender inequality, creating an environment is necessary through implementation of positive economic and social policies for full development of women to enable them to realize their full potential. Thus need for customized service is vital in utilizing the credit. Service need fulfilment will help women to get the best possible return from their investment. However, this requires changing practices by active participation and involvement of both men and women in deciding their specific service needs.

No rigorous method for measuring and tracking the changes in levels of empowerment has been developed by the World Bank or any other major development agency to check which determinants can or cannot contribute it. As a result, hundreds of studies have been conducted on women empowerment. Malhotra et al. (2003) provided many ways in which empowerment can be measured with six dimensions: economic, socio-cultural, familial-interpersonal, legal, political, and psychological. A number of studies have shown that women may not be fully empowered in all areas of life (Malhotra et al., 2003; Kishore and Gupta, 2004; Hashemi et al. 1996). Williamson (1983) and Jejeebhoy and Sathar (2001) have studied women empowerment in different countries with special emphasis on demographic determinants. Mahendra (2004) has studied the impact of economic participation and health and education on empowerment. Some researchers have attempted to measure women empowerment with a variety of determinants (such as education, health care, voting, participation, food intake, etc.) and dimensions (especially on economic, social, religious, etc) by different methods and techniques (Amin et al., 1998; Pradhan, 2003; Kishore and Gupta, 2004; Kabeer, 2005; Schüler, 2006; Klasen, 2006). Moreover the World Economic Forum's Gender Gap Index (GGI) also uses a broad range of dimensions and indicators (Lopez-Claros and Zahidi, 2005 and Klasen, 2006).

As can be seen, existing pieces of works on women empowerment mainly focus on exploring the economic, social, and political indicators of empowerment such as education, employment, participation, voice in decision making, etc (for more information, see for example the works of Kabeer, 2005; Schuler, Islam and Rottach, 2010). In addition, existing works explored the role of microcredit in creating or changing economic and social capital for women in order to reduce gender inequality (see for example, Sanyal, 2009; Hashemi, Schuler and Riley, 1996). However, we believe a potential source of gender inequality (as well as women empowerment) can be due to discrimination in service delivery mechanism – an important yet unexplored issue in the existing literature. This chapter intends to close that gap. Findings of this chapter are thus new to the existing literature as this chapter will explore specific service needs of men and women. It is hoped that effective delivery of those services can help the groups better utilize the borrowed money. Based on the items of the developed and validated multidimensional scale (developed in Chapter 5, see Table 5.11), this chapter explores the differences in opinion between male and female beneficiaries in assessing service delivery effectiveness of GOs and NGOs.

6.1.1 Gender inequality and women empowerment in Bangladesh

The concept of 'Division of labour' is often misused in societies that assume men will naturally work outside home and that women can do so, if and only if, they can combine outside work with inescapable and unequally shared household duties – a cruel form of gender discrimination. In more general terms, this is in fact 'forced accumulation of female labour' where rights and opportunities are not equally shared between men and women in a family as well as in society. Sen's (2001) work on the 'theory of households' represents the household not as an undifferentiated unit but as a unit of cooperation as well as inequality and internal discrimination.

The poverty experience in Bangladesh is a good example of gender inequality leading to social exclusion of women resulting in more poverty among them. Statistical evidence suggests that women generally receive less household resources for their food, education, health, and clothing than do men (Siddique, 1998). Bangladesh is one of four least positioned countries in the world where more girls than boys die before the age of five (Ahmad, 1995). A household survey by the Bangladesh Bureau of Statistics (BBS) reported that in rural areas boys receive 172% more money than girls for their education, and rural women receive 27% less medical support than men (HIES-BBS, 2000). The daily wage for female labour is much lower[2] than for males. A logical question to ask at this stage is: 'Who will initiate strength-enhancing activities for women, and how can this be done so that they can better combat poverty?'

The Government of Bangladesh (GoB) has been working for women's empowerment since independence in 1971. Bangladesh is a member of the Nairobi Forward Looking Strategies (NFS) and the United Nations Convention on the Elimination of Discrimination Against Women (CEDAW). The GoB has implemented free education up to undergraduate level for women with special stipend programs introduced for female students. The GoB has enforced laws such as the 'Dowry Prohibition Act,1980' , 'Acid Crime Prevention Act 2002', 'Speedy Trial Tribunal Act of 2002', and 'Muslim Marriage and Divorces Act 2005' to protect women and to reduce child-marriage rates. The numbers of allotted seats for female members of parliament and local female members at the union level have increased. Despite all these efforts, GO agencies have been criticized for a lack of projects on social mobilization and empowerment building, poor coverage, and less monitoring and supervision towards women. Thus, NGOs have come forward to fill these gaps in Bangladesh.

NGOs have been working alongside the GoB for poverty alleviation since 1972 and their main beneficiaries are women[3]. NGOs have rightly pointed out that the main obstacles to women's development are: illiteracy, lack of income, absence of social agency, and lack of awareness about women's rights. Micro-financing has become a useful tool to alleviate poverty among women. It is expected that the provision of capital to women will have the additional effect of improving households in terms of nutrition, health[4], and education. In rural Bangladesh, NGO workers travel door to door to deliver credit to poor women because women usually stay at home due to cultural and religious restrictions. However, two important issues need to be discussed. First, even though a loan may be sanctioned in the name of the woman, it is mostly used by their husbands or other male members of the family (Goetz and Gupta, 1996). Second, NGOs tend to neglect any capability-building of women, particularly making no provision for training or consultation on the effective use of the loan. On the other hand, in India, Sanyal (2007) found that social agency of women (where women meet regularly with other women) expanded women's mental capacities and this is reflected in their new attitudes and actions, thus improving the associative effects as described in Sen's (2000) concept of capability.

In this chapter, we have explored whether the service providers (GO and NGOs) formulate customized strategies for women to better combat poverty in a society that discriminates against women believing them to be less capable. We have shown the demand priorities of women from their own perspective because it is important to see how women themselves view the provision for services in the poverty alleviation programs in Bangladesh. It is equally important to explore whether a significant difference in opinion exists between men and women in evaluating the service delivery from the participant organizations.

6.2 Exploring gender variation in opinion using the effectiveness scale

To address the above mentioned issues, we will be using the validated multidimensional 'effectiveness scale' developed in Chapter 5 (refer to Table 5.11). Deviating opinions on the scale items from male and female respondents have significant implications for the managers of government and NGOs in implementing poverty reduction programs. We proceed with the following hypothesis:

> H_1: Effectiveness scale items have significant positive and non-discriminatory relationships with gender issue. Or in other words, male and female beneficiaries do not vary in their opinions on scale items.

To conduct the study, author combined all data so far used in the scale development process, thus our sample size is 930 (refer to Table 4.5 in Chapter 4). We begin with the results of two-group discriminant analysis which is shown in Table 6.1.

Table 6.1: Discriminant analysis between male and female beneficiaries in combined study

Items	Mean for beneficiary Male	Mean for beneficiary Female	Mean Diff.	*Wilks' lambda*	*F Value* To enter	Sig.	Loading	Maldobis Min D Sq
I1	3.32	3.96	0.64	0.908	93.520	0.00	0.917	0.405
I2	3.38	3.97	0.59	0.919	81.539	0.00	0.795	0.353
I3	3.48	3.93	0.45	0.948	51.290	0.00	0.679	0.222
I4	3.50	3.90	0.4	0.960	38.797	0.00	0.637	0.168
I5	3.51	3.93	0.42	0.953	45.329	0.00	0.613	0.196
I6	3.46	3.89	0.43	0.952	46.495	0.00	0.610	0.201
I7	3.55	3.93	0.38	0.958	41.024	0.00	0.593	0.178
I8	3.61	3.92	0.31	0.976	22.736	0.00	0.573	0.098
I9	3.25	3.42	0.17	0.988	11.067	0.00	0.539	0.048
I10	3.21	3.45	0.24	0.980	19.369	0.00	0.513	0.084
I11	3.43	3.67	0.24	0.979	20.045	0.00	0.491	0.087
I12	3.38	3.78	0.4	0.954	45.221	0.00	0.405	0.196
I13	3.32	3.68	0.36	0.965	33.766	0.00	0.331	0.146
I14	3.21	3.51	0.3	0.982	17.207	0.00	0.246	0.074

Note: I1-I14 are the items of the effectiveness scale as labelled in Table 5.11 in Chapter 5. 'Timeliness in loan disbursement/providing other services' (I1); 'If you had a problem, how sincerely the service provider resolved it '(I2); 'Regularity of information sharing through field workers' (I3); 'Fairness in decision-making by the organization' (I4); How sincerely the service provider keeps their promise' (I5); 'Quality maintenance of the service by the provider' (I6); 'How good are the workers in answering your queries quickly' (I7); 'Transparency in transaction process of the service provider' (I8); 'How good the organization is in listening to any of your suggestion' (I9); 'How helpful the service provider has been in dealing with other org.' (I10); 'Attention of the service provider towards your welfare' (I11); 'Attention of the workers towards beneficiaries' (I12); 'Workers' understanding of the individual beneficiary's need' (I13); and 'Service provider's location is convenient' (I14).

The results show that there are five items (I1, I2, I3, I5 and I6) with large mean differences. Of them, I1 has the largest mean difference with 0.64. It can be seen that *F* values for these five variables are quite high with lower *Wilks' lambda* values. For example, item (I1) with the highest mean value has the largest *F* (93.520) and lowest *Wilks' lambda* (0.908) with a significance of 0.000. Significance below 0.10 indicates that there exists a high level of *multi-collinearity* between that variable and the others. These tests indicate that the five scale items are also the variables with significant univariate differences between the opinions of male and female beneficiaries. This result is further supported by larger *Maldobis minimum D square* values. For instance, I1 has higher mean and F values and thus, has a higher *Maldobis* value too. Results also show that there is another item (I12) that has a higher *Maldobis* value which is also supported by a higher *F* value (45.221) but has a high *Wilks' lambda* value and thus, may not be a good candidate as a discriminating item at this stage. As a step-wise estimation procedure is followed, we first consider adding item I1 ('Timeliness in loan disbursement/providing other services') in the discriminant model because of its significant group differences. The results of other items which are not included in the discriminant model in the first stage are shown in Table 6.2.

Table 6.2: Variables not in the analysis after the first stage discriminant method applied

Items	***Wilks' lambda***	***F Value* to enter**	**tolerance**	**Minimum tolerance**	***Maldobis* min D square**
I2	0.904	4.431	0.368	0.368	0.426
I3	0.898	10.601	0.824	0.824	0.455
I4	0.905	3.851	0.794	0.794	0.423
I5	0.902	6.874	0.806	0.806	0.437
I6	0.900	8.598	0.827	0.827	0.446
I7	0.902	6.823	0.838	0.838	0.437
I8	0.907	1.465	0.862	0.862	0.412
I9	0.907	1.335	0.951	0.951	0.411
I10	0.905	3.440	0.932	0.932	0.421
I11	0.906	2.153	0.903	0.903	0.415
I12	0.898	11.173	0.873	0.873	0.458
I13	0.902	7.005	0.891	0.891	0.438
I14	0.901	7.220	0.980	0.980	0.439

Note: I1-I14 are the items of the effectiveness scale as labelled in Table 5.11 in Chapter 5.

After I1 entered into the discriminant model, the remaining variables have been evaluated on the basis of their incremental discriminating ability. Results (see Table 6.2) show that there is a good change in the ranking of the preferred variable since it can be seen that in Table 6.1, I2 was the next candidate for the discriminant model which now reports significantly low value of F (4.431). On the other hand, I12 was in the less preferred part of the list according to Table 6.1 which is now the best candidate to enter the model as it has the largest *F value* of 11.173 with lowest *Wilks' lambda* value of 0.898, and highest *Maldobis* value of 0.458. Other candidates for the model at this stage are I3, I6 and I14 (*F values* of 10.601, 8.598 and 7.220 respectively) which were in our primary list (Table 6.2) as well.

Summary of the step wise estimation process

We then added I12 ('Attention of the workers towards you') in the discriminant model and re-ran the analysis to see the discriminating values of excluded items. Then item 3 ('Regularity of information sharing through field workers') was added in the discriminant model and we found that there was no significant discriminant items left based on *F values*, *Wilks' lambda*, *Madobis D* value and tolerance level (maximum *F value* is found to be 2.40 only). A summary of the final stage discriminant analysis is given in Table 6.3.

Table 6.3: Summary of discriminant analysis between male and female beneficiaries

Items	Discriminant coefficient	Classification function coefficient		Loadings	Rank	Canonical correlation	Eigen value
		Male	Female				
I1	0.707	1.665	2.156	0.917	1		
I2	Nil	Nil	Nil	0.795	2		
I3	0.274	2.055	2.245	0.679	3		
I4	Nil	Nil	Nil	0.637	4		
I5	Nil	Nil	Nil	0.613	5		
I6	Nil	Nil	Nil	0.610	6		
I7	Nil	Nil	Nil	0.593	7	0.739	0.620
I8	Nil	Nil	Nil	0.573	8		
I9	Nil	Nil	Nil	0.539	9		
I10	Nil	Nil	Nil	0.513	10		
I11	Nil	Nil	Nil	0.491	11		
I12	0.294	2.451	2.655	0.405	12		
I13	Nil	Nil	Nil	0.331	13		
I14	Nil	Nil	Nil	0.246	14		

Note: Discriminant items are 'Timeliness in loan disbursement/providing other services' (I1), 'Regularity of information sharing through field workers' (I3) and 'Attention of the workers towards you' (I12).

Our results reveal that that multicollinearity is not present among the discriminant items as their *Wilks' lambda* values and *F values* are quite diverse from each other (see Table 6.1 columns 5 and 6). We further observe that the individual standardized coefficient of each discriminant item (column 2 of Table 6.3) has a unique impact on discriminant function. The most powerful discriminating item is I1 (timeliness in service delivery) followed by item-3 (importance of information sharing by field level workers). Finally, the canonical correlation value for the analysis is 0.739 meaning around 55% (square of 0.759) of the variance in dependent variable can be accounted for by this model.

6.2.1 Combined differences in gender variation of opinion

It was found in the above analysis that the opinion on the effectiveness scale varies between male and female beneficiaries in three items. Thus, we can derive a combined discriminant equation using these three items as:

$$DF_{Male\&Female} = -4.608 + 0.707\ I_1 + 0.274\ I_3 + 0.294\ I_{12} \qquad (1)$$

This combined equation shows that the estimated coefficient value is maximum for item-1 (which means more emphasis should be put on, 'Timeliness in loan disbursement/providing other services') for both male and female beneficiaries, followed by item-3 'Regularity of information sharing with beneficiaries'. However, to be more precise, we need to check the individual discriminant functions for male and female beneficiaries.

$$DF_{Male} = -11.162 + 1.67\ I_1 + 2.05\ I_3 + 2.45\ I_{12} \qquad (2)$$
$$DF_{Female} = -14.379 + 2.15\ I_1 + 2.25\ I_3 + 2.65\ I_{12} \qquad (3)$$

As scores of the individual independent variables indicate more improvement on the item in question, we can now find the varied profiles between male and female beneficiaries based on effectiveness scale items. Considering the classification function coefficients (see equations 2 and 3) we can conclude[5] that:

- Female beneficiaries are more interested in seeing improvements in items I1 (Timeliness in loan disbursement/providing other services), I3 (Regularity in information sharing) and I12 (Attention of the workers towards beneficiaries).

- Male beneficiaries, on the other hand, would like to see improvements in all these items but without as strong a preference (as their coefficient values are less than that of women) in all three aspects compared to those of female beneficiaries.

One major finding from these equations is that the relative negative impact will be higher for the female beneficiaries in all aspects if no changes are made by the service providers. This indicates that women are more deprived showing the evidence of gender discrimination, and thus, our H_1 is rejected.

Among the three items listed above, the highest gap between the opinions of male and female beneficiaries is in item-1 (coefficient gap is 0.48) which means women suffer more from the delay in service delivery. This problem is evidenced in the case of getting services other than credit, such as family planning, maternal health care, sanitation, pure water facility, etc. This problem is less severe for male beneficiaries because they can travel long distances to meet the field workers anywhere they like. But female beneficiaries report that they can't go outside due to social and religious restrictions and therefore, they must wait for the workers to deliver the desired services. Thus, for rapid improvement in living standards, this item is more important to women. The delay in service delivery by GO agencies is mainly due to bureaucratic red tape, whereas for NGOs this problem arises as the number of female beneficiaries becomes too large compared to the number of field workers available who can travel door to door.

As most of the poor beneficiaries are illiterate, and particularly women are less able, they require individual 'Attention from the officials as well as field workers' (I12) to maximize output from the borrowed money. This is supported by the results (see equation-3), as we can see this is the single largest item (coefficient value is 2.655 in equation-3) on which the female beneficiaries place more emphasis. While serving female beneficiaries, it is important that the participants ensure individual attention to women which will lead to their empowerment as well. There are many personal issues that female beneficiaries can't discuss in group meetings, and thus, the need for customized attention is crucial. Many female beneficiaries appreciate the employment of female field workers with whom they can more comfortably interact. At the time of our field survey, many female beneficiaries expressed that they have several ideas about investing their borrowed money. However, due to a lack of personalized consultation and training, they are unable to undertake those projects. It has also been suggested that disadvantaged female beneficiaries, particularly disabled/less-able women, widowed, aged, acid victims and minors need to be treated considerately in terms of charging interest on borrowing.

Validation of the result

To validate the findings of discriminant analysis we used a holdout sample which in our case comes from the original data. The results are given in Table 6.4.

Table 6.4: Classification results between male and female discriminant analysis

Gender	Predicted group members	
	Male	**Female**
Original data		
Male	62.1	37.9
Female	33.1	66.9
Holdout sample		
Male	62.1	37.9
Female	33.3	66.7

Our results show that 62.1% of the original group cases are correctly classified in the combined study and the result for the cross-validated sample is 62.1% which necessarily signifies the internal and external validity with these classification accuracy and hit ratios.

6.2.2 Estimating variations in discriminant items in different areas of Bangladesh

To check whether there is any variation in the opinions of male and female beneficiaries of different areas, we ran discriminant analysis on three other areas namely North area, South area and Central area (see chapter-4 for details of the areas). The summary of the discriminant functions for these three areas is demonstrated below:

$$DF_{North} = -3.39 + 0.59\ _{I1} + 0.69\ _{I3} - 0.37\ _{I14} \quad (4)$$
$$DF_{NorthMale} = -13.16 + 1.89\ _{I1} + 2.38\ _{I3} + 2.58\ _{I14} \quad (5)$$
$$DF_{NorthFemale} = -15.78 + 2.35\ _{I1} + 2.92\ _{I3} + 2.29\ _{I14} \quad (6)$$
$$DF_{South} = -4.84 + 0.65\ _{I7} + 0.69\ _{I9} \quad (7)$$
$$DF_{SouthMale} = -11.08 + 2.17\ _{I7} + 4.19\ _{I9} \quad (8)$$
$$DF_{SouthFemale} = -15.01 + 2.69\ _{I7} + 4.74\ _{I9} \quad (9)$$
$$DF_{Central} = -5.16 + 0.51\ _{I1} + 0.41\ _{I4} + 0.35\ _{I5} + 0.30\ _{I12} \quad (10)$$

$$DF_{CentralMale} = -12.39 + 2.12_{I1} + 0.96_{I4} + 2.54_{I5} + 2.13_{I12} \quad (11)$$
$$DF_{CentralFemale} = -17.06 + 2.58_{I1} + 1.33_{I4} + 2.86_{I5} + 2.39_{I12} \quad (12)$$

One common finding from the above equations is that in all the areas female beneficiaries are in need of more improvement in each and every item compared to male beneficiaries (see the coefficient values for male and female). This finding substantiates the existence of gender discrimination in the service delivery process. Opinions on item-wise improvement expectation of the beneficiaries (based on individual discriminant equation of 5 to 12) of different regions are listed in Table 6.5.

Table 6.5: Area wise discriminating scale items for male and female beneficiaries

Area	Beneficiary	Item of the Effectiveness scale chosen for improvement
North	Female	Timeliness in loan disbursement/providing other services (I1)
		Regularity of information sharing through field workers (I3)
	Male	Location of the service provider is convenient (I14)
South	Female	How good are the workers in answering your queries quickly (I7)
		How good the organization is in listening to any of your suggestion (I9)
	Male	None
Central	Female	Timeliness in loan disbursement/providing other services (I1)
		Fairness in decision making by the organization (I4)
		How sincerely the service provider keeps their promise (I5)
		Attention of the workers towards you (I12)
	Male	None

The findings shown in Table 6.5 further justify that there is significant difference in the opinions of male and female beneficiaries and thus, H_1 is rejected.

In the Northern area, the most important item pointed out by the female beneficiaries is ‘Lack of regularity in information sharing with beneficiaries and incorporating their suggestions’ (I3) (it has the highest coefficient value of 2.92 in Equation-6 and has maximum coefficient gap of 0.54 between male and female). As male members spend a large portion of their day outside home, and meet others at leisure time, they have a better chance of being informed about new rules, regulations or policies. But, as women are mostly deprived of that special attempts should be made to deliver timely information to women particularly regarding health, job, natural disaster, and education-related information.

The results from the Southern area (see equations 8 and 9) show that ‘Service provider’s intention to listen to beneficiaries’ (I9) has the highest coefficients of 4.74 for females and 4.19 for males, which are also the highest coefficient values among all the regional discriminant equations (equations 4 to 12). This means that both male and female beneficiaries feel that they are deprived of opportunities for participation in the decision-making process. However, female beneficiaries believe that they are more isolated and discouraged from the decision-making process of the service providers as the gap of coefficient values between male and female beneficiaries on this issue is the highest (0.55). This finding also conflicts with the major goal of the NGOs towards ‘women’s empowerment’. Sanyal’s (2007) study of women involved in microfinance in India found that it was really not money that was the source of the reversal of inequality, but the association (termed as ‘associative mechanism of microfinance’) of women in a culture that was repressive towards them. Policy-makers and regional managers of service providers should consider taking steps to involve female beneficiaries more in the development of the organisation by ensuring there are opportunities for involvement in decision-making especially through performance feedback (with complaint management and evaluation), project planning and operations, strategy making, and policy formulation.

In the Southern region, even though both male and female beneficiaries noticed a lack of ‘Knowledge of the field workers in answering their queries’ (I7), this complaint comes more from women (coefficient values are 2.69 for females and 2.17 for males), particularly from those who are receiving other special services (like family planning, immunization, sanitation). Therefore, they require more assistance from better-trained workers. It should be noted that due to generally lesser mobility of women, they depend totally on field workers for all answers to their queries. Thus, their requirement for knowledgeable staff members is more than that for male beneficiaries. Periodic training of the officials and workers based on findings from nationwide (across areas) problems may help policy formulation on this issue. Edwards (1989) reports that many projects in Zambia or Malawi have suffered due to inadequate training of the field staff in project implementation, which creates barriers to women’s empowerment (see also Edwards and Hulme, 1992).

Similar patterns of gender discrimination have been found in the Central area also, as coefficient values for women in each and every discriminant item are greater than that for men (see equation 11, 12 and Table 10). It was found that 'Issues related to promise keeping' (I5) is of the highest priority in the Central area and as usual women require more improvement in this field (coefficient value is 2.54 for men and 2.86 for women). Many female beneficiaries reported that service providers do not keep their promises in delivering necessary services to women because they have less power when it comes to raising their voices against the providers; field workers also know that the female beneficiaries are also psychologically weaker. Moreover, many female beneficiaries believe that they were given loans not with the intention of making them more economically well-off or to empower them, but rather because it is easier to collect instalments from women than from men. The poor are bankable, but poor women are unfailingly more bankable.

Even though beneficiaries in the Central areas believe that the service providers work for their wellbeing, women beneficiaries always question (coefficient value is 0.96 for male and 1.33 for female) the 'fairness' (I4) of GO agencies in choosing borrowers and approving loans. Most female beneficiaries noticed that GO agencies prefer to disburse loans to men or to more solvent people generally. In addition, they report the existence of large-scale corruption in GO agencies in the process of approving loans. Favouritism, bribery, pressure from the local elites and political leaders and pressure from fundamentalist groups are the main obstacles for women in getting loans from GO agencies. On the other hand, most male beneficiaries report that it is harder for them to get loans as NGOs prefer women, and GOs prefer collateral. Thus, the marginally poor males are in a disadvantaged position being rejected by both service providers. Male beneficiaries argue that the loan should be given based on need not on gender issues or solvency status. It has been reported during our survey that the wives of male family members borrow money on behalf of the men, which means women are utilized as 'loan receiving agents'.

As women are more disadvantaged (see equations 3, 6, 9, 12 and their coefficient values), more concentration towards women while understanding their specific needs can be made if: repayment schedules and interest rates are set in such a way so as to maximize the impact on income; registrations of assets purchased with loans in women's names or in joint names; incorporating strategies for women's graduation to larger loans; multiple choice options for women including loans for new activities like health care, education of the children, housing etc.;

increased savings patterns with high interest deposits and more restricted access.

6.3 Comparative analysis between Government and NGOs: Gender based study

In this section, we will identify which service provider is relatively more effective in delivering services for the poor based on the opinions of male and female beneficiaries according to the scale items as validated in Table 5.11 (see Chapter 5). The findings from this exercise will help beneficiaries choose their desired service providers and help the policy makers of GOs and NGOs better understand the deficiencies in their service delivery in each item of the validated scale.

6.3.1 Examining the group profile and verifying the assumptions

Multivariate Analysis of Variance (MANOVA) was used to examine the differences and assess the extent to which these differences are significantly different. Thus, it is important to test the homogeneity of variance of the dependent variables and normality of data.

The independence of the respondents is ensured as the data have been collected through a simple random sampling procedure from 12 districts. A second assumption employed for the MANOVA was the homogeneity of the variance-covariance between GOs and NGOs. Results of the univariate tests for all the scale items except for the two are non-significant (significance greater than 0.05) [6]. Thus, the equality of variances is supported for all items except those two. *Box's M* test for equality of the covariance matrices shows a slightly significant value (0.048 < 0.050; the expectation is non-significance). There could be two reasons for this finding: 1) two significant items in the dependent list; and 2) inequality in the sample sizes of the two groups[7]. However, *Bartlett's test for Sphericity* shows that a significant degree of inter-correlation does exist (significance = 0.000 found). Thus, normality of the dependent variables along with their homogeneity is guaranteed. For the problematic items (significance less than 0.050 for 'Regularity of information sharing' and 'Promise keeping by the providers') it has been decided to conduct a step by step modification process to identify the reasons behind the problem.

At the outset, skewness and kurtosis of the scale items are tested. Results show that all the variables are normally skewed and have satisfactory kurtosis values[8] and that is even true for the above problematic items (their skewness values are -0.492 and -0.481; kurtosis are -0.119 and -0.159). Testing through Q-Q plot and Box plot analyses also identified that the distribution of data is quite normal for both the variables with the presence of a few outliers. We then dropped these 7 outliers from the list and re-ran the homoscedasticity test. The revised results are displayed in Table 6.6.

Table 6.6: Multivariate and univariate measures for testing homoscedasticity of scale items

Part-A: Multivariate test of homoscedasticity

Box's M Test of equality of Covariance Matrices	
Box's M	331.135
F	2.435
df1	105
df2	151420.17
Sig.	0.053

Part-B: Univariate tests of homoscedasticity

Levene's test of equality of error variances				
Scale items	F	df1	df2	Sig.
I1	0.628	1	832	0.428
I2	2.152	1	832	0.143
I3	3.791	1	832	0.052
I4	1.299	1	832	0.255
I5	22.400	1	832	0.001
I6	0.087	1	832	0.769
I7	3.189	1	832	0.074
I8	3.082	1	832	0.080
I9	0.231	1	832	0.631
I10	0.158	1	832	0.691
I11	2.052	1	832	0.152
I12	0.511	1	832	0.475
I13	2.765	1	832	0.097
I14	1.407	1	832	0.236
Test for correlation among the dependent variables				
Bartlett's Test of Sphericity				
KMO Sampling adequacy	0.855			
Approx. Chi-Square	8250.321			

df	91
Sig.	0.000

The revised results indicate that the removal of outliers made 'Regularity of information sharing through field workers' (item-3) non-significant (value increased from 0.020 to 0.052), but the other problem variable still remains significant (value is 0.001). Interestingly, it was found that the *Box's M test* (Table 6.6, part-A) for equality of the covariance matrices now shows a non-significant value (0.053), indicating no significant difference between the two groups (GO and NGO) on thirteen dependent variables collectively. To solve the non-significance problem of the 'promise keeping' (item-5) variable, we attempted for variance stabilizing transformations sequentially. In all three cases of transformations (square root, logarithmic and inverse), no change has been observed in the level of significance for the problem variable. But *Bartlett's test* for sphericity still remains in line with the preferred analysis (significance is 0.000). Thus, by considering all the stated modification results, we conclude that this problem is due to unequal sample sizes of the groups under investigation. However, existing results are good enough to conclude that assumption of normality, outliers and homoscedasticity are met for each individual variable separately and fourteen variables collectively. Thus, all the assumptions to conduct MANOVA are satisfied.

6.3.2 Efficacy comparison based on opinions of male and female beneficiaries

In addition to MANOVA, *Kruskal Wallis* test of group ranking has been conducted to justify the findings of MANOVA. Our findings (column-7 of Table 6.7) suggest that in all cases $p < 0.01$ which guarantees there are significant differences in the opinions of male and female beneficiaries. Thus, H_1 can be rejected.

Table 6.7: Results of MANOVA and Kruskal Wallis test on the opinions of male and female beneficiaries on scale

Effectiveness determinants	Beneficiary	Provider	Results of MANOVA		Results of Kruskal Wallis Test	
			Mean	Std. Dev.	Mean Rank	Sig.
	Male	GO	3.30	0.975	213.64	0.000
I1		NGO	3.72	1.035	256.49	
	Female	GO	3.67	0.958	206.73	0.003
		NGO	3.77	1.056	237.93	
	Male	GO	3.37	0.963	214.29	0.001

Effectiveness determinants	Beneficiary	Provider	Results of MANOVA		Results of Kruskal Wallis Test	
I2		NGO	3.74	0.998	255.49	
	Female	GO	3.81	0.923	224.97	0.008
		NGO	3.76	1.082	233.65	
I3	Male	GO	3.27	0.924	208.55	0.000
		NGO	3.73	0.967	264.33	
	Female	GO	3.90	0.871	231.98	0.004
		NGO	3.86	0.892	234.35	
I4	Male	GO	3.29	0.974	255.75	0.001
		NGO	3.68	1.095	214.12	
	Female	GO	3.68	0.970	207.92	0.004
		NGO	3.77	1.064	237.65	
I5	Male	GO	3.57	0.930	183.83	0.000
		NGO	4.03	0.840	247.97	
	Female	GO	3.92	0.894	201.13	0.006
		NGO	4.01	0.828	214.94	
I6	Male	GO	3.07	0.902	208.81	0.000
		NGO	3.47	0.899	260.36	
	Female	GO	3.45	0.688	224.55	0.003
		NGO	3.47	0.729	231.87	
I7	Male	GO	3.75	0.864	216.11	0.002
		NGO	3.61	1.040	252.69	
	Female	GO	3.52	0.852	195.99	0.003
		NGO	3.78	0.901	240.45	
I8	Male	GO	3.92	1.010	274.09	0.000
		NGO	3.31	1.062	202.22	
	Female	GO	3.92	0.828	235.26	0.001
		NGO	3.85	0.934	218.09	
I9	Male	GO	3.17	0.814	222.88	0.001
		NGO	3.30	0.819	242.24	
	Female	GO	3.44	0.707	224.78	0.008
		NGO	3.50	0.718	233.69	
I10	Male	GO	3.06	0.965	209.84	0.000
		NGO	3.46	0.811	262.34	
	Female	GO	3.48	0.669	230.76	0.006
		NGO	3.46	0.773	232.29	
I11	Male	GO	3.30	0.900	211.73	0.000
		NGO	3.66	0.880	259.43	
	Female	GO	3.69	0.653	235.39	0.002
		NGO	3.64	0.794	217.55	
I12	Male	GO	3.23	0.958	206.92	0.000
		NGO	3.72	0.930	266.85	
	Female	GO	3.63	0.808	212.93	0.001
		NGO	3.72	0.882	236.48	
I13	Male	GO	3.16	0.912	211.67	0.000
		NGO	3.59	0.991	259.52	
	Female	GO	3.48	0.852	197.91	0.005
		NGO	3.68	0.903	240.00	
	Male	GO	3.02	1.143	206.94	0.000
		NGO	3.58	1.119	266.81	

Effectiveness determinants	Beneficiary	Provider	Results of MANOVA		Results of Kruskal Wallis Test	
I14	Female	GO	3.23	1.149	199.27	0.008
		NGO	3.51	1.039	239.68	

Note on Table-6.7: N for male GO = 225, N for female GO = 73, N for male NGO = 158 and N for female NGO = 348. Timeliness in loan disbursement/providing other services (I1); 'If you had a problem, how sincerely the service provider resolved it' (I2); 'Regularity of information sharing through field workers' (I3); 'Fairness in decision-making by the organization' (I4); 'How sincerely the service provider keeps their promise' (I5); 'Quality maintenance of the service by the provider' (I6); 'How good are the workers in answering your queries quickly' (I7); 'Transparency in transaction process of the service provider' (I8); 'How good the organization is in listening to any of your suggestions' (I9); 'How helpful the service provider has been in dealing with other org.' (I10); 'Attention of the service provider towards your welfare' (I11); 'Attention of the workers towards beneficiaries' (I12); 'Workers' understanding of the individual beneficiary's needs' (I13); and 'Service provider's location is convenient' (I14).

Even if there are significant differences in item-wise satisfaction between men and women, in one item ('Transparency in transaction process', item-8) both groups consider government to be more trustworthy than NGOs (mean values for male between GOs and NGOs are 3.92 and 3.31 respectively, whereas these are 3.92 and 3.85 for female beneficiaries). Several cases of NGO bankruptcy (for instance, Jubo Karmasangsthan Society (Jubok) and Islamic Trade and Commerce Ltd (ITCL)) or cancellation of registration[9] in earlier years may be the reason behind such perceptions. Due to charging higher rates of interest along with a reduction in the provision for additional services, a negative image of NGOs persists regarding microfinance and this makes them seem less transparent to the beneficiaries. In addition, women believe (see Table 6.7) that government agencies perform better than NGOs in four more fields namely, 'If you had a problem, how sincerely the service provider resolved it' (item-2), 'Regularity of information sharing through field workers' (item-3), 'How helpful the service provider has been in dealing with other organizations' (item-10) and 'Attention of the service provider towards your welfare' (item-11). It was mentioned by many of the beneficiaries surveyed that neither GOs nor NGOs provide them with the information required regularly (about such matters as interest rates, natural calamity, new diseases, etc.); whatever information they get, however, is through government agencies. Many believe that NGOs are not prompt in solving problems because there are too few workers compared to the number of beneficiaries. As a consequence, there is a long wait to get the required services, creating dissatisfaction among the beneficiaries. On the other hand, due to the comparatively small number of beneficiaries, government agencies are performing better than NGOs in solving problems. NGOs need to increase the number of field workers or open new service counters to ensure prompt delivery of services.

Beneficiaries also believe that as most NGOs are either foreign funded (national NGOs) or borrow money from larger NGOs, and their prime intention is in gaining their own financial sustainability that NGOs have little intention of maximizing welfare benefits to the beneficiaries. Conversely, this issue is not relevant to government agencies and so they seem to care more about their beneficiaries' welfare (for female respondents, the mean values of GOs and NGOs for item-11 are 3.69 and 3.64 respectively). This is exemplified by the fact that GOs charge lower interest rates than NGOs and they (GOs) are flexible with respect to loan repayment. Occasionally, GO agencies waive repayments if there is a severe natural calamity or economic shock.

As shown in Table 6.7, our study suggests that the largest gaps in the level of efficacy between GOs and NGOs exist in three items ('Location', item-14; 'Attention of the workers towards beneficiaries', item-12; and 'Promise keeping by the provider', item-5). These are the items that government needs to consider seriously. Among these, the government's first attempt to improve should be to increase coverage to reach the more destitute who live in the remotest corners of the country and who are deprived of the services provided by both GOs and NGOs. In addition, even if NGOs can reach them, those people will be neglected because of a higher likelihood of defaulting. Thus, GOs are possibly the only option for these disadvantaged people to fight poverty. A large number of beneficiaries have expressed a preference to borrow money from government organizations; however, the absence of convenient branches of government agencies in their areas deprives them of getting services from GO field workers. On the other hand, due to their wide coverage, NGOs gain a large number of beneficiaries.

Corruption and rent seeking by the GO agencies are also major problems that have been identified at the time of survey causing the belief that they can't keep their promises (item-5) and do not deliver the services timely. Beneficiaries pointed out that bribing the middlemen (who work on behalf of the managers and workers of the GO agencies) is quite common when getting loans from the GO agencies. Furthermore, beneficiaries also observed delays in disbursement due to unavailability of funds. In delivering timely services and keeping promises, GO policy-makers need to consider ways of eliminating corruption by removing middlemen and reducing bureaucratic barriers to fund disbursement.

Interestingly, it was observed that in a few fields ('Quality maintenance', item-6; 'Fairness in decision making', item-4 and 'Listening the suggestions of the beneficiaries', item-9) the difference between GO and NGO efficacy is minor. This is a positive note for poverty alleviation programs in Bangladesh, particularly as having their suggestions heard not only empowers the beneficiaries but also guarantees the service providers' interest in incorporating local issues in the decision-making process.

Our results reveal that male beneficiaries are more satisfied than their female counterparts when evaluating NGOs; they ranked NGOs most highly in 12 out of 14 items (see column-6, Table 6.7 and compare the rank values of NGOs for male and female). On the other hand, female beneficiaries reported their higher preference for government agencies in 8 items while male beneficiaries are happier with government agencies than are the female beneficiaries in 6 other items. These findings have three major implications:

First, women, who are the main (in some cases the only) beneficiaries of NGOs, are not happy with the services provided by NGOs;

Second, NGOs discriminate between male and female beneficiaries in providing quality services; and

Third, NGOs need to expand their credit facility towards marginally poor male beneficiaries. It is important to remember that the service provider's vision is supposed to be the reduction of poverty irrespective of gender, and the process of sanctioning credit should not be biased towards females only.

6.4 Conclusion

This chapter has shown that gender discrimination is evidenced in the poverty alleviation programs in Bangladesh and that female beneficiaries particularly are disadvantaged in receiving less attention from the managers and field staff of GOs and NGOs. Following are a few noticeable findings supporting our argument:

- For three items (timeliness in providing services, sharing information regularly, and workers' help towards the beneficiaries) there are discrepancies in opinions between male and female beneficiaries; improvement in all three items is demanded by female beneficiaries on the grounds that women are receiving lower standards of service.

- Similar results have been observed in the region-specific studies. For instance, in the Southern and Central areas, female beneficiaries feel there is a strong need for improvement in all discriminating items. In the Northern area, improvement in two out of three discriminating items is required by females, while males want an improved level of service on the other. All these results could be seen as evidence of gender discrimination regionally.
- Demand for improvement in service items by the female beneficiaries varies among the regions. For instance, in the Northern area, female members see the need for further improvement in 'timeliness in service delivery' along with workers' skills, whereas in the Southern area more attention is required to empowerment issues, particularly in listening and incorporating the suggestions from the beneficiaries in the decision-making processes of the service providers. Finally, in the Central area, more concentration is demanded on the items related to trustworthiness of the organizations, particularly fairness in the decision-making process, keeping the promises properly, and more attention from the workers towards the female beneficiaries.
- The results show that the target beneficiary group (women) is dissatisfied due to the reduction of additional services such as family planning, immunization, safe water, etc., and the lack of appropriate training in utilizing the loan more productively. Furthermore, the service providers need to reconcile whether women's empowerment should be given more emphasis in the short term rather than being just the long-term goal of reducing the head count in poverty through unisex credit delivery processes.

Our findings indicate that as the more disadvantaged segment of the population, women need more customized policy formulation which is fair, attentive, timely, and participative in nature.

A number of policies have been suggested in Chapters 5 and 6 to improve service delivery effectiveness of GOs and NGOs based on the opinions of beneficiaries. It is worth noting that this improvement needs to be on-going, and each and every development partner should be aware of their position against the position of others with respect to delivery efficacy. This efficacy appraisal process needs to be monitored regularly so that donors can make better-informed decisions about their fund disbursement channels.

In Chapter 5, we have developed a two-dimensional multi-item service delivery effectiveness scale and then compared the efficacy of GOs and NGOs based on the scale items (Chapters 5 and 6) to conform to the first and second objectives of the study. These studies are all *process-based* comparisons between GOs and NGOs. However, as mentioned in Chapters 1 and 2, it is equally important to compare the relative efficacy of GOs and NGOs with respect to their contribution in creating opportunities for the people to increase their capabilities for raising living standards – an *outcome-based* study. Chapter 7 addresses this issue.

Notes

[1] (Guidelines on Women's Empowerment UN Population Division, Department of Economic and Social Affairs, with support from the UN Population Fund (UNFPA), please also refer to, Islam and Rottach, 2010; Sanyal, 2009; Mayoux, 2006; Salwa and Furuta, 2006; Johnson and Desai, 2005; Vidler, 2005; Cecelski, 2005; IFAD, 2000; Bourgia, 1998)

[2] In general, women get 21% lower wages than men with this rate being much higher in rural areas (Kapsos, 2008).

[3] For instance, the proportion of female beneficiaries of Grameen Bank and BRAC are 97% and 96% respectively.

[4] In last two decades the fertility rate in Bangladesh has declined from 6.1 to 3.0, which is a major improvement (World Human Development report, 2006).

[5] These statistically significant conclusions are made based on score of independent variables on individual service provider, higher mean value differences and larger standard deviations

[6] Detailed results are available from the author upon request.

[7] In many cases if the group sizes differ more than 1.5 times, the significance levels of *Box's M* test may not be within acceptable levels (Hair et al., 2010).

[8] 'If the kurtosis and skewness are not between -2 and +2, the data is too far away from a normal distribution' (Hair et. al, 2010).

[9] According to the statistics of the Microcredit Regulatory Authority, 'there are 4200 NGOs working with microcredit among which only 453 have a licence to operate' (The Daily Janakantha, May 16, 2010).

CHAPTER SEVEN

ASSESSMENT OF MULTIDIMENSIONAL POVERTY AND EFFECTIVENESS OF MICROFINANCE-DRIVEN GOVERNMENT AND NGO PROJECTS IN THE RURAL BANGLADESH

7.1 Introduction

In this chapter, a multidimensional model is developed that can be used in assessing the economic, social, political and cultural dimensions of poverty in rural Bangladesh. By employing the developed model, a comparative analysis between the microfinance-driven projects of Government (GOs) and Non government organizations (NGOs) is performed to explore their relative effectiveness in poverty reduction programs in rural Bangladesh. Results of the analysis show that GO projects are more effective in enhancing the 'economic wellbeing' of the poor, whereas NGOs contribute more to the 'social' aspects of poverty. Findings also revealed that on the whole, GO projects perform 42% better than NGOs in improving living standards for the rural poor, and this contradicts findings in the existing literature of poverty reduction projects in developing countries.

Microfinance has been used as an effective tool for poverty alleviation around the world for decades. This approach has created not only the poor's access towards capital but also allowed them to improve their business which in turn increased personal income and increased personal spending on children's education, family healthcare, and improved housing, and nutrition (Morduch, 2000; Coleman, 2005). However, several studies also found unconvinced results about the economic benefit of microfinance (Hoque, 2004; Coleman, 2005). Study by Hossain (1988) found that microfinance also has impact on social indicators such as opportunity for empowerment and decision making rights which increases confidence and self-esteem. Study by Pitt and Khandker (1998) revealed that there is a positive correlation between use of microfinance and investment in human capital (such as choice of schooling and the contraceptive behaviour). But again, several other studies (Kabeer and Noponen, 2005) found the impact of microfinance on social indicators inconclusive. Even though it can be said that microfinance organizations targets the economic solvency of the poor, this operation has several other multiplier effects (social, cultural, political, etc.) in the lives of the poor which made microfinance institutions more appealing in the development context. However, as the outcomes of microfinance driven projects are mixed, one primary question at the foundation of this chapter is:

1) What should be the strategies for success of the microfinance driven projects?

In general, the studies (Epstein, 2005) focused on number of borrowers, borrower retention rate, financial stability of the projects, and most notably repayment rates (please refer to Chapter-1 for discussion on other criteria). However, a quick look to the stated criteria shows that all these are from the organizational perspective and do not measure the aggregate impacts of borrowers' living standard. Why is this lacuna? Is it because the target/appropriate indicators of poverty are not explored according to the opinion of the borrowers? It is worth mentioning that whether microfinance providers really benefit the poor or not that depends on how poor people define poverty and how effective are the organizations in contributing to the lives of the poor. Thus, this chapter will address two research questions.

a) What are the indicators of poverty and living standard opined by the poor in rural Bangladesh? (third task of the study)
b) To what extent could credit providers contribute to those living standard determining items? (fourth focus of the study)

Decades of studies on human wellbeing have revealed that poverty is multidimensional, and various approaches[1] have been used to monitor and assess these different dimensions. Despite this fact, poverty in Bangladesh is still viewed narrowly in official assessments, mostly in terms of direct caloric intake[2] (DCI) and food energy intake[3] (FEI) (GoB, 2010). A cost of basic needs (CBN) method has been introduced in the mid-1990s (see Chapters 1 and 3 for details). In the CBN method, the cost of a food basket that is required to meet predetermined nutritional requirements of households is calculated, and then an allowance for basic non-food consumption is added (BBS, 2005). Other than measuring income[4], there are two non-income indicators of poverty, namely 'infant mortality rate' and the 'school enrolment ratio' used in Bangladesh. The infant mortality rate reflects the state of primary health care system of the country, and the pace of its improvement over time, while the school enrolment ratio indicates to what extent the country is able to deliver universal education to its people. Like the government agencies, NGOs have been working for poverty reduction in Bangladesh since 1971. Even though the NGOs claim (Mahmud, 2008) that they work for social mobilization, women's empowerment and income generation, their main activities, as with the government agencies, are limited to basic needs fulfilment[5] through the delivery of microcredit and other social services to the poor. Other than CBN, NGOs do not use any official poverty model that can address other dimensions of wellbeing/poverty in Bangladesh. A head-count ratio (HCR) based on DCI or CBN methods provides a change in the monetary poverty rate for the whole or regional Bangladesh, but is unable to capture changes in social, political and cultural dimensions of poverty for a specific year. This is one important limitation of the poverty assessment methods used in Bangladesh.

Furthermore, whilst HCR is based on DCI/CBN methods, it does not split the individual contribution of GOs and NGOs or other development partners in improving living standards for the poor. NGOs claim (Ravallion et al, 1999) that they contribute more to eradicating poverty because of their higher disbursement of microcredit, larger number of field workers, and greater coverage of geographic areas compared to government agencies. However, no statistics are available on the relative performance of GOs and NGOs[6] with respect to contributions made to poverty reduction and improving living standard in any given year.

Like the Sen's (1985) human capability approach[7], the sustainable livelihoods model[8] (Chambers and Conway, 1992) is also based on the belief that people require a range of assets (or capital) to achieve positive livelihood outcomes (such as economic solvency or social inclusion), and no single category of asset is sufficient to ensure overall livelihood outcomes (refer to Fig-2.3 in Chapter 2). Considering this fact, the role of government and other development partners is to endow citizens with the required conditions necessary for actualizing capacities and opportunities. Thus, both the multidimensionality of deprivation and the role institutions play in poverty alleviation are increasingly being recognized in the livelihoods approach. However, Serrat (2008) has suggested that the sustainable livelihoods approach is just one way of integrating the complex issues that surround poverty and this model needs to be customized to local circumstances taking into account local priorities[9] (see gap 1 and 2 in Fig-2.3 in Chapter 2). Due to the absence of any multidimensional wellbeing model for Bangladesh, it is not possible to compare the effectiveness of microfinance-driven GoB and NGO projects from the outcomes perspective. In summary, it can thus be argued that there is no validated and group-invariance[10] checked multidimensional poverty model for Bangladesh available in the literature[11] that can be used to: (a) capture different dimensions of poverty; and (b) judge the effectiveness of various microfinance providers (such as Government and NGOs) based on whether they contribute to the achievement of the wellbeing indicators that people consider important.

This chapter will address these lacunas by developing a multidimensional poverty model by applying the sustainable livelihoods approach such that the needs priorities of the people of the stated area for different types of assets can be better understood. Development agencies then can help people become more capable of fulfilling those asset/capital needs. The model will also help make a comparative analysis between the efficacy of alternative microfinance-driven poverty reduction programs provided by GoB and NGOs. This effectiveness assessment is required for at least three reasons: a) existing studies[12] show that all of the stated effectiveness determinant issues are *process-relevant* factors and assessments of institutional efficacy based on *livelihood outcome-relevant* factors are mostly neglected in the studies. We strongly feel that any evaluation of institutional efficacy based on repayment and disbursement rates will contribute little unless a targeted approach is formulated to identify the asset needs (outcome factors) of specific sub-groups for improving their wellbeing or livelihood; b) finding out which development partner contributes more to improving the living standards of the beneficiaries; and c) helping the managers of GOs and NGOs identify specific wellbeing indicators that show where more effort could be concentrated.

7.2 Definition of poverty and effectiveness

7.2.1 Dimensions of poverty

For this study we define[13] poverty simply yet broadly as

> "the inability or less capability to participate in society, economically, socially, culturally and politically (as used by Hunzai et al. and ICIMOD, 2010, pp. 2)".

Multidimensionality of poverty based on the stated definition is explored and explained in details in Chapter 2.

With the intention of developing a multidimensional poverty model, our primary task is to explore indicators that reflect the economic, social, cultural, and political aspects of poverty. By reviewing the available literature[14] (for details see Section 2.3, 2.4, 2.5 and 2.6 in Chapter-2), lists of poverty indicators relevant to the lives of the rural poor in Bangladesh are prepared and a summary of those indicators is provided in Table 7.1.

7.2.2 Conceptualizing outcome based effectiveness

In general, effectiveness is determined by an input-output ratio which is expressed through profit and rate of return in the case of for-profit organizations. In the social sector, particularly in poverty reduction projects, the efficacy of the microfinance deliverers is measured by the number of beneficiaries reached, amount of credit delivered, the financial sustainability of the project, and most importantly, by repayment rates of microcredit[15]. However, in analysing effectiveness-based on outcomes of the microcredit driven projects of GOs and NGOs in poverty alleviation programs, it is important to examine the extent to which the development partners could support the poor for income generation (people always seek to increase the return to the activities they undertake by using the microfinance as increased income is the security of economic wellbeing), increased wellbeing (material goods such as food security, non material goods such as self esteem, sense of control and inclusion, physical security of the household members, health status, political enfranchisement, cultural works), build the *capability* of the people (adequate training, continuous monitoring and support services), reduce vulnerability (savings to cope with that shock time support), and mobilize them in social activities. All of these aspects go beyond the quantity of profit made through disbursing microcredit to the poor.

Even though the effectiveness of the agency is measured through its contribution to the social and economic wellbeing of the poor, the indicators of these aspects (see Table 7.1) do not affect effectiveness directly, rather the effect is indirect[16]. On the other hand, as most of the development partners use microcredit as the main (or in some cases only) tool to enhance the capability of the poor, the loan repayment rate, frequency of defaulting, repeat borrowing rate, size of the loan, length of borrowing, etc. are direct and micro-level indicators of effectiveness. A list of these indicators is presented in Table 7.1.

Table 7.1: Dimensions and items for the multidimensional poverty model

Outcome factors	Influential and outcome indicators/items
Economic wellbeing	Items related to: food intake by family members, income, savings, access to electricity, sanitary latrine and safe water, home and land ownership, land holding size, other household assets, average sick days of the family members, morbidity status, capacity to work in daily life, shortage time food intake, degree of vulnerability with respect to land and asset ownerships, etc.
Social wellbeing (includes social, cultural and political aspects)	Influential indicators are: access to information about natural disasters, loans, education, health and job, information about politics and local and central government, health care, education, schooling, freedom to do social, cultural, religious and political works, participation in society and politics and voting behaviour, decision-making in the household and work place, experience of robbery and theft, mental stress and feelings of insecurity, etc.
Effectiveness of development partner	Indicators like, loan repayment capability of the beneficiaries of that provider, amount of loan provided, length of borrowing from a particular provider with repeat borrowing, etc.

7.3 Model building process

At the primary stage of developing the model, we included 56 livelihood asset and six support service-related items (each as one question as discussed in Chapter-4) with two broader livelihood dimensions (economic and social wellbeing) and one effectiveness dimension. Note that all 56 items do not directly influence economic or social wellbeing dimensions (as can be seen the direction of arrows in Fig-7.1). This means that there will be a few additional dimensions (as labelled as intermediary dimension in Fig-7.1) which are directly influenced by several of these 56 items, and those dimensions directly affect economic or social wellbeing (refer to Fig-7.1). For instance, average sick days or morbidity status (items) of the person may not be directly related to economic wellbeing, rather they have a direct relationship with human capability building (an intermediary dimension). This capability in turn affects the economic wellbeing (dimension) of the person because the more physically capable people can earn more and are, as a consequence, economically better-off.

On the other hand, the levels of income and savings are the items (assets) that are direct outcomes of economic wellbeing (arrow from items to economic dimension in Fig-7.1).

Summarily, we hypothesize that many of these 56 items (or individual assets) will be grouped into different intermediary dimensions which influence economic and social dimensions of wellbeing. And the level of achievements of the aspects (assets) of economic and social wellbeing by the respective beneficiaries (of GO and NGOs) is the outcome-based measures of effectiveness dimension. Thus these 56 items (assets) influence the effectiveness dimension indirectly through their respective intermediary dimensions. These intermediary dimensions affect the final two dimensions (economic and social) that determine the level of outcome-based effectiveness. On the other hand, there are six other items (as listed in row-4 of Table 7.1) that directly affect process-based effectiveness of GO and NGOs.

The following flow chart (Fig-7.1) describes the model in short. It can be seen in the flow chart that there are arrows coming towards effectiveness dimension. Arrows from the left, towards the effectiveness dimension show how different items (assets) and living standard-relevant dimensions determine the level of effectiveness. On the other hand, the arrow from the, towards effectiveness, shows that it is a process-based assessment of effectiveness.

To estimate the proposed model empirically, Structural Equation Modelling (SEM) is used to explore those indirect and unobserved relationships. Unlike the traditional multivariate analysis tools (such as regression), SEM makes it possible to answer a set of interrelated research questions in a systematic way by modelling the relationships among multiple independent (such as intermediary dimensions in Fig-7.1) and dependent dimensions (Economic, Social and Effectiveness dimensions) simultaneously. This capability for simultaneous analysis differs greatly from most traditional regression models, such as linear regression, LOGIT, ANOVA, and MANOVA, which can analyse only one layer of linkages between independent and dependent items at a time (such as the relation between items and intermediary dimensions or relation between economic and social dimension with effectiveness). Furthermore, SEM allows the researchers to combine multiple observed items of a dimension (through exploratory factor analysis) and then model the causal relationships amongst these dimensions rather than amongst single observed items which are merely proxies for those dimensions.

Figure 7.1: Hypothesized model for asset identification and effectiveness assessment

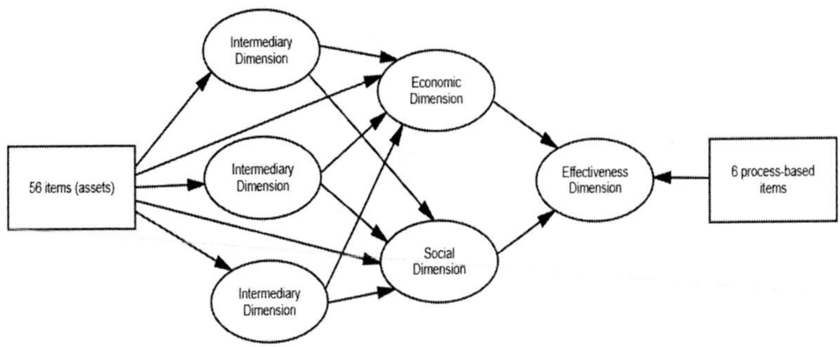

Our estimation process (SEM) begins with Exploratory Factor Analysis (EFA)[17] to explore the relevance of items with specific dimensions. EFA detects: a) items that influence social and economic dimensions directly; b) items that have an indirect relationship to social and economic wellbeing, but have direct relationships to other intermediary dimensions that directly affect social and economic dimensions; and c) items that are less relevant to the study of livelihood asset in Bangladesh according to the opinions of the beneficiaries. As a next step, Confirmatory Factor Analysis[18] (CFA) is used to test if the relationships between grouped items and their corresponding dimensions truly exist. This step confirms that a specific item belongs to only one dimension and has no relation with other dimensions of the model. And finally, measurement model and structural model are used to track the relationships among the explored intermediary dimensions and the social and economic wellbeing dimensions with effectiveness dimension.

Stage-1: *Model purification through Exploratory Factor Analysis (EFA)*

At the primary stage of development of the model, we have 56 wellbeing and six support service-related items (each is one item/variable) with two broader wellbeing dimensions/factors (economic and social wellbeing) and one effectiveness factor.

We began by testing the level of data and sample adequacy to perform the factor analysis. The results show that the *Kaiser-Meyer-Olkin* (KMO) measure of sample adequacy (MSA) value is 0.763 which is a better indication[19] of data adequacy. In addition, an individual MSA value for the items ranges from 0.544 to 0.925, which is another positive indication of data adequacy. Based on the *eigenvalue* rule[20], these 62 items can belong to 16 individual factors. To identify the most relevant items and dimensions, we used a *moderately strict* decision rule of deleting items with cross loading or loading less than 0.50 on any factor[21] and those carrying less communality values (<0.50). In addition, we dropped factors with fewer items in order to run CFA in the next step (see Arbuckle, 2009 for the number of acceptable items). As a result, a total of nine items and three factors have been dropped from the raw model.

The results of the second-stage factor analysis show that the remaining items belong to 13 individual factors and as a whole they explain 66.90% of the total variation (a 2 percent improvement from previous stage). At this stage, cross loaded items, and items having loading less than 0.50, have been dropped from the model. This purification process through EFA has been continued until each and every item fulfilled the suggested requirements. Finally, a total of 11 factors represented by 43 items have been selected with 68.34% of total variance explained.

Stage-2: Individual Confirmatory Factor Analysis (CFA)

The remaining 43 items and 11 factors are now subject to individual CFA to test the hypothesis that a direct relationship exists among the selected items and their corresponding factors. We started with Factor-1 containing seven items as shown in Fig-7.2.

Figure 7.2: Individual CFA for Factor-1

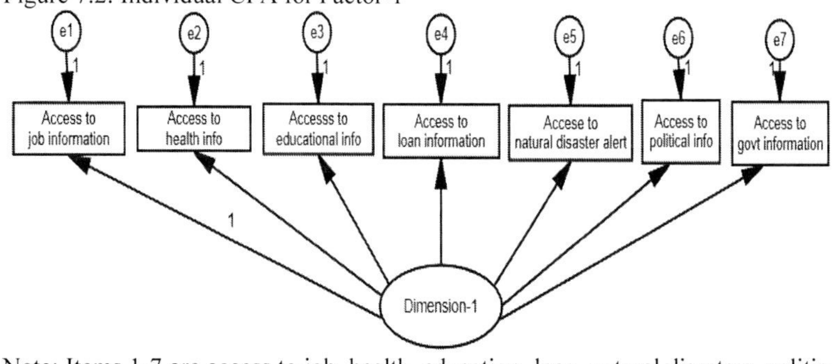

Note: Items 1-7 are access to job, health, education, loan, natural disasters, politics and government related information respectively.

Results show that the critical values of this CFA range from 15.129 to 50.153 which are all statistically significant. However, the Comparative

Fit Index (CFI), Goodness-of-Fit Index (GFI), *p* and Root Mean Square Error Estimation (RMSEA) values are 0.847, 0.821, 0.000 and 0.275 respectively suggesting that at this stage the model is a bad fit[22]. It has been observed through the modification index that a large covariance (349.85) exists between items 6 and 7 (i.e., political- and governance-related information). In addition, items 6 and 7 have comparatively low loading values of 0.609 and 0.555 respectively, whereas other items in the model have quite high loading values ranging from 0.79 to 0.96. Thus items 6 and 7 are re-grouped (as shown in Fig-7.3) and this two-group CFA has been run again.

Figure 7.3: Re-grouping the items of Factor-1

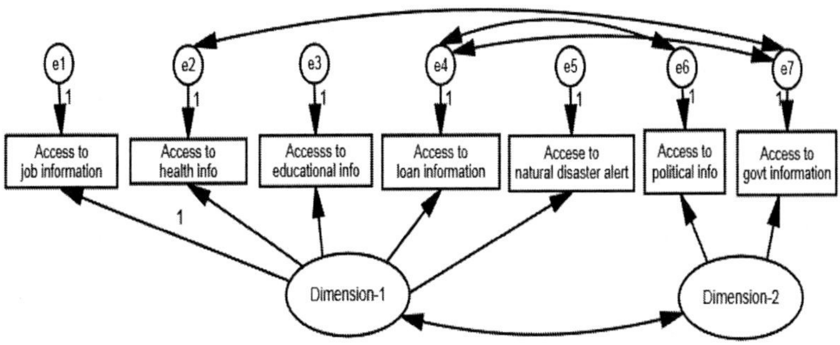

As a result of the re-grouping, the *chi-square* value dropped to 12.77 from 608.8 with a significant *p* value of 0.120. In addition, CFI, GFI and RMSEA values were found to be 0.999, 0.993, and 0.033 respectively which also guarantee a satisfactory fit. Moreover, loading values for items 6 and 7 have now increased to 0.964 and 0.882 respectively which indicate significant improvement in this two-factor model.

We followed the same procedure for the remaining 36 items and 10 factors with a restricted rule of deleting items with a loading less than 0.40 and accepting the individual CFA models with good fit statistics[23]. Subjective views have been taken into consideration because it is important to determine the significance of droppable variables based on the existing literature and qualitative observations from field study, besides judging only through loading values identified in the statistical process. Following the stated criteria, a total of seven items[24] have been dropped from further study through whole CFA. At this stage there are 36 items belonging to 11 factors/dimensions.

Naming the factors: It was found that there are five items related to access of information that are incorporated into a single factor. As these aspects of information are diverse in nature (for example, health or education or natural disaster or loan information), we have decided to name the factor 'Access to General Information'. Two more information-related items were then grouped into another factor; access to information about politics and government. By looking to similarities in the nature of information, we named the resulting factor as 'Access to Governance Information' which means that these two items help people make informed decisions about power or the decision-making bodies in the country. There are three items that express the extent to which people are free to perform their political, social, and cultural works, and thus, naturally this factor should be titled 'Freedom'. The next three items (land ownership, land size, house ownership) are all related to asset creation for poor beneficiaries and so that factor is called 'Asset Building'. Items that include average sick days for male and female, morbidity, and the capacity to work are grouped in to one factor. Naturally these items reflect the physical aspects and are thus named 'Human Capability Building' factors, being outcomes of human capability building. For instance, if human or physical capability was improved, there would be less sick days, less morbidity and more capacity to work. The next items (food intake by members) are quite straight forward and related to the 'Core or Basic Needs' and so the dimension is named accordingly. We then have four items that measure income, savings, and access to electricity and sanitary latrine. It is logical to assume that all of these are the outcomes of economic solvency. For instance, whether an individual is economically well off or not is reflected by his or her income, savings, and the utilities used, thus, we named this group 'Economic Wellbeing'. In the next factor, there are three measured variables (Decision-making at home, Experience of theft and Food intake at the shortage time). All of which are outcomes of 'Vulnerability'. The next three items: decision-making at work, mental stress, and feelings of insecurity demonstrate to what extent an individual is socially better off. For instance, a socially well-off person will have less mental stress and can make decisions at work, and often experience greater security. This group is then labelled 'Social Wellbeing'. Finally, we have items like loan repayment rate and length of borrowing which are logically explained as process-relevant outcomes of the efficacy of the service provider. For example, higher repayment rates by beneficiaries are of course considered outcomes of the performance of the service provider. This dimension was then given the title 'Effectiveness'. These items and their corresponding factors are displayed in Table 7.2.

Table 7.2: Factors and their outcome items after CFA

Items (outcomes) retained through CFA	Proposed name of the factor/dimension
Access to natural disaster, loan, education, health and job related information	Access to general information
Sharing political and government information	Access to governance information
Freedom of performing cultural, religious and political works	Freedom
Home ownership, land holding size and status	Asset building
Average sick days of male and female, morbidity and capacity to work normally	Human capability building
Food intake per day by male, female and kids	Core need fulfilment
Decision at household, experience of theft and robbery and shortage time food consumption	Vulnerability
Monthly income and savings, access to electricity and sanitary latrine	Economic wellbeing
Decision at job, mental stress and feeling of insecurity	Social wellbeing
Loan repayment status, amount of loan taken and length of borrowing by the beneficiaries	Effectiveness
Voting by male and female beneficiaries, choice of preferred candidates	Empowerment

Stage-3:
The measurement model: Construction and purification

The measurement model shows how the dimensions (factors) are operationalized by sets of measured items and enables an assessment of construct validity. This model also assesses the extent to which all factors and measured items as a whole are operational and compatible as a model. After running the first measurement model with 11 factors and their corresponding 36 items, the result was found to be non-admissible due to negative covariance of the 'Empowerment factor' with other factors of the model[25]. In addition, loading values of the items of the 'Empowerment' factor are too low when grouped in the model with other factors and items. One probable reason for non-significance of the 'Empowerment' factor is the lesser relevance of its items.[26] Based on statistical results and evidence of less relevance, the 'Empowerment' factor and its corresponding three items have been dropped from further study. The purified measurement model with ten factors and 33 items is shown in Fig-7.4.

This time the model is operational; however, goodness of fit and other statistics of the revised measurement model were below the satisfactory level (*chi-square* is 1564.578 with *GFI*, *CFI*, *PCLOSE* and *RMSEA* values are 0.851, 0.881, 0.000 and 0.066 respectively), even though all items have loading values above the reference value (0.40) with significant critical ratio values (all values greater than ±1.96) (see detailed results in Table A7.1 in the Appendix). These results have two implications: 1) all items shown in the measurement model may be kept intact; and 2) some further adjustment of the model is needed by considering the large modification and error index values (especially the ones greater than 20) (see Table A7.2).

As expected, there is a large modification index found (refer to Table A7.2 in appendix) for the model given in Fig-7.4. In the beginning, there is a correlation shown between e25 (Decision at household) and the factor Freedom. It is quite obvious that they are correlated because decision making at household level enhances freedom for individual persons. In the similar way, e27 (Loan repayment rate) is related to the factor Human capability building as we know better the capability of the individual, better would be the loan repayment capacity. Again e21 (Income per month) is correlated to other variables like e27 (Loan repayment rate), e19 (Save per month) and e20 (electricity usage) meaning higher income will ensure better loan repayment rate, more savings, and electricity use. This is considered a luxury for many poor beneficiaries. And for that reason most of these correlated items are grouped into single factor (Economic wellbeing). It was found that e8 (Freedom of political work) is correlated to items such as Vulnerability and social wellbeing meaning that vulnerability hinders the freedom of political involvement and social wellbeing is expressed by political participation as well. One large modification index is between e9 (House ownership pattern) and vulnerability that signify that the ownership of prime assets is highly influenced by the proximity of vulnerability. More vulnerable people are more homeless as always seen practically. Similar interpretation can be made for the correlation between e10 (Land holding status) and Vulnerability. Result shows that they are negatively correlated and is quite true indeed as landless people become more vulnerable in the society. Another large modification index is between e14 (Morbidity status) and social wellbeing which demonstrate that more sick people are more detached from the society and deprived of social well off. Highest correlation in the modification index was found between e1 (Access to natural disaster information) and Vulnerability, and this is very logical that most of the poor people become vulnerable due to the impact of natural calamities which result mainly from lack of information about natural disasters in their areas. Poor people can't move to safe places or can't save their assets or properties from the natural disasters as they are not well informed about the impact time of most natural calamities such as cyclone, flood, and even drought. Another large modification index has been observed between e2 (Access to loan related information) and e32 (Access to government information) which state that government source of information regarding credit for the poor is unavailable or doesn't reach the poor people. Now by considering all these justified correlations, we re-ran the purified measurement model shown in Fig-A7.1 in appendix. With this new measurement model, our chi-square dropped to 1005.461 with a PCLOSE value of 0.090. In addition, result shows that *GFI*, *CFI*, *RMSEA* and *Hoelter* values are 0.901, 0.927, 0.049 and 243, and 254 respectively. Thus, this purified measurement model is not only a good fit but also better than the independence model (as *Hoelter* values are greater than 200 and *AIC* values are less for our model). This gives us a guarantee that we can proceed to the next level of structural model building based on this modified measurement model (We have 10 factor and 33 items).

Figure 7.4: Measurement Model for Effectiveness Analysis

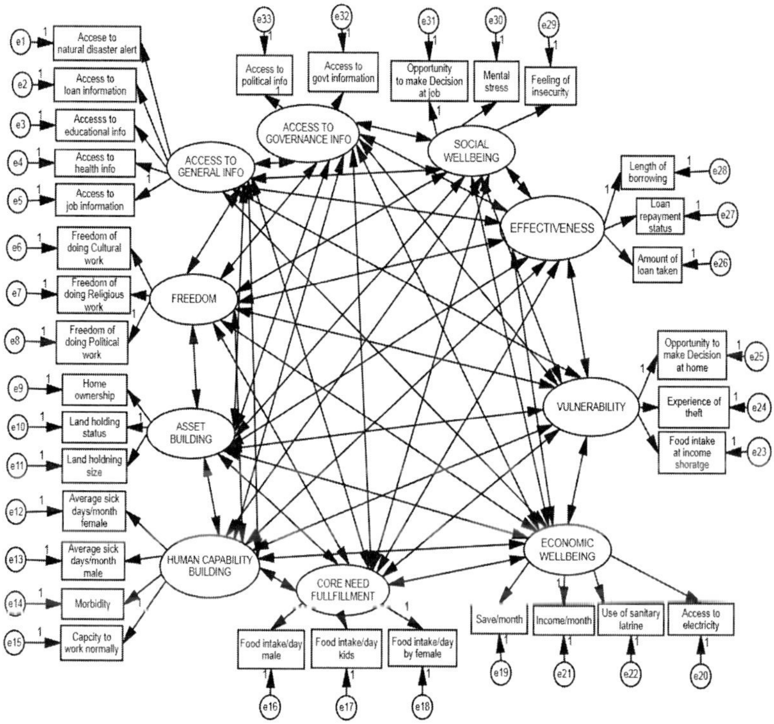

Stage-4:
Validity of the measurement model

For the construct validity of the model, we checked the convergent validity, discriminant validity and nomological validity. Results for the convergent validity analysis[27] are shown in Table 7.3. All items except 'decision making at household level' have loading values greater than 0.40 (acceptable level) which satisfy the factor loading criteria. Except 'Vulnerability', all other factors have average variance extracted values more than 40% (range is from 43% to 85%) that necessarily guarantee the evidence of convergent validity. Finally, construct reliability values range from 0.49 to 0.94 except 'Vulnerability' factor, suggesting adequate reliability of the measurement model. However, we did not check discriminant and nomological validities for the measurement model due to unsatisfactory 'construct reliability' of the 'Vulnerability' factor. The

'Vulnerability' factor is relatively less significant, perhaps because of its less-relevance to other factors and items. For example, (a) our result shows that more than 91% of 'household decisions' are made jointly; thus, this item has less importance in the whole model and (b) because of low income level of the respondents, nothing valuable is available to be 'theft from their home' and thus, this item seems less important for the model too. Two out of three items of 'vulnerability' factor has been found to be less important. This made this factor less significant for the model. Therefore, at this stage, 'Vulnerability' factor and its corresponding items have been dropped due to low extracted value of average variance (36.98%) with less construct reliability (0.27). Deletion of 'Vulnerability' factor further proves that vulnerability is not a *dimension* of poverty rather it is a *symptom* of poverty[28].

Table 7.3: Factor loadings, Average Variance Extracted and Construct Reliability for the Measurement Model

Dimen. Items	Access to General Info	Access to Govern. info	Human Capital Building	Asset Building	Freedom	Econ. Well Being	Core Need Fulfilment	Social Well Being	Vulnerability	Effectiveness
Access to Job info	0.945									
Access to Health info	0.965									
Access to Educat info	0.922									
Access to Loan info	0.787									
Access to natural disaster alert info	0.739									
Access to political info		0.955								
Access to govt info		0.891								
Capacit to work normaly (5 hours at stretch)			0.882							

Dimen. Items	Access to General Info	Access to Govern. info	Human Capital Building	Asset Building	Freedom	Econ. Well Being	Core Need Fulfilment	Social Well Being	Vulnerability	Effectiveness
Morbidity			0.801							
Averg sick days/ month for male (in last 6 months)			0.456							
Averag sick days/ month for female (in last 6 months)			0.463							
Land holding status				0.879						
Home ownership				0.695						
Land size owned				0.906						
Freedom to perform Politic work					0.662					
Freedom to perform Religious work					0.647					
Freedom to perform Cultural works					0.924					
Income/ month						0.751				
Access to electri.						0.589				
Saving/ month						0.693				
Use of sanitary latrine						0.590				
Food intake/ day by male							0.904			
Food intake/ day by female							0.957			

Dimen. Items	Access to General Info	Access to Govern. info	Human Capital Building	Asset Building	Freedom	Econ. Well Being	Core Need Fulfilment	Social Well Being	Vulnerability	Effectiveness
Food intake/ day by kids							0.902			
Opportunity to make Decision at job place								0.463		
Mental stress								0.708		
Feeling of insecurity								0.766		
Opportunity to make decision at home									**0.334**	
Experience of theft									0.528	
Income Shortagtime food intake									0.848	
Length of credit borrowing										0.594
Loan repayment status										0.673
Amount of loan taken										0.807
Average variance extracted (%)	76.79	85.29	46.04	69.21	57.02	43.48	84.88	43.41	36.98	48.56
Construct reliability	0.876	0.923	0.494	0.912	0.823	0.567	0.945	0.581	0.271	0.648

Stage-5:
Validity testing for the finalized Measurement Model

In the revised measurement model, item named 'Access to electricity' has been decided to be dropped due to a critical ratio of 1.47 (which is less than acceptable value of 1.96) and low factor loading value. Probably this particular utility service is still considered a luxury good by the poor beneficiaries in Bangladesh. With the above modifications, our finalized measurement model has *chi-square* value of 733.018 with *GFI*, *CFI*, *PCLOSE*, *RMSEA* and *Hoelter* values of 0.918, 0.953, 0.837, 0.047 and 283 and 297 respectively which indicate a better fit.

Notable results (see Table 7.4) of the purification are: a) all items have satisfactory factor loadings with average variance extracted values greater than 45%, b) construct reliability values ranging from 0.736 to 0.981 (which is another indication of construct validity) and c) construct reliability of the factor titled 'Economic wellbeing' has increased to 0.831 from 0.567 (comparing Table 7.3 and 7.4) due to the elimination of the item 'Access to electricity'.

Table 7.4: Factor loadings, Average Variance Extracted and Construct Reliability of the Purified Measurement Model

Dimens. Item	Access to General Info	Access to Gov info	Human Capability Building	Asset Building	Freedom	Econ Well Being	Core Need Fulfilment	Social Well Being	Effectiveness
Access to Job info	0.945								
Access to Health info	0.966								
Access to Educationinfo	0.922								
Access to Loan info	0.796								
Access to Natural Disaster alert info	0.727								
Access to political info		0.961							
Access to govt info		0.882							
Capacity to work normally (5 hours at stretch)			0.880						
Morbidity			0.729						
Average sick days/month for male (in last 6 months)			0.479						

Dimens. Item	Access to General Info	Access to Gov info	Human Capability Building	Asset Building	Freedom	Econ Well Being	Core Need Fulfilment	Social Well Being	Effectiveness
Average sick days/month for female (in last 6 months)			0.461						
Land holding status				0.869					
Home ownership				0.695					
Land size owned				0.919					
Freedom to perform Political work					0.650				
Freedom to perform Religious work					0.647				
Freedom to perform Cultural work					0.946				
Income/ month						0.727			
Save/ month						0.679			
Use of sanitary latrine						0.578			
Food intake/day by male							0.903		
Food intake/day by female							0.957		
Food intake/day by kids							0.903		
Opportunity to make Decision at job place								0.463	
Mental stress								0.720	
Feeling of insecurity								0.766	
Length of credit borrowing									0.575
Loan repayment status									0.671
Amount of loan taken									0.792

Dimens. Item	Access to General Info	Access to Gov info	Human Capability Building	Asset Building	Freedom	Econ Well Being	Core Need Fulfilment	Social Well Being	Effectiveness
Average variance extracted	76.76%	85.07%	47%	69.42 %	57.86 %	45%	84.88%	45%	51.03%
Construct reliability	0.972	0.979	0.787	0.970	0.928	**0.831**	0.981	0.736	0.808

Discriminant validity shows to what extent one dimension is truly different from other and captures some phenomena other measures do not. Evidence of discriminant validity can be found in Table 7.5. In this table, values below the diagonal are correlation estimates among dimensions; diagonal values are dimension variance; and values above the diagonal are squared correlations. It can be observed that all average variance extracted values estimated in Table 7.4 are greater than the corresponding inter-dimension squared correlation estimates in Table 7.5 (above the diagonal). Therefore, this test indicates that there are no problems with discriminant validity for this effectiveness measurement model. However, one important issue to be noted that there are two values (between economic wellbeing and effectiveness and access to general information) are a bit high even though less than average variance extracted showing that in this big model there may be a chance that few variables are related to other dimensions that do not belong to. But that rate of correlation would be very less as well.

Nomological validity can be explained with the aid of Table 7.5. As our main intention is to assess the effectiveness of the service providers, we need to check the correlations among effectiveness and other factors. It can be seen from the table that all dimensions other than Freedom are positively correlated with effectiveness dimension. That means, a positive social and economic wellbeing, core need fulfilment, asset building, and creation of better access to information are the key to service provider's effectiveness in uplifting living standard of the poor beneficiaries. This is true in reality. Thus face validity and the nomological validity of the measurement model are justified. Even though correlation between freedom and effectiveness is negative, a smaller value of that and consistent positive relation status of other dimension will lead us to conclude that this one exception is not a major concern.

Table 7.5: Measurement model dimension correlation matrix (Standardized)

	Effectiveness	Social Well Being	Core Need Full	Eco Well Being	Freedom	Asset Building	Human Capab Build	Accesto Gov info	Access to Gen Info
Effectiveness	1.000	0.0289	0.014	**0.428**	0.0009	0.098	0.0001	0.09	0.104
Social Well Being	0.170	1.000	0.069	0.106	0.0002	0.010	0.007	0.011	0.073
Core Need Full	0.120	0.264	1.000	0.167	0.001	0.012	0.047	0.020	0.044
Eco Well Being	0.727	0.326	0.409	1.000	0.036	0.264	0.000	0.248	**0.422**
Freedom	-0.031	0.015	0.032	0.192	1.000	0.013	0.002	0.004	0.0002
Asset Building	0.314	-0.104	-0.112	-0.514	-0.117	1.000	0.002	0.058	0.063
Human Cap Build	0.031	-0.086	-0.218	-0.006	0.050	-0.046	1.000	0.012	0.003
Access to Gov info	0.300	-0.109	-0.143	-0.498	0.070	0.241	0.114	1.000	0.379
Access to Gen Info	0.324	-0.272	-0.210	-0.709	-0.017	0.252	-0.059	0.616	1.000

Note: Values are significant at 0.05.

Stage-6: Constructing the Structural Poverty model for effectiveness assessment

The preliminary structural model is constructed in a way that 'Effectiveness' of the development partners is measured by their contribution in improving 'Economic' and 'Social' wellbeing of the beneficiaries. In one hand, 'Economic wellbeing' is influenced by 'Core need fulfilment', 'Human capability building' and 'Asset building capability' of the beneficiaries. On the other hand 'Social wellbeing' is the result of 'Access to general information', 'Access to governance information', and 'Freedom'. Similar explanations can be given to demonstrate the relation among measured items and their corresponding factors[29]. This preliminary structural poverty model is shown in Fig-7.5.

By running the preliminary structural model, we have explored several new correlations between a few factors and measured items which require specific interpretations.

(a) *Relations between length of borrowing (item-28) and loan repayment rate (item-27) with 'Human capability building' factor*. The rate of repayment depends heavily on an individual's physical and intellectual capabilities. For example, less sick days and better capacity to work will ensure more work days, thus more earning and consequently better repayment rate.

(b) We found a *relation between the factor 'Freedom' and 'income per month' (item-21).* This means people believe that freedom of doing things depends on the level of income. That means better earned people are freer than an insolvent person, or better earning people are less socially excluded.

(c) We have identified correlation *between 'Social wellbeing' factor and 'freedom to do political works' (item-8).* This relation justifies that freer engagement in political activities is an indicator of social wellbeing.

Figure 7.5: Preliminary structural model for effectiveness assessment

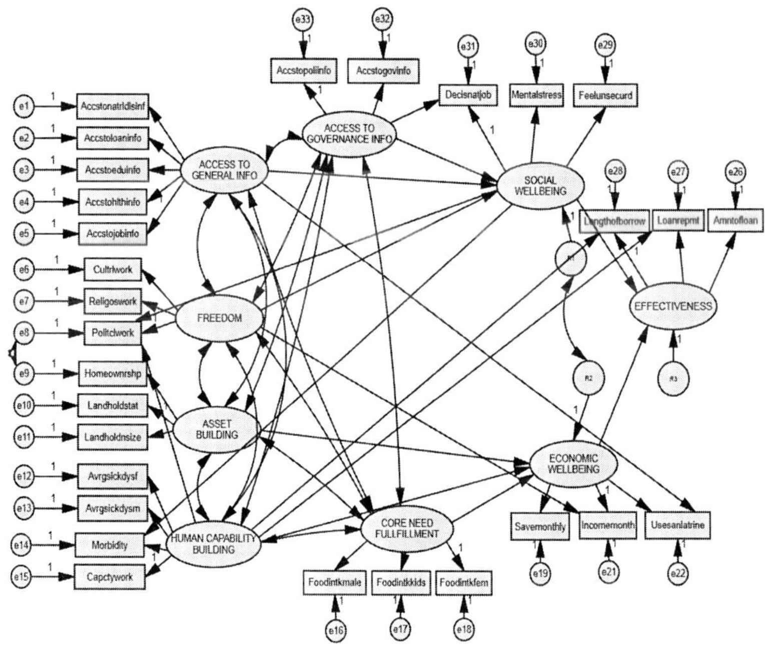

In our preliminary model (Fig-7.5), GOF results have chi-square of 1115.859 with 348 degrees of freedom and *RMR*, *GFI*, *CFI*, *RMSEA* and *PCLOSE* values have been found to be 0.077, 0.878, 0.912, 0.063 and 0.000 respectively. *Hoelter* values have been found to be 198 and 203. All these results show that the model is moderately good fit based on *GFI*, *CFI* and *Hoelter* values but bad fit based on *RMSEA* and *PCLOSE* values. However, the critical ratio (t-values) values for the variables are all significant (greater than ±1.96) with all loading values greater than 0.40.

Thus, we have decided to keep all the variables at this stage of model building and for further purification we have checked the modification index.

After checking the modification index (see Table A7.3 in appendix) and by making other necessary modifications (additional correlations are shown in Fig-7.6), the goodness of fit values have been compared between before and after the modifications. Result shows that chi-square value significantly dropped to 687.553. Finalized structural poverty model (shown in Fig-7.6) demonstrates satisfactory fit values with *CFI*, *GFI*, *RMR*, *RMSEA* and *P value* of 0.959, 0.922, 0.067, 0.044 and 0.983 respectively[30].

Figure 7.6: Final Multidimensional Poverty Model for Effectiveness Assessment

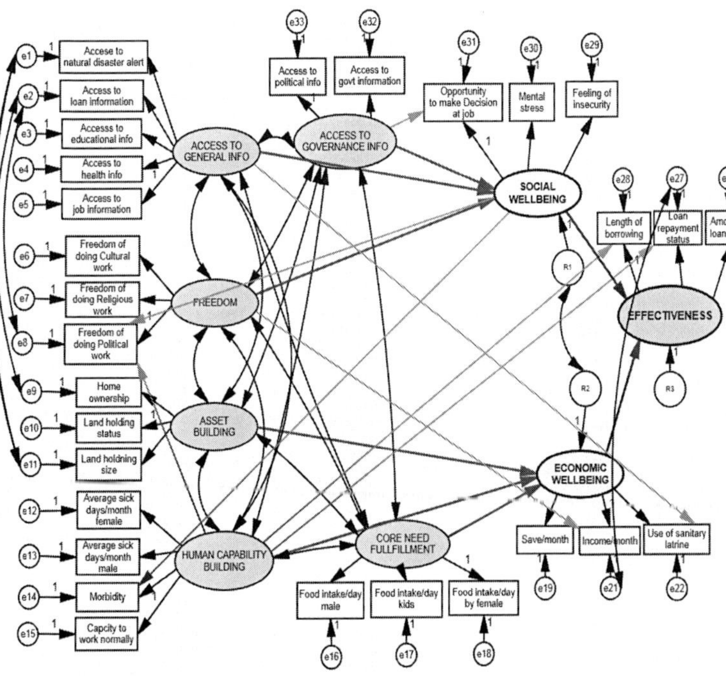

In the finalized model, all loading values were reported to be greater than 0.45 with *Coefficient-H reliability*[31] value of 0.909. In addition, newly correlated variables have low loading values which demonstrate that there is a relation between those variables and other dimensions but

that is not significantly very high, thus, discriminant validity of the structural model is further satisfied.

Relating our model to the livelihood assets of SL approach: Table 7.6 compares the livelihood assets of our model with DFID's sustainable livelihoods approach and thus, justifies the applicability of the SL approach for Bangladesh. However, it is important to mention that all the items listed in the livelihoods approach are not present (nor applicable) in our model as our model is customized to the need preferences of the people in rural Bangladesh.

Table 7.6: Comparing various concepts of capitals: The livelihoods approach and our model for Bangladesh

Asset category in Livelihoods model	Factor/asset category in our model
Human capital	Human capability building (4 items)
Social capital	Social wellbeing comprised of access to information and freedom (10 items)
Physical capital	Core need fulfilment and some part of economic wellbeing (4 items)
Financial capital	Economic wellbeing and some part of asset building plus items covered in Effectiveness factor (7 items)
Natural capital	Asset building (3 items)

7.4 Testing the model for invariance across GOs and NGOs for comparative study

We have accomplished our first objective of developing and validating the multidimensional poverty model in the last section. Now in order to fulfil the second objective (comparing effectiveness of GOs and NGOs), it is important to check whether this model and its individual items and factors are equally applicable for both GO and NGO beneficiaries. Simultaneous multiple group method (dividing the whole data into two groups of beneficiaries of GOs and NGOs) has been performed for this purpose and a summary is presented in Table 7.7 (shown as *configural invariance*). Remaining fit statistics were found to be satisfactory[32] as well. In addition to these, to check the equivalency of the model between GOs and NGOs, we have conducted a number of invariance tests. The results of these tests are displayed in Table 7.7.

Table 7.7: Structural Invariance tests for GOs versus NGO Beneficiaries

	Model Fit Measures					Model Differences		
Model tested	**Chi-square**	**DF**	***P***	***CFI***	***RMSEA***	**$\Delta\chi^2$**	**ΔDF**	**Δp**
Configural Invariance	1150.092	658	0.00	0.944	0.037			
Metric Invariance	1241.517	686	0.00	0.937	0.037	92.42	28	0.147
Scalar Invariance	1316.385	687	0.00	0.929	0.040	166.29	29	0.136
Factor Cov. Invariance	1232.868	688	0.00	0.938	0.038	82.71	30	0.013
Factor Var. Invariance	1173.684	666	0.00	0.943	0.037	23.59	8	0.098
Error Var. Invariance	1428.080	687	0.00	0.916	0.044	277.98	29	0.767

Note: Results for configural invariance are the fit values of two group poverty model.

- Configural invariance: Configural invariance is supported as we are using exactly the same structural model (shown in Fig-7.7) for both the groups. Thus the number of items, factors and parameters are exactly the same. Moreover, *GOF* results in Table 7.6 (2nd row) are the guarantee of configural invariance.
- Metric invariance[33]: This is the first empirical comparison between GO and NGO projects based on the equivalence of factor loadings. Table 7.7 shows that the change in *chi-square* is only 92.42 with 28 degrees of freedom and the change in *p* value indicates a non-significant difference. Thus, two models exhibit full metric invariance.
- Scalar invariance[34]: Here the $\Delta\chi^2$ is 166.29 with a change in df of 29 which is not statistically significant (as the change in *p* value is 0.136); thus, scalar invariance between the model is supported too.
- Factor covariance invariance[35]: Results from Table 7.7 show that $\Delta\chi^2$ is 82.71 with change in df of 30 and this result is partially significant as Δp is 0.013 (which is less than 0.05 but greater than 0.01). It is suggested (Hair et al., 2010) that the covariance invariance can be partially supported to compare the structural model between groups. Thus, reasonable grounds are there to compare this model between GO and NGO projects.
- Factor variance invariance[36]: A $\Delta\chi^2$ of only 23.59 with change in 8 degrees of freedom shows only a little difference indicating that factor variances are almost identical between the groups.

- Error variance invariance: The model has a high $\Delta\chi^2$ of 277.98 due to higher $\Delta\chi^2$ in the scalar invariance test. However, this result is highly non-significant as Δp is 0.767. Thus it supports that in two groups the presence of structural errors are similar.

Given these findings, all factor loadings, variances, and covariances with additional error covariances of the structural poverty model are invariant[37] across GO and NGO's poverty reduction projects.

7.5 Comparing effectiveness between credit driven GO and NGO projects

In this section, validated and invariance checked structural model (shown in Fig-7.6) has been used to compare the efficacy of GOs and NGOs driven poverty reduction projects in enhancing the living standards of the poor beneficiaries in rural Bangladesh. The two-group structural poverty model has the following parameter information:

Number of variables (total): 70

Number of observed variables: 29

Number of unobserved variables: 41

Number of exogenous variables: 38

Number of endogenous variables: 32

Parameter summary (For GO Beneficiaries)

	Weights	Covariances	Variances	Means	Intercepts	Total
Fixed	41	0	0	0	0	41
Labelled	28	0	0	0	29	57
Unlabeled	8	32	38	0	0	78
Total	77	32	38	0	29	176

Parameter summary (For NGO Beneficiaries)

	Weights	Covariances	Variances	Means	Intercepts	Total
Fixed	41	0	0	0	0	41
Labelled	28	0	0	6	29	63
Unlabeled	8	32	38	0	0	78
Total	77	32	38	6	29	182

Sample size of GO and NGO beneficiaries = 207 and 355.

Of major interest, the number of labelled (which is latent variables) parameters is different for two groups. In this study we have taken GOB projects as the controlled group and NGO projects as the estimated group for mean comparison among living standard issues. As GOB projects were considered the controlled group, factor means (6 exogenous variables) of the stated project were fixed to zero. Thus, the number varies here between GOB and NGO projects by 6. Remaining information is the variable and parameter summary which shows that the model is over-identified with adequate sample size.

Model assessment: Fit index results of this two-group model are given in Table 7.8. Results show that the multidimensional poverty assessment model exceptionally fits these two sets of data as *CFI* and *RMSEA* values are 0.932 and 0.039 respectively. While comparing our model, it has been observed that both *AIC* and *ECVI* values of our model are smaller than that of Saturated or Independence model. In addition, loading values were above the acceptable range (shown in Table 7.10). While checking the critical ratios and standard errors for measured variables, dimensions and covariance for both GOB and NGO projects, it was found that all of them are highly significant with low error values (refer to Table A7.4 to A7.7 in appendix). Thus, we can conclude that our model is appropriate for the efficacy comparison between GO and NGO projects.

Table 7.8: Summary of Goodness of fit Statistics for the GO-NGO Structural Model

Fit index	Effectiveness model	Saturated model (Competing model)	Independence model
NPAR	219	928	116
CMIN (Chi-Square)	1312.869	0.000	9669.639
DF	709	0	812
P	0.000	-	0.000
NFI	0.864	1.000	0.000
IFI	0.933	1.000	0.000
TLI	0.922	-	0.000
CFI	0.932	1.000	0.000
RMSEA	0.039	-	0.140
AIC	1750.869	1856.000	9901.639
ECVI	3.127	3.314	17.681
Hoelter 0.05	331	-	52

7.5.1 Comparison based on individual factors and items

We begin the comparison based on the main factors (exogenous) reported in Table 7.9. It is important to remember that the mean values for GO projects were fixed at zero, as we have taken GO projects as the controlled group (mean = 0) and NGO projects as the estimated group. These mean values reported in Table 7.9 are for the NGO projects only.

Table 7.9: Comparative Means of Factors for NGO Projects

	Estimate	S.E.	C.R.	P
Effectiveness	-0.425	.122	-3.492	***
Access to_general info	0.489	0.076	6.415	***
Access to governance info	0.403	0.073	5.533	***
Human capability building	-0.187	0.062	-3.037	.002
Asset_building	0.384	0.051	7.607	***
Freedom	-0.006	0.064	-.091	.927
Core need_fullfillment	-0.072	0.034	-2.132	.033

In spite of the large investment, wider coverage and larger workforces of NGOs, statistically significant results suggest that out of six poverty and wellbeing indicators, NGOs perform better in three fields (see second column with positive values), whereas GOs perform better in three other fields (denoted by negative signs). However, in one field ('Freedom') the gap is marginal and insignificant[38]. Thus, even though government projects are better in empowering poor people's freedom, this difference is too small to notice.

It can be readily observed that NGOs are around 49% more effective compared to government projects in delivering 'general information' (such as natural disaster, job related, education related, loan related and health related information) to the rural poor, whereas this rate is around 41% in sharing governance related information. Interestingly, it was found that the NGO projects are more effective (39% more) in helping their beneficiaries to create assets. This is certainly a positive sign of improvement because ownership of assets (particularly land and houses) reduces the level of vulnerability of the rural poor.

GO projects perform comparatively better (19% more) in 'Human capability building', especially in reducing morbidity and physical sickness. This result is quite justified as more rural poor take healthcare services from government hospitals (even though hospitals are remotely located) due to their limited access to NGO and private healthcare centres caused by financial constraints. However, the GO-NGO effectiveness difference in this field is comparatively small (19%) due to the presence of 'village doctors'. Many rural poor visit village doctors instead of GO or NGO healthcare centres to avail prompt service at the lowest cost, or to get the services on credit.

It can be observed that GO projects perform 8% better in fulfilling 'Core needs of the family' particularly in food intake and providing education. Government's continuing 'Food for Work and Education' projects is responsible for this result as NGOs do not operate such projects. In addition, government's allowance for elderly, poor allowance and pension policy helped in this respects.

To check the overall performance of the organizations, we estimated the mean value of the 'Effectiveness' factor for NGOs where Effectiveness is determined by Economic and Social Wellbeing and their respective indicators (such as human capability building, core need fulfilment, freedom etc.) and credit related issues (such as loan repayment rate, amount of loan, length of borrowing etc.) (see Fig-7.6). The result (-0.425) concludes (see Table 7.9, 1st row) that as a whole, GO projects are more effective (at least 42%) than the operations of NGOs in improving living standards of the rural poor in Bangladesh. This contradicts the existing literature which stresses NGO domination over Government in poverty reduction projects in developing countries.

The comparative statistics on the remaining dimensions and individually measured asset items are reported in Table 7.10 which shows that out of 30 remaining fields (excluding the 'Effectiveness' dimension), NGOs are superior in 17 fields, whereas GO agencies lead in 13 other fields. Detailed discussion for each item is provided in Section 7.6.

Table 7.10: Standardized Regression Weights for GO and NGO Poverty Reduction Projects

Measured assets		Dimensions in the model	Estimates for			Comments
			GO	NGO	GO/ NGO Ratio *	
EFFECTIVENESS	<---	ECONOMIC_WELLBEING	.863	.454	1.90	GOs are twice effective
EFFECTIVENESS	<---	SOCIAL_WELLBEING	.014	.238	0.05	NGOs are 17 times better, however, values are low
ECONOMIC_WELLBEING	<---	HUMAN CAPABILITY_BUILDNG	0.384	0.016	24	GO agencies are much better
ECONOMIC_WELLBEING	<---	ASSET_BUILDING	0.482	0.440	1.09	Marginal difference
ECONOMIC_WELLBEING	<---	CORE NEED_FULLFILLMENT	0.436	0.370	1.17	GO agencies are more effective
Access to job information	<---	ACCESS TO_GENERAL INFO	.927	.948	0.97	Marginal difference
Access to health information	<---	ACCESS TO_GENERAL INFO	.950	.970	0.97	Almost same

Measured assets		Dimensions in the model	Estimates for			Comments
			GO	NGO	GO/ NGO Ratio *	
Access to educational information	<---	ACCESS TO_GENERAL INFO	.898	.928	0.97	Similar performance
Access to loan information	<---	ACCESS TO_GENERAL INFO	.747	.804	0.93	Similar performance
Access to natural disaster alert information	<---	ACCESS TO_GENERAL INFO	.657	.763	0.86	NGOs are more effective
Access to political information	<---	ACCESS TO_GOVERNANCE INFO	.966	.963	1.00	Equal effectiveness
Access to government information	<---	ACCESS TO_GOVERNANCE INFO	.850	.889	0.95	Similar performance
Capacity to work normally	<---	HUMAN CAPABILITY_BUILDNG	.931	.801	1.17	GOs are more effective
Morbidity**	<---	HUMAN CAPABILITY_BUILDNG	**-.685**	**-.727**	**0.94**	**GOs are better**
Average sick days/month for male**	<---	HUMAN CAPABILITY_BUILDNG	.359	.450	0.79	GOs perform much well
Average sick days/month for female**	<---	HUMAN CAPABILITY_BUILDNG	.579	.570	1.01	GOs are marginally effective
Land holding status	<---	ASSET_BUILDING/PHYSICL	.800	.855	0.93	Similar effectiveness
Home ownership	<---	ASSET_BUILDING/PHYSICL	.656	.614	1.17	GOs are more effective
Freedom of performing Political work	<---	FREEDOM	.672	.647	1.03	GOs are more effective
Freedom of performing Religious work	<---	FREEDOM	.645	.623	1.04	GOs dominance
Freedom of performing Cultural work	<---	FREEDOM	.866	.983	0.88	NGOs are better
Income/month	<---	ECONOM_WELLBEING	.452	.510	0.88	NGOs perform better
Save/month	<---	ECONOM_WELLBEING	.415	.610	0.68	NGO's dominance
Use of sanitary latrine	<---	ECONOM_WELLBEING	.309	.353	0.87	NGOs are better
Food intake/day by kids	<---	CORE NEED_FULLFILLMENT	.941	.894	1.05	GOs are better
Food intake/day by adult male	<---	CORE NEED_FULLFILLMENT	.918	.891	1.03	GOs are effective
Opportunity of decision making at job place	<---	SOCIAL_WELLBEING	.358	.616	0.58	NGOs are far effective
Mental stress**	<---	SOCIAL_WELLBEING	**.430**	**.677**	**0.63**	**GOs are much effective**
Length of borrowing	<---	EFFECTIVENESS	.595	.460	1.30	GOs are more effective
Loan repayment status	<---	EFFECTIVENESS	.544	.454	1.20	GOs are far better

Measured assets		Dimensions in the model	Estimates for GO	Estimates for NGO	GO/NGO Ratio *	Comments
Amount of loan borrowed	<---	EFFECTIVENESS	.553	.793	0.69	NGOs are much better
Land holding size	<---	ASSET_BUILD/PHYSICAL	.885	.960	0.92	Similar effectiveness
Feeling of insecurity	<---	SOCIAL_WELLBEING	.644	.811	0.79	NGOs are more effective

*Values bigger than one show GO domination and vice versa. ** For average sick days, morbidity and mental stress, ratio lower than one means GOs effectiveness and vice versa.

7.5.2 An asset-pentagon-based comparison between GOs and NGOs

In this section, a schematic asset-pentagon (like the one shown in Fig-2.3 part-2) based comparison has been made between GOs and NGOs from the findings as shown in Tables 7.6, 7.9 and 7.10. For each capital, the maximum possible loading value is 1. The frontier of the pentagon for a best possible situation is drawn accordingly. This 'best frontier' is now compared with the estimated values of various capitals. Thus, the sides of the new pentagons are drawn based on the loading values (regression coefficient reported in Table 7.10), which show the degree of access to that particular asset by the beneficiaries of GOs and NGOs. For example, in Table 7.6 we have shown that social capital of the livelihood model is represented in our model by the indicators of social wellbeing. Thus, the loading values of social wellbeing for GO (0.014) and NGOs (0.238) reported in Table 8 are their respective value in the social capital endowment line of the asset pentagon (in Fig-7.7). Again, Table 7.6 linked financial capital of SL model with the items of economic wellbeing dimension of our model. Loading of economic wellbeing for GO and NGOs are 0.863 and 0.545 respectively (in Table 7.10) and thus, these are the values of the financial capital endowment of asset pentagon (in Fig-7.7). Similar explanation can be given for the values of natural (asset building in Table 7.10), human (human capability building in Table 7.10) and physical capital (Core need fulfilment in Table 7.10) endowment (respective loading are reported in Table 7.10). A bigger pentagon inside the frontier represents the higher level of resource utilization which represents maximization of access of the poor to that particular capital. Gaps between the corner points of the pentagon of GO and NGO from the frontiers (from the value 1) show the dead weight loss in utilizing resources for poverty reduction programs. In Fig-7.7, dotted and solid line pentagons are used for NGOs and GOs respectively.

Figure 7.7: GOs and NGOs compared by livelihood capital pentagon

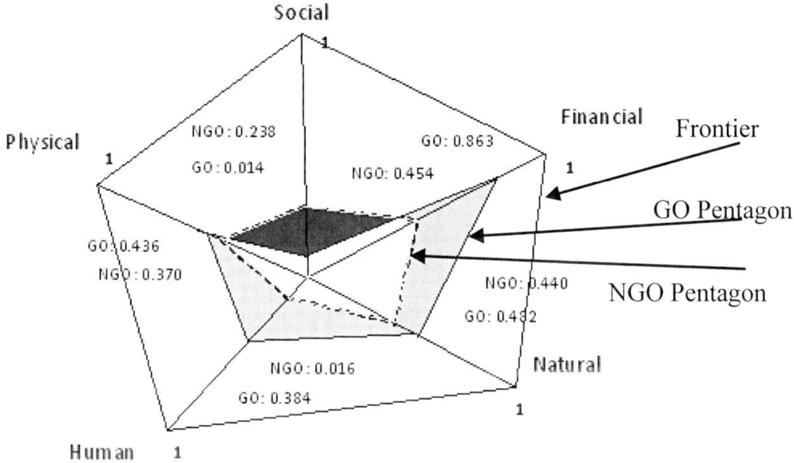

It can be seen that NGOs are more effective in enhancing social assets to the poor in rural Bangladesh (based on our results presented in Tables 7.9 and 7.10) than GOs. The gap (see the loading values) between the GO and NGO pentagons point over social capital endowment line is particularly notable. It shows that NGOs are contributing more to social inclusion and mobilization of the poor; an issue that GO agencies need to consider more closely in order to enhance the effectiveness of their performance. Fig-7.7 also shows that GO agencies are more efficient in creating the human and financial capital of the rural poor (see the loading values). The GOs dominance is in creating physical assets, and this is quite logical since most of the rural infrastructures are built by them. However, the NGOs contribution to creating awareness of using sanitary latrines and pure water sources is worth noting. GOs also perform better in asset-building (natural); however, the contribution of both GOs and NGOs is still low in this important aspect of livelihood outcome.

When combined we get a complete picture of the effectiveness of GOs and NGOs in enhancing livelihood assets from their respective pentagons in Fig-7.7. Green filled areas (big areas) show the dominance of GOs while the blue areas demonstrate the superiority of NGOs in social works. Two major comparative results can be deduced from this figure:

a) Priority should be given towards social capital-building (existing values are 0.238 and 0.014 for NGO and GOs respectively); and
b) As the respondents believe that poor people mostly depend on their physical labour for earnings and natural capital, more resources need to be channelled towards the creation of natural and human capital to make poverty reduction sustainable.

7.6 Discussion and Policy implications

The final column of Table 7.10 reveals that GO projects are more effective in improving 'Economic wellbeing' of the rural poor compared to NGOs (loading value of 0.863 for GO and 0.454 for NGOs), whereas NGOs are better in 'Social issues' (loading of 0.238, whereas GO loading value is 0.014). But the alarming issue is that both GO and NGO projects have less impact on social issues as can readily be seen from absolute magnitudes of loading values. This finding further proves the domination of policies aimed at enhancing economic wellbeing in Bangladesh that by-passeses social aspect of poverty.

NGOs perform better in providing all types of general information (job, health, education, natural disaster information, etc.) to the rural poor, especially information regarding loan sources and natural disasters even though the loading values for GOs and NGOs are quite close (loading differences are 0.057 and 0.106 respectively). GO projects lead in providing political information to the rural poor; however, the variation (only 0.003) is not that much wide with NGO projects. Our result also shows that poor people obtain better information about the activities of government from the NGOs (loading value is 0.889 for NGO and 0.850 for GO). Noticeable results are the higher loading values of both GOs and NGOs in providing education and health information to the rural poor (all values are higher than 0.89). This demonstrates that both the service providers perform exceptionally well in these social dimensions. For instance, Bangladesh Rural Advancement Committee (BRAC) schooling[39], free primary and secondary education by government, hospitals and clinics of *Gonoshashto Kendra,* and government's '*Surjer Hashi*[40]' (major funding by USAID), and '*Sobuj Chata*' clinics are responsible for these findings.

GO projects were superior in building 'human capabilities' among the rural poor. The results show that the beneficiaries of GO projects (loading 0.931) have better 'capacity to work' compared to NGO beneficiaries (loading of 0.801). Similar results have been found in the case of items such as 'morbidity' and 'average sick days per month' for male members of the family. This finding is in line with our previous findings of GOs domination in core need fulfilment. However, one interesting finding is that ‘average sick days per month for female beneficiaries’ is less for NGO beneficiaries (with loading 0.570) compared to that of GO beneficiaries (loading: 0.579). This necessarily proves NGOs’ higher concentration on women.

NGOs dominate in ‘asset building’ aspects, particularly in ‘land holding size’ (loading is 0.960 compared to GOs’ 0.885) and ‘land holding status’ (0.855 compared to GOs’ 0.800). This means more poor beneficiaries supported by NGOs could buy new land compared to those supported by GOs. On the other hand, it was found that the ‘home ownership pattern’ is better in the case of GO (loading 0.656) beneficiaries compared to the recipient of NGO benefits (loading 0.614). This is an indication that the GO projects target solvent beneficiaries with more assets which are used for the collateral purposes.

Results show that GO beneficiaries enjoy more ‘freedom in performing their political and religious activities’, whereas NGO beneficiaries are better off in cultural works (loading 0.983 compared to 0.866 of GOs). This is because NGOs conduct formal group meetings more frequently; thus their beneficiaries have more opportunity for social and cultural engagement. Therefore, we recommend that GO projects need to concentrate more on this particular social issue as group meetings can also explore suggestions from the beneficiaries that can be useful for various development partners. Similar recommendations have been made by the study of the Goldin Institute (2007) and Bunning (2004) for other countries.

It was found that NGOs are more effective in ‘creating employment’, thus helping to generate more income to the beneficiaries (loading is 0.510 compared to 0.452 for GOs). However, smaller loadings suggest that both GOs and NGOs need to improve this particular aspect. Development partners should provide consultation and training for the beneficiaries about better utilization of the loan amount such that better output can be expected from the projects. NGOs are found to be more effective than GO projects in creating not only income generation but also in ‘creating savings’ of the beneficiaries (loading is 0.610 compared to 0.415). This is because NGOs have mandatory saving scheme per week for the beneficiaries.

Interestingly it has been observed that in all cases of ‘core need fulfilment’ (particularly food intake by the family members), GO projects perform better than NGOs. This is primarily because the rate of interest charged by NGOs is much higher than the GOs (Fernando, 2006)[41]. Thus,

NGO beneficiaries are less fed despite their higher earnings because a major portion of their income leaks away on higher interest payments. In addition, we have found in one of our earlier cases that the beneficiaries of GO projects are more capable of work; thus they earn more and feed family members better.

Results show that provision for health and hygiene (use of 'sanitary latrine') is quite small by both GOs (loading is 0.309) and NGOs (loading of 0.353). We recommend that more emphasis should be given to the awareness and conscious building programs among beneficiaries with respect to health and hygiene.

It is observed that in 'decision making process at job place', NGO beneficiaries are more empowered compared to GO beneficiaries (loading value is 0.616 compared to 0.358). Two explanations can be offered. First, more NGO beneficiaries run their own small businesses or invest in farming; thus their decision making opportunity is more. Second, due to more social engagement through group meetings, NGO beneficiaries are better informed about their social rights.

Interestingly, it has been observed that the 'mental stress' is more apparent among NGO beneficiaries (loading 0.677) than that of GOs (loading 0.430). This may be due to the excessive repayment pressure imposed by the NGO field workers on the beneficiaries. At the time of survey, many NGO beneficiaries reported that they had to repay the instalment even if this means they go without food. It has also been observed at the time of survey that to tackle the repayment problem and to pay the instalment of one NGO, many beneficiaries have borrowed money from rural money lenders (called *Mohajon*). They have argued that *mohajons* are flexible than NGOs as they don't ask for a weekly repayment. However, the end result is not welcome as the beneficiaries cannot repay to either NGOs or money lenders and are trapped in chronic poverty with endless mental stress.[42]

Our results also show that the 'length of borrowing' is larger in the case of GO beneficiaries (loading is 0.595 compared to 0.460). That means there is at least 30% more repeat borrowing in the case of GO beneficiaries compared to NGOs. This is an important message for the development partners that charging higher interest may cause less number of beneficiaries and more defaulters in the long run. All these explanations are further supported by another finding that the loan repayment rate is higher in GO projects (loading 0.544) compared to NGOs (loading 0.454). Perhaps GOs' flexible loan repayment schemes and lower interest burden have made beneficiaries less loan defaulter. NGOs need to revise their interest rates in line with GO rate and in addition, NGOs need to consider re-scheduling their loan repayment process. It has also been observed that the NGOs deliver more loans and larger amounts of loans to the beneficiaries (loading value is 0.793 compared to 0.553). However, our previous findings suggest that there is no direct correlation between loan size and living standard enhancement of the beneficiaries. Thus, loan size may not matter to all beneficiaries; rather its better utilization with flexible repayment schedule would be more effective.

In summary, it can be claimed that GO projects need to concentrate more on 'social wellbeing' issues, whereas NGOs need to be careful about 'economic issues' particularly interest burdens and core needs fulfilment. It should be noted that social sides of poor beneficiaries are often ignored and both GOs and NGOs require more investment (with additional donor support) in social sides of living, particularly building awareness about social, cultural, religious, and political rights.

7.7 Conclusion

This chapter has developed and validated a multidimensional model of poverty to explore asset or capital need of the poor beneficiaries of GO and NGOs in Bangladesh. As invariance analysis has been successful for the model, it was utilized to compare the effectiveness of GO and NGOs. It has been observed that as whole GO agencies are more effective in improving welfare of the poor beneficiaries than NGOs. However, our survey results show that GO agencies need to concentrate more on social issues, especially on empowerment building of the poor through group meeting processes and employment creation. On the other hand, to reduce the mental stress of the beneficiaries, NGOs need to concentrate more on their loan delivery, rate of interest, and repayment schedules such that these would not be a burden for the beneficiaries. Both GOs and NGOs need to consider human capability building to make beneficiaries more capable of earning throughout the year as it is always believed that economic solvency is more important to the poor people. In addition, both GOs and NGOs' less contribution to social aspects of poverty is disturbing. However, their remarkable contribution to health and education in rural Bangladesh should be appreciated.

Appendix D

Table A7.1: Regression weights of the measurement model

Item	Factor	Estimate	S.E.	C.R.	P
Accstojobinfo	<--- Access to General_Info	1.000			
Accstohlthinfo	<--- Access to General_Info	1.023	.020	51.200	***
Accstoeduinfo	<--- Access to General_Info	.979	.023	42.232	***
Accstoloaninfo	<--- Access to General_Info	.779	.029	27.091	***
Accstonatrldisinf	<--- Access to General_Info	.850	.036	23.309	***
Accstopoliinfo	<--- Access to_Govern Info	1.000			
Accstogovinfo	<--- Access to_Govern Info	.924	.036	25.860	***
Capctywork	<--- Human Capability_Building	1.000			
Morbidity	<--- Human Capability_Building	-1.197	.112	-10.680	***
Avrgsickdysm	<--- Human Capability_Building	1.034	.196	5.272	***
Avrgsickdysf	<--- Human Capability_Building	.602	.178	3.382	***
Landholdstat	<--- Asset Building	1.000			
Homeownrshp	<--- Asset Building	.491	.029	16.853	***
Politclwork	<--- Freedom	1.000			
Religoswork	<--- Freedom	.426	.032	13.393	***
Cultrlwork	<--- Freedom	.889	.066	13.367	***
Incomemonth	<--- Economic_Wellbeing	1.000			
Accsstoelectr	<--- Economic_Wellbeing	-.308	.062	-4.962	***
Savemonthly	<--- Economic_Wellbeing	1.080	.162	6.664	***
Foodintkfem	<--- Core Need_Fullfillment	1.000			
Foodintkkids	<--- Core Need_Fullfillment	.904	.024	37.989	***
Foodintkmale	<--- Core Need_Fullfillment	.980	.025	38.413	***
Decisnatjob	<--- Social_Wellbeing	1.000			
Lengthofborrow	<--- Effectiveness	1.000			
Loanrepmt	<--- Effectiveness	.091	.065	3.402	.161
Amntofloan	<--- Effectiveness	1.044	.198	5.275	***
Landholdnsize	<--- Asset Building	-.860	.037	-23.148	***
Usesanlatrine	<--- Economic_Wellbeing	-.767	.108	-7.115	***
Mentalstress	<--- Social_Wellbeing	.895	.105	8.528	***
Feelunsecurd	<--- Social_Wellbeing	1.732	.207	8.366	***
DecsnatHH	<--- Vulnerability	1.000			
Exprncoftheft	<--- Vulnerability	-1.753	.291	-6.025	***
Foodintkinshortg	<--- Vulnerability	-4.107	.701	-5.855	***

Table A7.2: Covariances: Modification index for measurement model

			M.I.	Par Change
e25	<-->	Freedom	30.390	-.147
e27	<-->	Human Capability_Building	21.504	-.126
e21	<-->	e27	28.956	.246
e21	<-->	e19	15.920	.127
e21	<-->	e20	24.098	-.082
e6	<-->	e25	25.256	-.087
e8	<-->	Vulnerability	20.002	.047
e8	<-->	Social_Wellbeing	27.492	-.085
e8	<-->	e31	20.915	-.132
e9	<-->	Vulnerability	40.994	.028
e9	<-->	e23	23.078	-.082
e9	<-->	e16	22.243	.015
e9	<-->	e8	22.417	.059
e10	<-->	Vulnerability	22.958	-.025
e13	<-->	Freedom	20.549	-.305
e14	<-->	Vulnerability	16.334	.033
e14	<-->	Social_Wellbeing	30.858	.069
e15	<-->	Social_Wellbeing	27.544	.057
e1	<-->	Vulnerability	59.631	-.070
e1	<-->	e23	23.538	.168
e1	<-->	e9	15.995	-.043
e2	<-->	e8	28.590	-.105
e2	<-->	e10	11.236	.032
e2	<-->	e32	43.576	.067
e2	<-->	e33	17.731	-.041

Table A7.3: Final structural model Regression Weights

Items and factors			Estimate	S.E.	C.R.	P
ECONOMIC_WELLBEIN	<---	HUMAN CAPABILITY_BUILDIN	.146	.056	-2.596	.009
ECONOMIC_WELLBEIN	<---	ASSET_BUILDING	.430	.063	-6.851	***
SOCIAL_WELLBEING	<---	ACCESS TO_GOVERN INFO	.011	.036	2.298	.066
SOCIAL_WELLBEING	<---	ACCESS TO_GENERAL INFO	.170	.036	-4.702	***
SOCIAL_WELLBEING	<---	FREEDOM	.015	.034	3.449	.054
ECONOMIC_WELLBEING	<---	CORE NEED_FULLFILLMENT	.296	.082	3.624	***
EFFECTIVENESS	<---	ECONOMIC_WELLBEING	.969	.228	4.247	***
EFFECTIVENESS	<---	SOCIAL_WELLBEING	.401	.154	2.601	.009
Accstojobinfo	<---	ACCESS TO_GENERAL INFO	1.000			
Accstohlthinfo	<---	ACCESS TO_GENERAL INFO	1.024	.020	51.588	***
Accstoeduinfo	<---	ACCESS TO_GENERAL INFO	.978	.023	42.150	***

Items and factors			Estimate	S.E.	C.R.	P
Accstoloaninfo	<---	ACCESS TO_GENERAL INFO	.782	.028	27.805	***
Accstonatrldisinf	<---	ACCESS TO_GENERAL INFO	.836	.036	23.326	***
Accstopoliinfo	<---	ACCESS TO_GOVERNANCE INFO	1.000			
Accstogovinfo	<---	ACCESS TO_GOVERNANCE INFO	.886	.035	25.311	***
Capctywork	<---	HUMAN CAPABILITY_BUILDING	1.000			
Morbidity	<---	HUMAN CAPABILITY_BUILDING	-.920	.081	-11.401	***
Avrgsickdysm	<---	HUMAN CAPABILITY_BUILDING	.932	.173	5.396	***
Avrgsickdysf	<---	HUMAN CAPABILITY_BUILDING	.557	.157	3.561	***
Landholdstat	<---	ASSET_BUILDING	1.000			
Homeownrshp	<---	ASSET_BUILDING	.492	.028	17.555	***
Politclwork	<---	FREEDOM	1.000			
Religoswork	<---	FREEDOM	.422	.031	13.726	***
Cultrlwork	<---	FREEDOM	.929	.065	14.182	***
Incomemonth	<---	ECONOMIC_WELLBEING	1.000			
Savemonthly	<---	ECONOMIC_WELLBEING	.860	.122	7.075	***
Foodintkfem	<---	CORE NEED_FULLFILLMENT	1.000			
Foodintkkids	<---	CORE NEED_FULLFILLMENT	.906	.024	38.190	***
Foodintkmale	<---	CORE NEED_FULLFILLMENT	.977	.025	39.028	***
Decisnatjob	<---	SOCIAL_WELLBEING	1.000			
Mentalstress	<---	SOCIAL_WELLBEING	.721	.078	9.253	***
Lengthofborrow	<---	EFFECTIVENESS	1.000			
Loanrepmt	<---	EFFECTIVENESS	.083	.061	1.966	.172
Amntofloan	<---	EFFECTIVENESS	.822	.176	4.686	***
Landholdnsize	<---	ASSET_BUILDING	-.853	.035	-24.056	***
Feelunsecurd	<---	SOCIAL_WELLBEING	1.527	.165	9.246	***
Politclwork	<---	HUMAN CAPABILITY_BUILDING	.315	.059	5.309	***
Incomemonth	<---	FREEDOM	-.356	.062	-5.770	***
Usesanlatrine	<---	ECONOMIC_WELLBEING	.292	.055	-5.317	***
Usesanlatrine	<---	ACCESS TO_GENERAL INFO	.182	.022	8.415	***
Lengthofborrow	<---	HUMAN CAPABILITY_BUILDING	.595	.167	3.563	***
Loanrepmt	<---	HUMAN CAPABILITY_BUILDING	-.519	.084	-6.208	***
Decisnatjob	<---	ACCESS TO_GOVERNANCE INFO	.243	.044	5.501	***
Politclwork	<---	SOCIAL_WELLBEING	-.697	.235	-2.966	.003
Morbidity	<---	SOCIAL_WELLBEING	.516	.080	6.462	***

Table A7.4: Regression Weights for GO beneficiary

			Estimate	S.E.	C.R.	P
Accstojobinfo	<---	ACCESS TO_GENERAL INFO	1.000			
Accstohlthinfo	<---	ACCESS TO_GENERAL INFO	1.022	.020	52.069	***
Accstoeduinfo	<---	ACCESS TO_GENERAL INFO	.984	.023	42.782	***
Accstoloaninfo	<---	ACCESS TO_GENERAL INFO	.785	.028	28.094	***
Accstonatrldisinf	<---	ACCESS TO_GENERAL INFO	.858	.034	24.889	***
Accstopoliinfo	<---	ACCESS TO_GOVERN INFO	1.000			
Accstogovinfo	<---	ACCESS TO_GOVERNCE INFO	.892	.033	26.627	***
Capctywork	<---	HUMAN CAPABILITY_BUILDING	1.000			
Morbidity	<---	HUMAN CAPABILITY_BUILDING	-.933	.074	-12.648	***
Avrgsickdysm	<---	HUMAN CAPABILITY_BUILDING	.932	.170	5.486	***
Avrgsickdysf	<---	HUMAN CAPABILITY_BUILDING	.582	.156	3.737	***
Landholdstat	<---	ASSET_BUILDING	1.000			
Homeownrshp	<---	ASSET_BUILDING	.494	.028	17.484	***
Politclwork	<---	FREEDOM	1.000			
Religoswork	<---	FREEDOM	.417	.030	13.828	***
Cultrlwork	<---	FREEDOM	.906	.063	14.487	***
Incomemonth	<---	ECONOMIC_WELLBEING	1.000			
Savemonthly	<---	ECONOMIC_WELLBEING	.865	.121	7.163	***
Foodintkfem	<---	CORE NEED_FULLFILLMENT	1.000			
Foodintkkids	<---	CORE NEED_FULLFILLMENT	.941	.020	46.474	***
Foodintkmale	<---	CORE NEED_FULLFILLMENT	.980	.023	42.748	***
Decisnatjob	<---	SOCIAL_WELLBEING	1.000			
Mentalstress	<---	SOCIAL_WELLBEING	.699	.072	9.663	***
Lengthofborrow	<---	EFFECTIVENESS	1.000			
Loanrepmt	<---	EFFECTIVENESS	.057	.057	3.995	.020
Amntofloan	<---	EFFECTIVENESS	.841	.170	4.943	***
Landholdnsize	<---	ASSET_BUILDING	.880	.036	24.655	***
Feelunsecurd	<---	SOCIAL_WELLBEING	1.492	.151	9.914	***
Politclwork	<---	HUMAN CAPABILITY_BUILDING	.286	.058	4.951	***

			Estimate	S.E.	C.R.	P
Incomemonth	<---	FREEDOM	-.355	.061	-5.805	***
Usesanlatrine	<---	ECONOMIC_WELLBEING	.324	.058	-5.536	***
Usesanlatrine	<---	ACCESS TO_GENERAL INFO	.175	.022	7.989	***
Lengthofborrow	<---	HUMAN CAPABILITY_BUILDING	.574	.167	3.434	***
Loanrepmt	<---	HUMAN CAPABILITY_BUILDING	-.522	.082	-6.397	***
Decisnatjob	<---	ACCESS TO_GOVERNANCE INFO	.247	.045	5.537	***
Politclwork	<---	SOCIAL_WELLBEING	-.444	.203	-2.191	.028
Morbidity	<---	SOCIAL_WELLBEING	.488	.073	6.667	***

Table A7.5: Intercepts for GO beneficiary

Items	Estimate	S.E.	C.R.	P	Label
Accstojobinfo	2.727	.061	44.610	***	i5
Accstohlthinfo	2.646	.062	42.760	***	i4
Accstoeduinfo	2.649	.061	43.542	***	i3
Accstoloaninfo	2.910	.053	55.297	***	i2
Accstonatrldisinf	2.598	.060	43.512	***	i1
Accstopoliinfo	3.045	.061	50.085	***	i29
Accstogovinfo	3.111	.057	54.793	***	i28
Capctywork	2.038	.050	40.436	***	i15
Morbidity	2.574	.054	47.546	***	i14
Avrgsickdysm	5.562	.105	53.176	***	i13
Avrgsickdysf	6.270	.093	67.529	***	i12
Landholdstat	1.976	.040	49.267	***	i10
Homeownrshp	1.159	.023	50.405	***	i9
Politclwork	1.945	.059	33.072	***	i8
Religoswork	1.137	.025	45.898	***	i7
Cultrlwork	1.258	.046	27.192	***	i6
Incomemonth	5.536	.052	107.303	***	i20
Savemonthly	1.626	.041	39.885	***	i19
Foodintkfem	2.846	.025	113.368	***	i18
Foodintkkids	2.859	.025	116.021	***	i17
Foodintkmale	2.854	.026	109.998	***	i16
Decisnatjob	2.309	.040	57.406	***	i27
Mentalstress	1.834	.024	77.842	***	i26
Lengthofborrow	4.286	.103	41.762	***	i24
Loanrepmt	3.331	.053	63.024	***	i23
Amntofloan	2.603	.054	47.904	***	i22
Landholdnsize	1.868	.033	56.080	***	i11
Feelunsecurd	2.928	.039	75.340	***	i25
Usesanlatrine	1.400	.025	56.816	***	i21

Table A7.6: Regression Weights for NGO beneficiaries

Item		Factor	Estimate	S.E.	C.R.	P
Accstojobinfo	<---	ACCESS TO_GENERAL INFO	1.000			
Accstohlthinfo	<---	ACCESS TO_GENERAL INFO	1.022	.020	52.069	***
Accstoeduinfo	<---	ACCESS TO_GENERAL INFO	.984	.023	42.782	***
Accstoloaninfo	<---	ACCESS TO_GENERAL INFO	.785	.028	28.094	***
Accstonatrldisinf	<---	ACCESS TO_GENERAL INFO	.858	.034	24.889	***
Accstopoliinfo	<---	ACCESS TO_GOVERNANCE INFO	1.000			
Accstogovinfo	<---	ACCESS TO_GOVERNANCE INFO	.892	.033	26.627	***
Capctywork	<---	HUMAN CAPABILITY_BUILDING	1.000			
Morbidity	<---	HUMAN CAPABILITY_BUILDING	-.933	.074	-12.648	***
Avrgsickdysm	<---	HUMAN CAPABILITY_BUILDING	.932	.170	5.486	***
Avrgsickdysf	<---	HUMAN CAPABILITY_BUILDING	.582	.156	3.737	***
Landholdstat	<---	ASSET_BUILDING	1.000			
Homeownrshp	<---	ASSET_BUILDING	.494	.028	17.484	***
Politclwork	<---	FREEDOM	1.000			
Religoswork	<---	FREEDOM	.417	.030	13.828	***
Cultrlwork	<---	FREEDOM	.906	.063	14.487	***
Incomemonth	<---	ECONOMIC_WELLBEING	1.000			
Savemonthly	<---	ECONOMIC_WELLBEING	.865	.121	7.163	***
Foodintkfem	<---	CORE NEED_FULLFILLMENT	1.000			
Foodintkkids	<---	CORE NEED_FULLFILLMENT	.941	.020	46.474	***
Foodintkmale	<---	CORE NEED_FULLFILLMENT	.980	.023	42.748	***
Decisnatjob	<---	SOCIAL_WELLBEING	1.000			
Mentalstress	<---	SOCIAL_WELLBEING	.699	.072	9.663	***
Lengthofborrow	<---	EFFECTIVENESS	1.000			
Loanrepmt	<---	EFFECTIVENESS	.057	.057	2.995	.120
Amntofloan	<---	EFFECTIVENESS	.841	.170	4.943	***
Landholdnsize	<---	ASSET_BUILDING	.880	.036	-24.655	***
Feelunsecurd	<---	SOCIAL_WELLBEING	1.492	.151	9.914	***
Politclwork	<---	HUMAN CAPABILITY_BUILDING	.286	.058	4.951	***

Item		Factor	Estimate	S.E.	C.R.	P
Incomemonth	<---	FREEDOM	-.355	.061	-5.805	***
Usesanlatrine	<---	ECONOMIC_WELLBEING	-.324	.058	-5.536	***
Usesanlatrine	<---	ACCESS TO_GENERAL INFO	.175	.022	7.989	***
Lengthofborrow	<---	HUMAN CAPABILITY_BUILDING	.574	.167	3.434	***
Loanrepmt	<---	HUMAN CAPABILITY_BUILDING	-.522	.082	-6.397	***
Decisnatjob	<---	ACCESS TO_GOVERNANCE INFO	.247	.045	5.537	***
Politclwork	<---	SOCIAL_WELLBEING	-.444	.203	-2.191	.028
Morbidity	<---	SOCIAL_WELLBEING	.488	.073	6.667	***

Table A7.7: Intercepts for NGO beneficiaries

Item/factor	Estimate	S.E.	C.R.	P	Label
EFFECTIVENESS	-.425	.122	-3.492	***	int
Accstojobinfo	2.727	.061	44.610	***	i5
Accstohlthinfo	2.646	.062	42.760	***	i4
Accstoeduinfo	2.649	.061	43.542	***	i3
Accstoloaninfo	2.910	.053	55.297	***	i2
Accstonatrldisinf	2.598	.060	43.512	***	i1
Accstopoliinfo	3.045	.061	50.085	***	i29
Accstogovinfo	3.111	.057	54.793	***	i28
Capctywork	2.038	.050	40.436	***	i15
Morbidity	2.574	.054	47.546	***	i14
Avrgsickdysm	5.562	.105	53.176	***	i13
Avrgsickdysf	6.270	.093	67.529	***	i12
Landholdstat	1.976	.040	49.267	***	i10
Homeownrshp	1.159	.023	50.405	***	i9
Politclwork	1.945	.059	33.072	***	i8
Religoswork	1.137	.025	45.898	***	i7
Cultulwork	1.258	.046	27.192	***	i6
Incomemonth	5.536	.052	107.303	***	i20
Savemonthly	1.626	.041	39.885	***	i19
Foodintkfem	2.846	.025	113.368	***	i18
Foodintkkids	2.859	.025	116.021	***	i17
Foodintkmale	2.854	.026	109.998	***	i16
Decisnatjob	2.309	.040	57.406	***	i27
Mentalstress	1.834	.024	77.842	***	i26
Lengthofborrow	4.286	.103	41.762	***	i24
Loanrepmt	3.331	.053	63.024	***	i23
Amntofloan	2.603	.054	47.904	***	i22
Landholdnsize	1.868	.033	56.080	***	i11
Feelunsecurd	2.928	.039	75.340	***	i25
Usesanlatrine	1.400	.025	56.816	***	i21

Figure A7.1: Purified measurement model with good fit

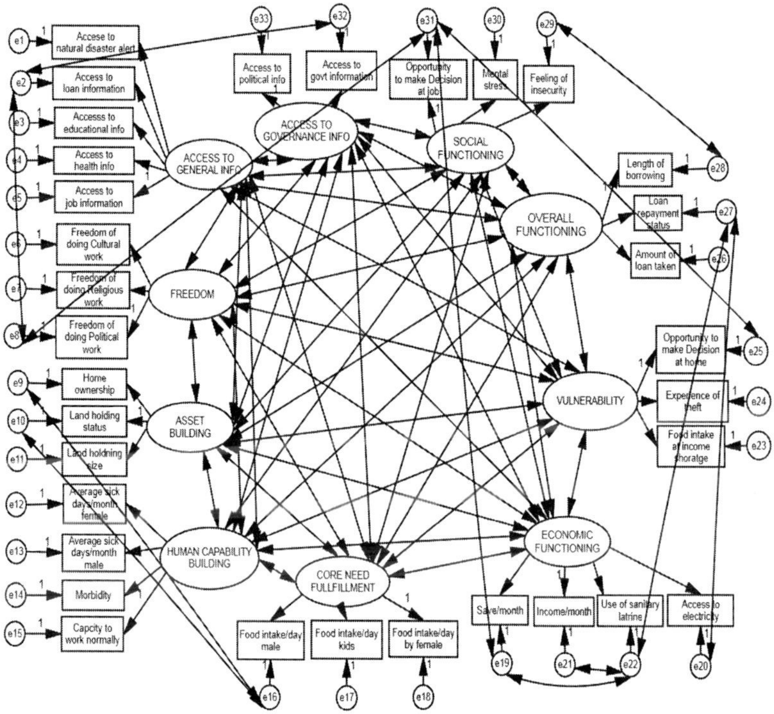

Notes

[1] For example, Rowntree's (1901) *physiological approach, basic needs* approach as discussed by Streeten (1975); the *social exclusion* approach by Townsend (1979); the sustainable livelihoods model by Chamber (1989) and DFID; the study of '*capability*' forwarded by Sen (1985); and UNDP's *human development* approach and *human rights* approach. For further details, see works of Booysen (2002); McGillivray and Noorbakhsh (2007).

[2] According to DCI, poor households are defined as those with per capita energy intake less than the standard per capita requirement of energy (1805 kilo calorie for extreme and 2112 kilo calorie for moderate poverty line)

[3] The FEI method sets the poverty line as the income or consumption level at which basic needs are met (Ahmed, 2004).

[4] In income poverty analysis, statistics on land ownership, consumption and savings pattern are available.

[5] This includes income generation, healthcare and education support.

[6] How many poor beneficiaries of government and NGOs separately could break the cycle of poverty.

[7] Amartya Sen (1985), in his human capability approach, 'outlined the need for assets, commodities and services for an acceptable standard of living, and an inability to access or acquire the stated requirements as the main cause of poverty'.

[8] For a list of works, see, Neely et al. (2004); Scoones (1997).

[9] Sustainable livelihoods guidance sheets also recommended that the asset or capital requirement should be investigated case by case.

[10] Usability of a single model between different groups without any modification for individual group.

[11] Available studies only explored few indicators and didn't offer any validated model for the effectiveness comparison. See Nabi (1999); Mahbub and Roy (1997); Moore, Choudhury and Singh (1998).

[12] See for instance, Kevane and Wydick, 2001; Mayoux, 1999; Goetz and Gupta, 1996; Mahmud and Ahmed, 2003; McGhee, 1999; Chao, 2003; Morshed, 2000.

[13] Similar approach was used by Silver (2007).

[14] See, Poggi and Devicienti (2007); Nussbaum (2000, 2003); Robeyns (2002); Ruggeri-Laderchi (2001); Narayan et al. (2000, 1999); Alkire and Black (1997); Doyal and Gough (1991); Sen (1982, 1983).

[15] See for instance, NGOAB and PKSF websites and Goldin Institute survey (2007).

[16] For example, income and savings will determine the level of economic wellbeing. Freedom to do political and cultural works will determine the level of social wellbeing, whereas economic and social wellbeing will determine the level of effectiveness. That means the relationship is indirect between income and savings with effectiveness..

[17] Exploratory factor analysis (EFA) is a statistical method that helps determining underlying dimension for a set of measured items (or assets).

[18] CFA allows the researcher to test the hypothesis that a relationship between the observed items and their underlying dimension(s) exists. CFA tests whether a specified set of dimensions is influencing responses in a predicted way.

[19] Acceptable range of MSA is above 0.50 (Hair et al., 2010, p.132).

[20] By considering the total number of factors until the *eigenvalue* drops below 1.

[21] Similar rules were followed in Marketing literature by Shimp and Sharma, 1987; in Psychology literature by MacCallum and Austin, 2000; in Research methodology by Hair et al, 2010).

[22] For a good fit, preferred CFI value is closer to 0.95 and RMSEA value should be less or equal to 0.05.

[23] For instance, small and significant chi-square values, p values greater than 0.05, *GFI* and *CFI* greater than 0.90, *RMSEA* less than 0.05 and *Hoelters* value more than 200 (Byrne, 2001).

[24] All these items have loading less than 0.30.

[25] The problem with the factor,'Empowerment' has been identified by a trial and error process when checking the GOF values of the model by deleting one factor and its items at a time.

[26] For example, our survey result explored that about 96.3% of the respondents cast their vote regularly and 98% of the regular voters vote for their preferred candidate. This shows that from the voting point of view, beneficiaries are quite empowered thus these items and the 'Empowerment' factor were identified as less relevant to the model.

[27] It includes factor loading testing, average variance extracted test and construct reliability measures.

[28] Similar findings can be seen in DFID's Sustainable Livelihoods Model, where vulnerability is not considered itself as a dimension of poverty.

[29] For example, outcome of economic wellbeing are income per month, savings per month and use of sanitary latrine; outcome of asset building is home ownership pattern, land holding size and land holding status (whether bought new or sold or owned by inheritance).

[30] Chi-square value dropped to 687.553 from 1115.859 of preliminary model. Hoelters values are 304 and 320 which are greater than 200. AIC and ECVI are both lower than independence model.

[31] In case of structural model, *Cronbach's Alpha* is always underestimated or under-reported (Arbuckle, 2009) thus we used *Coefficient H* value.

[32] *RMR*, *GFI*, *Hoelter* are 0.076, 0.902, 315 and 364 respectively. *AIC* value (1574) and *ECVI* value (2.811) were found to be less than that of saturated model (*AIC* is 1740 and *ECVI* is 3.107)

[33] Metric invariance establishes the equivalence of the basic meaning of the construct because the loadings denote the relationship between indicators and latent factor (Hair et al., 2010).

[34] It tests for the equality of the measured variable intercepts (means) on the construct. It allows the relative amount of latent factors to be compared between groups.

[35] It shows whether the factors are related to each other in a similar fashion across the groups.

[36] It assesses the equality of variances of the factors across the groups.

[37] Invariance of this model was further tested between male and female beneficiaries and in all cases results were found to be satisfactory which argues that this model is robust in comparing between different groups.

[38] *C.R* value is only -0.091.

[39] As of December-2009, 32,000 primary schools with 32,937 teachers were in operation to cater to the needs of 984,440 children where 65% were girls. Among these, 5,500 schools with 164,835 students (72% girls) were operated by other NGOs with our support. Additionally, 1,415 BRAC primary schools were operated in urban areas with 47,539 students and 2,250 ethnic schools with 57,645 learners were operated in remote areas.

[40] They have coverage on 61 districts in Bangladesh with 320 static clinics.

[41] Also see, Interest rates policy for MFIs streamlined in *The Financial Express* on April 29, 2009. Check, *The Independent* on March 5, 2004.

[42] As study by the Goldin Institute (2007) found that it is not uncommon for families to carry as many as five loans, most used to cover old debts, rather than to purchase new assets.

CHAPTER EIGHT

SUMMARY CONCLUSION, POLICY PRESCRIPTION AND FURTHER RESEARCH IMPLICATIONS

Effectiveness comparison between microcredit-driven government and NGO projects has been continuing for decades with a common myth of NGO effectiveness domination in the stated programs. This study argues that in general, effectiveness of the microfinance driven poverty reduction projects in developing countries such as Bangladesh is assessed by repayment rates, the number of beneficiary, area coverage, the amount of loan disbursed, and the cost of operation which are all narrow ways of effectiveness measurement as none of them reflect the perceptions of the poor people towards the efficacy of the projects. Even though poor people's participation is considered the most important aspect of poverty reduction as well as empowerment, in most cases their opinions in the decision making and performance appraisal of the projects are ignored. This study also argues that large scale credit delivery (which is one of the indicators of project's effectiveness) cannot contribute a lot to changing the poverty condition of the households unless proper and customized support services are provided for them so that the beneficiaries can utilize the loan more productively. In addition, donor's and regulatory authority's effectiveness assessment of the poverty reduction projects based on repayment rate is a misleading judgement as it is evidenced that majority of the borrowers take loans from another loan provider (both formal and informal) to repay loans and thus, the funds used for repayment may not necessarily be generated from a productive venture. Similar results have been found in a recent study by Hoque (2010) which reported that 81% of the female borrowers and 86% of the male borrowers took loans from multiple sources to repay loan. Due to this multi-lending behaviour of the clients, most of the credit driven projects have a large number of beneficiaries. This necessarily proves that a single beneficiary is covered by multiple projects; thus, the number of beneficiary is not a viable criteria for effectiveness assessment either. However, there are still a large number of marginal poor unserved as the credit driven projects find it costly to serve them.

Our argument is that to accelerate the poverty reduction rate by utilizing the credit more effectively, there is a need for effective and customized service delivery based on the need preferences of the credit borrowers. Even though the existing development theories (such as capability approach and sustainable livelihoods model) stressed the need for effective service delivery, the development partners (such as GO and NGOs) have never been compared based on their service delivery effectiveness – a processed based comparison – which is crucial to poverty reduction. This study has, thus, offered a different dimension of comparing GO and NGO credit-driven projects. This is a significant contribution to addressing the effectiveness debate. As there is no set of parameters suggested in the existing literature which can be utilized to evaluate service delivery efficacy, this study has offered a methodology to develop a scale, and items which can be used for the performance evaluation of credit-driven GO and NGO projects.

Expected outcome of the credit driven poverty reduction projects are supposed to begin with the degree of employment creation and income generation which in turn facilitate other economic and social need fulfilment. Thus, an outcome relevant comparison among the poverty reduction projects should be based on their relative contribution to uplifting living standard of the poor. However, in reality most outcome relevant comparison is grounded on loan recovery rate, profitability, and financial sustainability of the projects that only reflect the benefit of the projects and donors and neglect welfare aspects. There are few studies available which compared the efficacy of government and that of NGO projects based on few pre-determined criteria and those criteria were not selected based on the opinions of the beneficiaries. Thus, we argue that a more authentic living standard-relevant comparison can be done if a composite and customized poverty model can be developed by utilizing the opinion of the concerned beneficiaries. As Sen (1990) also argued that a poverty reduction project can be effective only if the local needs of the poor are identified first. We, thus, feel that it would be rational to explore the need preferences (or poverty indicators) first and then compare the efficacy of GO and NGO credit-driven projects with respect to their contribution to the explored indicators. In this book, we have proposed a new methodology to develop customized poverty model that can capture economic, social, political, religious, and cultural aspects of poverty. The model is then utilized to compare the effectiveness of credit-driven GO and NGO projects based on a large set of poverty indicators. This extensive comparison is another new way to contribute to the effectiveness debate.

By utilizing the scale items (process-based comparison), our study shows that in many important fields of service delivery dimensions, GO is performing more effectively than NGOs. Even though NGOs have much higher investment, wider coverage and large workforce compared to GO and better performance in several fields, items relating to trustworthiness in financial issues and caring more for beneficiary's social welfare are in favour of GO projects.

This process based comparative study also shows that *gender discrimination* is evident in the poverty alleviation programs in Bangladesh. Female beneficiaries are in disadvantageous position not only for cultural or religious customs but also due to less attention towards them by the services provided by GOs and NGOs. Following are few noticeable findings supporting our argument:

- As a whole for several items, there is discrimination in opinions between male and female beneficiaries; in all of these items more improvement is demanded by the female beneficiaries on the ground of standard of services received compared to the male beneficiaries.
- Similar results have been observed in the case of region specific studies (refer to Table 5.12 for detailed characteristics). For instance, in the South and Central areas, improvement in all discriminating items is demanded by the female beneficiaries. In the North area, out of three discriminating items, improvement in two items is required by the females while males require improvement on the other. All these results support the evidence of gender discrimination regionally.
- Demand for improvement in service items by the female beneficiaries varies among the regions. For instance, while in the North area, female members look for further improvement in timeliness in service delivery along with worker's skills, whereas, in the South area more attention is required in the empowerment issues, particularly in listening and incorporating the suggestions of the beneficiaries in the decision making process of the service providers. Finally, in the Central area, more concentration is demanded on the items related to trustworthiness of the organizations, particularly fairness in the decision making process, keeping the promises properly and more attention of the workers towards the female beneficiaries.

Our findings indicate that as more disadvantageous segment of the population, women need more customized policy formulation which is fair, attentive, timely, and participative in nature.

Comparative study on poverty model (outcome based) shows that credit-driven government agencies are more effective in creating economic wellbeing of the poor, whereas NGOs are better in social aspects of poverty. Our study also shows that NGOs are superior in creating access to general, financial and governance related information to the poor even though the gaps between GO and NGOs are marginal. Government agencies were found to be more capable of reducing morbidity and average sick days of the poor in the households. One main reason for that finding is the better access of the beneficiaries to government hospitals and clinics. Even though private NGO hospitals and clinics are there, the poor beneficiaries can't afford those services to buy. In building assets, a mixed result has been observed. GO agencies were seen to be more effective in creating assets such as home and other households, whereas, NGO beneficiaries reported that their land holding size increased. Results found that GO agencies are better in creating political and religious awareness among people, whereas NGOs are performing better in enhancing cultural freedom of the poor. It is believed that NGOs' group meeting process has contributed a lot in such respect. Our field observation and results suggest that NGO workers put excessive pressure on beneficiaries while asking for the repayment instalments and thus, NGOs are responsible for creating more mental stress to the people compared to GO agencies – one major problem that NGOs need to address. Furthermore, it was also found that loan repayment rate in GO agencies is much better than that in NGOs. This necessarily contradicts the existing literature.

8.1 Policy prescriptions

The above discussion shows that both GO and NGOs have their shortcomings while delivering services and uplifting living standards of the poor. We infer that by making the service delivery process more effective and customized the development partners can increase the productivity of the poor people and thus, can contribute more to reducing different dimensions of poverty. Based on the opinions of the beneficiaries and our analysis we offer the following policy prescription to the GO agencies and NGOs:

8.1.1. Policies for GO agencies

1) GOs require more improvement in the items related to beneficiary focus dimension, namely listening to the suggestions of beneficiaries and expanding coverage along with fairness in operation.
2) To maximize the interest of beneficiaries and the impact of poverty reduction, government projects need to expand their coverage, inject additional budget for infrastructure, and recruit more field workers with additional training.
3) In the case of regional analysis for GO agencies, improvement is required with respect to the location or coverage in the remote areas.
4) This study recommends the necessity of a cultural change in the service providers in rural Bangladesh by ameliorating the GO corruption through elimination of middlemen and by speeding up lending processes. Beneficiaries of Government agencies require more monitoring and liaison before and after loan approval. Furthermore, GOs need to invest more in infrastructure and coverage through employing more field workers and by setting up more branch offices.
5) GO agencies need to revise their service delivery chain by reducing the bureaucracy in the poverty reduction projects where prompt response is required. In addition, by reducing the political and elite pressures, GO agencies can make their distribution more pro-poor.
6) GO agencies need to invest heavily on human resources practices by conducting periodic training to the field workers. It has been observed at the time of field study that monitoring by the field workers of GO agencies is comparatively less; thus beneficiaries are deprived of services whenever needed. Better transport facilities need to be provided to the GO field staffs to ensure regular monitoring. Moreover, the remuneration package of the GO field staffs needs to be competitive such that the workers can be motivated to offer better services.
7) Based on the results, it is believed that GO agencies should re-negotiate with the donors to acquire more funds as it was found that a large number of beneficiaries rely more on government and they believe that only government works for their welfare. However, before the negotiation, GO agencies have to visibly prove that they could reduce corruption to a large extent and they are capable of delivering better services to the more marginal and neglected poor.

8) Study also reveals that more investment is required in the health sector or human capability building to reduce morbidity and average sick days per month of the poor. This policy has particular weight as most of the poor live on income based on physical labor. GO agencies need to build more health centres in remote rural areas.
9) GO agencies should focus on creating more income generating opportunities for the poor. In such respect, government can use their unused (*khas*) lands and water-bodies by leasing them to the poor people at a flexible condition. Moreover, special consideration is required to combat with seasonal and natural shocks (especially in the Northern part). Our study found that GO agencies waived the interest burden of the credit whenever there were any natural calamities – a special consideration that should be appreciated. GO agencies should encourage their clients to invest more money on off-farm activities which can ensure round the year employment and income.

8.1.2. Policies for NGOs

1) NGOs need to concentrate more on items belonging to credibility dimensions of the scale such as sincerity of the providers in solving problems, and requiring increased skills of the workers in dealing with individual problems.
2) To maximize the interest of beneficiaries and the impact of poverty reduction, NGOs need to consider restructuring customized rate of interest and building an image of voluntary social organization.
3) In the Northern region, NGOs need to concentrate on issues related to skills of the workers, whereas in the Southern region more attention should be paid to service quality maintenance; in the Central areas, NGOs need to devote more consideration to credibility related issues, particularly with regard to keeping their promises in service delivery by establishing transparency in transaction processes.
4) The NGOs need to re-schedule rates of interest and repayment processes. NGOs should change the image of 'workers as money collection agents' by investing more on human resources practices and training, and keeping in close and regular contact with the beneficiaries.

5) NGOs should increase the provision for complementary services, especially for those which are mostly demanded by the female beneficiaries.
6) In addition to credit delivery, NGOs need to put more emphasis on social mobilization projects as our outcome based study revealed that poor people are lagging behind in social aspects of poverty. NGOs should convince donors to channel more fund for the stated purpose.
7) NGOs should publish and circulate their annual reports to establish their transparency of operations. Periodic meetings with the beneficiaries are important to inform them about the recent changes and activities of the NGOs, especially about the interest rate, new services, new operating procedures, etc.
8) NGOs should consider revising their rate of interest to put reasonable pressure on the beneficiaries as our study revealed that mental pressure and stress are higher for NGO beneficiaries. NGOs usually start collecting their instalment just after two weeks of delivering the loan. In most cases, it is hard for the beneficiaries to accumulate return within that short time of span. In addition, the beneficiaries need to contribute to compulsory saving scheme which means they can't utilize the whole amount they are borrowing. However, the beneficiaries need to pay interest on the whole borrowed amount. All these issues need to be addressed by the NGOs.
9) To facilitate the people in getting better health care support, NGOs and private sector should focus on reducing the cost of health care services such that the poor can access to those facilities.
10) Credit driven projects of NGOs should introduce additional insurance and asset creating schemes for their beneficiaries such as medical insurance, future shock insurance, home loans, asset loans, etc as the projects have the compulsory savings schemes.

8.1.3 Policies for both GO agencies and NGOs

1) Both GO agencies and NGOs should involve the poor in their decision making process. It is believed that more area of origin relevant to policy package is fruitful while solving problems of that particular community. In addition, case study on the problems of other areas can be a strategic step for both the service providers.
2) Both GO and NGOs should introduce customized credit systems based on the physical (such as disability) and social status (such as

widowed) of the poor. Both the agencies may consider setting customized rate of interest according to the area of proposed investment as it is obvious that return from each venture cannot be the same.

3) Consultation with the client is a must before approving the loan so that actual requirement of the proposed business can be identified. In addition, after sanctioning the loan, monitoring is required to see whether any extra services are needed.
4) Outcome based study reveals that a strong monitoring is required to ensure that women lenders can use their funds, by themselves, which to a large extent are used by their male counterparts. The existing practice goes against the principles of women empowerment and should be monitored closely. However, our study also suggests that credit should be given according to the poverty status of the person, not based on their gender.
5) Both GOs and NGOs have to invest more in social aspects of poverty which necessitates special attention towards social, political, religious, and cultural consciousness building. It is believed that such projects can help the poor become more aware of their social and political rights; thus ensure pro-poor and democratic practices in the country.
6) Our study revealed that both GOs and NGOs have less focus on creation of assets for the clients. Both GO and NGOs should provide better consultation and after delivery services such that poor beneficiaries can accumulate savings with better productive ventures. It should be noted that these savings can be used to create assets, such as land and home which will not only reduce the vulnerability of the poor but reduce the inequality in the society.
7) Our study highly recommends that the poor's participation based periodic survey need to be conducted to get an updated idea about the effectiveness of the development partners in contributing to the poverty reduction projects. The results of those studies can help donors make more informed decision about the effective channels for fund delivery other than relying on traditional comparison tools, such as repayment rate or amount of loan disbursement.
8) This study recommends the potentiality of large scale GO-NGO collaboration in the poverty reduction sector in the developing countries. Governments' administrative power and long experience in the social sector with NGOs' dedicated workforce and state of the art mechanism may create revolution in poverty reduction.

8.2 Further research potentials

This study recommends the following research ideas to extend our proposed effectiveness scale and poverty model:

1. Application of the effectiveness scale and poverty model in hilly areas, islands and haor (water bodies) areas in Bangladesh.
2. Application of both scales and the model in other developing countries of the world with minor regional adjustments due to the fact that both the models are validated through discriminant validity, nomological validity, and convergent validity.
3. Updating models after a certain time period (for instance after 3-4 years).
4. Comparing the effectiveness of individual GO and NGO projects with GO-NGO collaborative projects by using the proposed models to explore the potential benefit of collaboration.
5. Setting benchmark for service delivery items in the same industry but in other developing countries. Based on those studies, a global (or regional) benchmark can be set.
6. Developing a multidimensional poverty model for children based on the methodology we have developed to address the issues of intra-household poverty.
7. Validation of the models for other emerging development partners, such as cooperatives, traditional rural lenders (*Mohajons*), etc.
8. In the study, we argue that still a large number of rural poor visit village doctors instead of GO and NGO hospitals/clinics. Testing this argument further with its probable underlying reasons through the beneficiary opinion can be a value addition.
9. Our study has shown that NGOs are charging a higher rate of interest and create excess pressure on the beneficiaries for instalment payment causing mental stress. Explore whether this particular finding has further justification that informal rural lenders may come back again.
10. Our study shows that the poor are borrowing loan from one development partner to repay the interest burden of another. Further research would be to find the leakage of funds due to this malpractice and how that affects vulnerability of the moderate poor in becoming extreme poor.

REFERENCES

Ackerman, R. S. 1996. Altruism, nonprofits, and economic theory, *Journal of Economic Literature,* 34, 2, pp. 701-28.

ADB. 1999a. *Fighting Poverty in Asia and the Pacific: The Poverty Reduction Strategy of the Asian Development Bank.* Manila, Philippines.

Ahluwalia, M. S., and Chenery, H. B. 1974. The economic framework, in Chencry *et al. Redistribution with Growth.* London: Oxford University Press, 1974. Chapter-2

Ahmad, N. 1995. Environment Development and Women. *Empowerment of Women*, Women for Women, Dhaka.

Ahmed, M. U. 2004. Socio-demographic Correlates Of Rural Poverty in Bangladesh: A Case Study of Gaibandha Sadar and Tanore Upazillas, *Bangladesh e-Journal of Sociology*. Vol. 1. No. 2. July, 2004, pp. 50-66.

Ahmed, N. 2009. The Sustainable Livelihoods Approach to the Development of Fish Farming in Rural Bangladesh. Journal of International Farm Management Vol.4. No.4 –February, pp. 2-18.

Akaike, H. 1987. Factor analysis and AIC. *Psychometrika*, 52, pp. 317-332.

Albrecht, K., and Zemke, R. 1985. Service America. Homewood, Ill: Dow JonesIrwin.

Alkire, S. 2002. *Valuing Freedoms. Sen's Capability Approach and Poverty Reduction*. Oxford: Oxford University Press.

—. 2007. Measuring freedoms alongside well-being, in GOUGH, I. and J. A. MCGREGOR (eds.) Well-being in developing countries: new approaches and research strategies. Cambridge: Cambridge University Press.

Alkire, S. and Black, R. 1997. A Practical Reasoning Theory of Development Ethics: Furthering the Capabilities Approach. *Journal of International Development*, 9(2), pp. 263-79.

Allardt, E. 1976. Dimensions of Welfare in a Comparative Scandinavian Study, *Acta Sociologica*, 19, pp. 227-39.

Aminuzzaman, S. 2000. Institutional Framework of Poverty Alleviation: An overview of Bangladesh experiences, online publications, pp. 1-14.

Amsden, A. 1989. *Asia's Next Giant: South Korea and Late Industrialization*, Oxford University Press, New York.

Arbuckle, J. L. 2009. *Amos 18 User Guide.* Amos Development Corporation, USA.

Asaduzzaman, M., and Huddleston, B. 1983. An Evaluation of Management of Food for Work Programme. *The Bangladesh Development Studies*. Vol-XI (Numbers 1 & 2), pp. 19-33. Dhaka. Bangladesh Institute of Development Studies.

Asian Development Bank (ADB). Annual Report: 2001, 2002, 2003, 2005, 2006.

Atkinson, A. 1998. *Poverty in Europe*, Blackwell

Azam, S. M., and Katsushi, I. S. 2009. Vulnerability and Poverty in Bangladesh, *ASARC Working Paper*-2009.

Babakus, E., and Boller, G.W. 1992. An empirical assessment of the SERVQUAL scale. *Journal of Business Research,* 24(3), pp. 253-68.

Balestrino, A. 1996. A Note on Functioning Poverty in Affluent Societies., *Notizie di Politeia*, 12, pp. 97-105.

Bandalos, D. L. (1993). Factors influencing cross-validation of confirmatory factor analysis models. *Multivariate Behavioural Research*, *28*, pp. 351-374.

Banerjee. L, 2008. Of Floods and Agricultural Wage rates in Bangladesh: Empirical Evidence from the recent past.

Bangladesh Bank, 2008. Comparative Statement of per capita expenditure (Districts and Divisions). Government of Bangladesh.

Bangladesh Bureau of Statistics (BBS), Government of Bangladesh. Annual Report 2005, 2002

Bangladesh Bureau of Statistics (BBS). 2011. *Welfare Monitoring Survey-2009.*

—. Statistical Yearbook of various years.

Bangladesh Bureau of Statistics. HIES BBS, 2000, 2002, 2005, 2006, 2007

Bangladesh Planning Commission; WFP, 2005. The Food Security Atlas of Bangladesh, 2005. pp. 78; HIES-BBS, 2005.

Barcellos, S. 2007. Benchmarking in the Public and Non-profit Sector. Centre for Leadership and Management, Graduate School, USDA

Bardhan, P., Bowles, S. and Gintis, H. 1999. Wealth Inequality, Wealth Constraints and Economic Performances, in A. Atkinson and F. Bourguignon (eds), Handbook of Income Distribution, Elsevier, Chapter-10, pp. 541-603.

Bawa, A., 2004. Consumer Ethnocentrism: CETSCALE Validation and Measurement of Extent. *VIKALPA*, 29 (3), pp. 43-55.

BBS, 2008. *Agricultural Census Report-2008*. Ministry of Planning, Government of Bangladesh.

—. 2008. *Demographic Characteristics by Zilla. B-12.*

—. 2008. *Household Income and Expenditure Survey-2005.*

—. Various Years. Year book of Agricultural Statistics of Bangladesh. Ministry of Planning, GOB.

BBS, WB and WFP, 2009. *Updating Poverty Maps of Bangladesh.*

Bebbington, A. and Farrington, J. 1992. *Private Voluntary Initiatives and Governments, NGOs and Agricultural Development*, London: ODI.

Ben-Ner, A. 1986. Non-profit Organizations: Why Do They Exist in Market Economies?, *In the Economics of Non-profit Institutions: Studies in Structure and Policy*, ed. Susan Rose-Ackerman. Oxford: Oxford University Press.

Bentler, P.M. 1990, Comparative Fit Indexes in Structural Models, *Psychological Bulletin,* 107 (2), pp. 238-46

Bergman, L. R., and Magnusson, D. 1995. Stability and Change in Patterns of Extrinsic Adjustment Problems, *in* Magnusson, D and Casaer, P (1995) *Longitudinal Research on Individual Development.* Cambridge: Cambridge University Press, pp. 1-25

Bhalla, A. S. and Lapeyre, F. 1997. Social Exclusion: Towards an Analytical and Operational Framework, *Development and Change*, Vol. 28, pp. 413-433.

Bollen, K.A. 1990. Overall Fit in Covariance Structure Models: Two Types of Sample Size Effects, *Psychological Bulletin*, 107 (2), pp. 256-59.

Booysen, F. 2002. Measuring poverty with data from the Demographic and Health Survey (DHS): An Application to South Africa. *Journal for Studies in Economics and Econometrics*, 26 (3), pp. 53-70.

—. 2002a. Poverty and health in Southern Africa: Evidence from the Demographic and Health Survey, in *South African Journal of Economics*, vol.70, no. 2: pp. 391-415.

—. 2002b. Financial responses of households in the Free State Province to HAV/AIDS-related morbidity and mortality, in *South African Journal of Economics*, vol.70, no.7, pp. 1193-1215.

Bossert, W., D'Ambrosio, C., and Peragine, V. 2007. Deprivation and Social Exclusion, *Economica*, vol-74, pp. 777-803.

Bourgignon, F. 1999. Absolute Poverty, Relative Deprivation and Social Exclusion, *Inclusion, Justice, and Poverty Reduction*, Berlin: Villa Borsig Workshop Series.

—. 1998. Crime as a Social Cost of Poverty and Inequality: a Review Focusing on Developing Countries.

Bowen, G. A. 2007. An Analysis of Citizen Participation in Anti-Poverty Programs, *Community Development Journal*, April 26, 2007, vol-43 (1), pp. 65-78.

Bozdogan, H. 1987b. ICOMP: A new model-selection criterion. Preprint paper in Hans H. Bock (Ed.), Classification and related methods of data analysis. Amsterdam: Elsevier Science (North-Holland).

Bradshaw, J., Kemp, P., Baldwin, S., and Rowe, A. 2004. *The drivers of social exclusion: A review of the literature for the Social Exclusion Unit in the Breaking the Cycle series*. London: Office of the Deputy Prime Minister.

Brandolini, A., and D'Alessio, G. 1998. Measuring well-being in the functioning space, Banca d'Italia Research Department.

Brinkerhoff, J. M., and Brinkerhoff, D. W. 2002. Government-non profit relations in comparative perspective: Evolution, themes and new directions. *Public Administration and Development*, 22 (1), pp. 3-19.

Brinkerhoff, J. M., Smith, S. C., and Teegen, H. 2007. NGOs and the Millennium Development Goals: Citizen Action to Reduce Poverty, by Palgrave Macmillan, New York.

Brown, S.W., and Swartz, T. 1989. A gap analysis of professional service quality. *Journal of Marketing,* 53(2), pp. 92-8.

Brown, T., Churchill, G., and Peter, J. 1993. Improving the measurement of service quality. *Journal of Retailing,* 69(1), pp. 127-39.

Browne, M. W., and Cuddeck. 1993. Alternative ways of assessing model fit. In Bollen, K. A., and Long, J. S. (eds), Testing Structural Equation Models, pp. 136-162, Newbury Park, CA: Sage

Buchanan, J. M. 1987. The Constitution of Economic Policy. *American Economic Review*, June-1987, vol-77, pp. 243-250.

Bunning, A, 2004. A microcredit success story: Women make the difference, *Development Bulletin*, no. 64, pp. 63-66.

Burra, N. 2005. Women and Microcredit: Some Challenges. Note prepared for the National Commission of Farmers in India.

Byrne, B. M. 2001. *Structural Equation Modelling with Amos-Basic Concepts, Applications and Programming.* Lawrence Erlbaum Associates, Inc. USA

—. 2009. *Structural Equation Modeling with AMOS: Basic Concepts, Applications, and Programming* (Multivariate Applications Series). Routledge Publications, ISBN: 0805863737.

Cahyat, A., Gonner, C., and Huag, M. 2007. Assessing Household Poverty and Wellbeing, A Manual with Examples from Kutai Barat, Indonesia. Published by Centre for International Forestry Research.

Camfield, L. 2006. They Why and How of Understanding Subjective Wellbeing: Exploratory Work by the WeD Group in Four Developing Countries, *WeD Working Paper-26*, ESRC Research Group.

Camfield, L. and Skevington, S. 2003. Quality of Life and Wellbeing, Paper, *ESRC Research Group on Wellbeing in Developing Countries*, University of Bath.

Camp, S. L., and Speidel, J. J. 1987. *The International Human Suffering Index*, Washington: Population Crisis Committee.

Centre for Policy Dialogue (CPD), 2008. Addressing Regional Inequality Issues in Bangladesh Public Expenditure. Occasional Paper series-71, November-2008.

—. Bangladesh. Annual Report-2003

Chakravarty, S and D'ambrosio, C. 2006. The Measurement of Social Exclusion, *Review of Income and Wealth*, 52-3, pp. 377-398.

Chambers, R. 1983. *Rural Development: Putting the Last First.* Harlow, Longman

—. 1995. Poverty and Livelihoods: Whose Reality Counts? *IDS Discussion Paper No. 347.*

—. 2006. Poverty Unperceived: Traps, Biases and Agenda. *IDS Working Paper No. 270.* Institute of Development Studies, University of Sussex, UK.

Chambers, R. and Conway, G. R. 1992. Sustainable Rural Livelihoods: Practical Concepts for the 21st Century, *Institute of Development Studies Discussion Paper, 296*. Cambridge.

Chao, D. 2003. Improving Health care Delivery in Bangladesh, Study conducted by Research Triangle Institute (RTI) funded by USAID.

Cheston, S., and Kuhn, L. 2002. Empowering Women through Microfinance. Research sponsored by the Women's Opportunity Fund and its funding partners: Elizabeth Foster and Michael Walsh, Gems of Hope USA, and the Morrow Charitable Trust. In: Daley-Harris, S, ed. *Pathways out of poverty: innovations in microfinance for the poorest families*. Bloomfield, CT: Kumarian Press, pp. 167-228.

Chowdhury, O., Islam, KM. 1999. Flood-1998: A Rapid Economic Appraisal. *Report prepared for Asian Development Bank.*

Clark, A., and Oswald, A. 1994. Unhappiness and Employment, *Economic Journal*, 104 (424), pp. 648-59.

Clark, D. 2000. Concepts and perceptions of development: Some evidence from the Western Cape. Working Paper no. 88. University of Cape Town, South Africa; Labour and Development Research Unit, Cape Town.

Clark, D. A. 2003. Concepts and Perceptions of Human Well-Being: Some Evidence from South Africa, *Oxford Development Studies*, 31(2), pp. 173-196.

—. 2005. The Capability Approach: Its Development, Critiques and Recent Advances, Global Poverty Research Group-WPS-032, 2005.

—. 2006. The Capability Approach: Its Development, Critiques and Recent Advances, *The Elgar Companion to Development Studies*, Cheltenham: Edward Elgar.

Clark, D. A. and Qizilbash, M. 2005. Core Poverty, Basic Capabilities and Vagueness: An Application to the South African Context. *GPRG Working Paper 26*, Universities of Manchester and Oxford, UK. Available online at http://www.gprg.org/pubs/workingpapers/pdfs/gprg-wps-026.pdf

Clark, D. A., and Qizilbash M. 2002. Core Poverty and Extreme Vulnerability in South Africa., *Discussion Paper No. 2002-3*, School of Economics, University of East Anglia, UK. Revised version: http://www.geocities.com/poverty_in_southafrica

Clark, J. 1991. Democratizing Development: The role of voluntary organizations, West Hartford: Kuamrian Press.

Cohen, G. A. 1993. Equality of What? On Welfare, Goods and Capabilities, *The Quality of Life,* Edited by Martha C. Nussbaum and Amartya Sen, Oxford University Press, pp. 9-29.

Coleman, I. 2005. Defending Microfinance. (Winter), *Fletcher Forum of World Affairs*.

Cooke, B., and Kothari, U. 2001. *Participation: The New Tyranny*? Published by Zed Books, London.

CPD-UNFPA, 2008. Gender related Development Index for 64 Districts of Bangladesh.

Crocker, D. A. 1998. Consumption, Well-Being and Capability in David A. Crocker and Toby Linden (eds), *Ethics of Consumption: The Good Life, Justice and Global Stewardship*, New York: Rowman and Littlefield Publishers, pp.366-90.

Cronbach, L. and Meehl, P. 1955. Construct validity in psychological tests. *Psychological Bulletin*, 52, 4, 281-302.

Cronbach, L., Thorndike, R. L. 1971. Test validation. Educational measurement , 2nd ed, pp. 443-507. American Council on Education , Washington, DC

Cronin, J. J., and Taylor, S. A. 1994. SERVPERF versus SERVQUAL: reconciling performance-based and perceptions-minus-expectations measurement of service quality. *Journal of Marketing,* 58(1), pp. 125-31.

Cummins, R. 1996. The Domains of Life Satisfaction: An Attempt to Order Chaos. Citation Classics from Social Indicators Research. Volume-26, pp. 20-36.

Dasgupta, P. 1993. *An Inquiry into Well-being and Destitution.* Oxford: Clarendon Press.

Dasgupta, P. S. 2001. *Human Well Being and the Natural Environment.* New Delhi: Oxford University Press.

Datt, G. and Ravallion, M. 1992. Growth and Redistribution Components of Changes in Poverty Measures: A Decomposition with Applications to Brazil and India in the 1980s, *Journal of Development Economics*, 38, pp. 275-295.

De Haan, G. 1997. *Skizzen zu einer lebensstilbezogenen Umweltbildung*, in: Lohmeyer, M. et. al.: *Ökologische Bildung im Spagat zwischen Leitbildern und Lebensstilen, Loccumer Protokolle 25* ,97, (Outlines to a lifestyle-driven environmental education. In: M Lohmeyer, et al. (Eds.)., *Ecological education in the twine between models and lifestyles, Loccumer journals 25,97*, Loccum.

Deng, G. 2008. Public donations to help disaster relief in the aftermath of the Sichuan earthquake in China. KOF Swiss Economic Institute in Zurich and the Radboud University in Nijmegen.

Deolalikar, A. B., Brillantes, A. B., Gaiha, R., Pernia, E. M., and Racelis, M. 2002. Poverty Reduction and role of institutions in Developing Asia, *ERD Working paper series* no. 10, Asian Development Bank.

Desai, M. 1995. Poverty and Capability: Towards An Empirically Implementable Measure in *Poverty, Famine and Economic Development*, Aldershot: Edward Elgar, pp.185-204.

Devicienti, F., Poggi, A. 2007. Poverty and social exclusion: two sides of the same coin or dynamically interrelated processes?, *LABORatorio R. Revelli Working Papers Series 62*, LABORatorio R. Revelli, Centre for Employment Studies.

DFID and World Bank. 2003. Perú: *Voces de los Pobres,* Lima: DFID / World Bank.

DFID Policy paper. 2005. Reducing Poverty by Tackling Social Exclusion, DFID Publication, September-2005.

DFID. 2002. DFID Rural Livelihoods Department, Annual Program Report.

Diener, E. 1995. A Value-based Index for Measuring National Quality of Life. *Social Indicators Research*, 36: pp. 107–27.

Diener, E., and Biswas-Diener, R. 2000. New Directions in Subjective Well-Being Research. Mimeo.

Disaster Management Bureau (DMB)-MFODM, 2009. Summary of Cyclonic Storm AILA. June 11, 2009.

Doyle, L., and Gough, I. 1991. *A Theory of Human Need.* London: Macmillan Education.

Doyle, L., and Gough, I. 1993. A Theory of Human Need, by Len Doyal and Ian Gough. NewYork: The Guilford Press, 365 pp.

Drewnowski, J., and Scott, W. 1966. *The Level of Living Index*. Geneva: United Nations Research Institute for Social Development, Report No. 4.

Dreze, J. And Sen, A. K. 1989. *Hunger and Public Action*, Oxford, Clarendon Press. UK

Dubois, J. L., and Rousseau, S. 2008. Reinforcing Household's Capabilities as a Way to Reduce Vulnerability an Prevent Poverty in Equitable Terms in *The Capability Approach: Concepts, Measures and Applications*, F. Comim, M. Qizilbash and S. Alkire (eds), Cambridge University Press, Cambridge, pp. 421-436.

Easterlin, R. A. 2001. Income and Happiness: Towards a Unified Theory. *Economic Journal*, 111 (July), pp. 465-84.

Edwards, M. 1989. Learning From Experience In Africa. Oxford: Oxfam; mimeo.

Edwards, M. and Hulme, D. 1992. Making A Difference: NGOs and Development In A Changing World. Earthscan, London.

Edwards, M., and Hulme, D. 1996. Beyond the Magic Bullet: NGO performance and accountability in the post cold war world, West Hartford, CT: Kumarian Press.

Eid, M. and Diener, E. 2003. Global Judgements of Subjective Well-being: Situational Variability and Long-term Stability, *Social Indicators Research*, 65: pp. 245–77.

Elbers, C., Lanjouw, J. O. and Lanjouw, P. 2003, Micro-level Estimation of Poverty and Inequality, Econometrica, 71(1): pp. 355-364.

Epstein, M. J., and Crane, A. 2005. Alleviating Global Poverty through Microfinance: Factors and Measures of Financial, Economic and Social Performance. Paper presented at Rice University seminar on poverty.

Evans, P. and Rauch, P. 2000. Bureaucratic Structure and Bureaucratic Performance in Less Developed Countries, Journal of Public Economics, 75, pp. 49-71.

Faaland, J., Parkinson, J. R. 1975. Bangladesh: The Test case of Development. Westview Press.

Fama, E., and Jensen, M. 1983. Agency problem and residual claims, Journal of Law and Economics, 26: pp. 327-50

FAO Policy Brief. 2003. Reclaiming Rights – Reclaiming Livelihoods Secure Land and Property Rights for Women in Sub-Saharan Africa in the Era of AIDS

Fernando, A. N. 2006. Understanding and Dealing with High Interest Rates on Microcredit: A Note to Policy Makers in the Asia and Pacific Region. *Asian Development Bank Publication*, May, 2006.

Flood Forecasting and Warning Centre (FFWC), 2007. Situation Report-Floods Engulf Villages of Several Districts'. Site Rep no. 07, Dhaka. July 22, 2007.

Francesco, D and Poggi, A. 2007. *Poverty and Social Exclusion: Two Sides of the Same Coin or Dynamically Interrelated Processes*? Centre for Employment Studies, working paper no. 62.

Frey, B., and Stutzer, A. 2002. What can economists learn from happiness research? *Journal of Economic Literature*, XL, 2: pp. 402-35.

Galor, O., and Zeira, J. 1993. Income Distribution and Macroeconomics. *Review of Economic Studies*, vol-60 (1), pp. 35-52.

Gasper, D. 1996a. Needs and Basic Needs: A Clarification of Meanings, Levels and Streams of Work. *ISS Working Paper No. 210.* The Hague: Institute of Social Studies.

—. 1996b. Culture and Development Ethics: Needs, Women's Rights and Western Theories. *Development and Change.* Vol. 27, pp. 627-661.

—. 2002. Is Sen's Capability Approach an Adequate Basis for Considering Human Development. *Review of Political Economy*. Vol. 14. No. 4, pp. 435-461.

—. 2003. Human Wellbeing: Concepts and Conceptualization, Paper for 3rd Conference on the Capability Approach, 7-9 September 2003, Italy.

—. 2007. Conceptualizing human needs and wellbeing. In I. Gough and J. A. McGregor (Eds.), Wellbeing in developing countries: From theory to research. Cambridge: Cambridge University Press.

Gerbing, D.W., and Anderson, J.C. 1993. Monte Carlo evaluations of goodness-of-fit indices for structural equation models. In K.A. Bollen, and J.S. Long (eds.), *Testing structural equation models.* Newbury Park, CA: Sage.

Gliem, J. A., and Gliem, R. R. 2003. Calculating, Interpreting, and Reporting Cronbach's Alpha Reliability Coefficient for Likert-Type Scales. 2003 Midwest Research to Practice Conference in Adult, Continuing, and Community Education

Goetz, SM., and Gupta, SR. 1996. Who Takes the Credit? Gender, Power and Control over Loan use in Rural Credit programs in Bangladesh. World Development, 24 (1), pp. 45-63.

Goldin Institute, 2007. Improving Microcredit Programs: Listening to Recipients. Research conducted jointly with Nijera Kori and Unnayan Onneshan.

Gordon, D. and Pantazis, C. 1997. Poverty and Crime, In Gordon, D. and Pantazis, C. (Eds.) *Breadline Britain in the 1990s,* Aldershot, Avebury.

Gordon, D. and Townsend, P. (Eds). 2000. *Breadline Europe: The Measurement of Poverty*, The Policy Press: Bristol.

Government of Bangladesh (GoB), 2005. Unlocking the Potential: National Strategy for Accelerated Poverty Reduction. General Economics Division, Planning Commission.

—. 2010. *Economic Review* by Ministry of Finance, Peoples Republic of Bangladesh.

—. 2009. Tropical Cyclone Bijli affected area report: Disaster Management Information Centre situation report. April 18, 2009.

Greenwald, B. and Stiglitz, J. E. 1986. Externalities in Economies with Imperfect Information and Incomplete Markets, *Quarterly Journal of Economics*, 101(2), pp. 229-264.

Grisez, G., Boyle, J. and Finnis, J. 1987. Practical Principles, Moral Truth and Ultimate Ends, *American Journal of Jurisprudence*, 32, pp. 99-151.

Hair, F. J., Black, W. C., Babin, B. J., Anderson, R. E. 2010. *Multivariate Data Analysis: A Global Perspective*, 7th Ed. Pearson Publication.

Hansmann, H. 1985a. The effect of tax exemption and other factors on competition between non-profits and for-profits enterprise. Yale University, Program on Non-profit organizations Working paper no. 65.

—. 1987. 'Economic Theories of Non-profit Organization' in The Non-profit Sector-A Research Handbook', New Haven, Yale University Press.

Hansmann, H. B. 1980. The role of non-profit enterprise. *Yale Law Journal*, *89*, pp. 835-901.

—. 1981d. The rationale for exempting non-profit organizations from corporate income taxation. *Yale Law Journal*, *91*, pp. 54-100.

Hargreaves, J. R., Morison, L., John S. S., Gear, J., Porter, D.H., Mzamani, B., Makhubele, J. C., Kim, J., Buzsa, C. W., and Paul, M. P. 2004a. Hearing the voices of the poor: Assigning poverty lines on the basis of local perceptions of poverty: a quantitative analysis of qualitative data from participatory wealth ranking in rural South Africa', paper presented to *Q-Squared in Practice: a conference on experiences combining qualitative and quantitative methods in poverty appraisal*, Toronto 15-16 May 2004.

Hashemi, S. M. 1995. NGO Accountability in Bangladesh: Beneficiaries, Donors and State in Edwards, M. and Hulme, D. (eds.) Non-governmental Organizations : Performance and Accountability Beyond the Magic Bullet. London: Earthscan Publications.

Herrera J. 2001. Subjective and objective poverty in Peru, Paper prepared for the Congreso Internacional de Americanistas, Santiago du Chile, 2003.

Herrera, J., Razafindrakoto, M. and Roubaud, F. 2006. The Determinants of Subjective Poverty: A Comparative Analysis between Madagascar and Peru, Document De Travail, DT/2006-01.

Hess, P. 1989. The Military Burden, Economic Growth, and the Human Suffering Index: Evidence from the LDCs. *Cambridge Journal of Economics*, 13: pp. 497–515.

Heyne, P. 2007. The Concise Encyclopaedia of Economics. USA.

Hickey, S., and Bracking, S. 2005. Exploring the Politics of Chronic Poverty: From representation to a politics of justice? *World Development*, 33(6): pp. 851-865.

Higham, S., Chadwick, R., McDonald, M., 1997. Learning Together – A Best Practice Project in Managing Diversity. *Community and Youth Training Services*, WA.

Hoelter, J. W. (1983a). The analysis of covariance structures: Goodness-of-fit indices. *Sociological Methods & Research, 11*, pp. 325-344.

Hoque, M. Z. 2010. Does Microfinance Alleviate Poverty?: Response from the Borrowers. Working Paper presented at 4th Asian Business Research Conference, 23-24 December, Dhaka-Bangladesh.

Hoque, S. 2004. Micro-credit and the Reduction of Poverty in Bangladesh. *Journal of Contemporary Asia*, Vol. 34 No. 1, pp 21-32.

Hossain, M. 1988, Credit for Alleviation of Rural Poverty: The Grameen Bank in Bangladesh. *IFPRI Research Report 65*, IFPRI, Washington, D.C.

—. 2009. Dynamics of Poverty in Rural Bangladesh, 1988-2007: An Analysis of Household Level Panel Data. Paper presented in the Conference on Employment, Growth and poverty reduction in developing countries. The Political economy research institute, University of Massachusetts.

Hossain, M., Sen, B. 1992. Rural poverty in Bangladesh: Trends and Determinants. Asian Development Review, 10(1), pp. 1-34

Hossain, Z. R., Hossain, M. (eds). 1995. Rethinking Rural Poverty: Bangladesh as a case study. Sage Publication, New York.

Howarth, C., Kenway, P., Palmer, G., and Street, C. 1998. Monitoring Poverty and Social Exclusion: Labour's Inheritance, York: York Publishing Services.

Hu, L., and Bentler, P. M. 1999. Cutoff criteria for fit indexes in covariance structure analysis: Conventional criteria versus new alternatives. *Structural Equation Modeling, 6*, pp. 1-55.

Hu, L.-T., and Bentler, P. 1995. Evaluating model fit. In R. H. Hoyle (Ed.), *Structural Equation Modeling. Concepts, Issues, and Applications* (pp. 76-99). London: Sage.

Hulme D, Edwards M (eds). 1997. NGOs, States and Donors: Too Close for Comfort? St Martin's Press, in association with Save the Children: New York.

Hunzai, K., Gerlitz, J., Hoermann, B., and Kollmair, M. 2010. Understanding Mountain Poverty, Paper developed for International Center for Integrated Mountain Development (ICIMOD).

International Federation of Red Cross and Red Crescent Societies, 2008. Operations Update on Cyclone SIDR in Bangladesh. Operations Update no. 07. Glide no: TC-2007-000208-BGD. January 9, 2008.

—. 2005. Bangladesh: Monsoon Floods Information Bulletin. October 13, 2005.

Islam, S. A. 2005. Sociology of Poverty; Quest for a New Horizon, *Bangladesh E-Journal of Sociology*, Vol. 2, No. 1, January-2005, pp. 1-8.

James, E. 1986.How nonprofits grow: A model. In S. Rose-Ackerman (Ed.), *The economics of nonprofit institutions: Studies in structure and policy* (pp. 185-204). New York: Oxford University Press.

James, L. R., Mulaik, S. A., and Brett, J. M. 1982. Causal analysis: assumptions, models, and data. Beverly Hills: Sage.

Jelinek E., 2006. A Study of NGO Relations with Government and Communities in Afghanistan, Special Report Funded by the European Commission.

Jennings, B. et al., 2003. *Access to Hospice Care* . Garrison, NY: Hastings Center.

Jock, A. R. and Roumasset, J. A. 1993. Food Insecurity and Stochastic Aspects of Poverty, *Asian Journal of Agricultural Economics,* vol. 2 (1), pp. 53-66.

Jöreskog, K. and Sörbom, D. 1996a, LISREL 8: User's Reference Guide. Chicago, IL: Scientific Software International Inc.

Juddy, C., Keysik., and Jerry, F. 2010. *Research for Effective Social Practice* (2nd ed.). Routledge, New York. ISBN: 0-415-80505-8.

Kabeer, N., and Noponen, H. 2005. Social and Economic Impacts of PRADAN's Self Help Group Microfinance and Livelihoods Promotion Program: Analysis from Jharkhand, India. *Imp-Act Working Paper No. 11.*

Kagan, S. 1994. Me and My Life. Summary in Ackerman et al. (eds.), pp. 194-6.

Kanbur, R. 1987. The Standard of Living: Uncertainty, Inequality and Opportunity, in Geoffrey Hawthorn (ed.), *The Standard of Living*, Cambridge: Cambridge University Press, pp. 70.93.

Kapsos, S. 2008. *The Gender Wage Gap in Bangladesh.* Asia-Pacific Working Paper Series. Geneva: ILO.

Kevane, M., and Wydick, B. 2001. Micro-enterprise Lending to Female Entrepreneurs: Sacrificing Economic Growth for Poverty Alleviation? *World Development*, 29, pp. 1225-1236.

Khondker, S. R, Hussain, A. Samad., and Zahid, H. Khan. 1998. Income and Employment Effects of Micro-credit Programs: Village-level Evidence from Bangladesh, *The Journal of Development Studies*, 35(2), pp. 96-124.

Kingdon, G G. and Knight, J. 2004. Wellbeing Poverty Versus Income Poverty and Capabilities Poverty in South Africa, Forum Paper-2004 for African Development and Poverty Reduction: The Macro-Micro Linkage, 13-15 October, 2004, South Africa.

Klasen, S. 1997. Poverty, inequality and deprivation in South Africa: an analysis of the 1993 SALDRU survey. *Social Indicators Research*, 41, pp. 51-94.

—. 2000. Measuring poverty and deprivation in South Africa., *Review of Income and Wealth*, 46(1), pp. 33-58.

Korten DC. 1990. Getting to the 21st Century: Voluntary Action and the Global Agenda. Kumarian Press: West Hartford, CT.

Kothari, R. 1995. Poverty: Human consciousness and the amnesia of development. Zed Books, London. ISBN 185649361X

Kozlowski, A. 1983. International Non-governmental Organizations as Operating Development Agencies. In Rice, A. E. (ed.) *The Role of Non-Government Organizations in Development Cooperation.* OECD-DAC, Paris.

Kramer, R. M. 1981. *Voluntary Agencies in the Welfare State*, Barkeley: University of California Press.

Lance, C. E., Butts, M. M., and Michels, L. C. 2006. The sources of four commonly reported cut-off criteria: What did they really say? Organizational Research Methods 9(2):202-220. Discusses Kaiser and other criteria for selecting number of factors.

Lane, R. E. 1998a. The Joyless Market Economy. In A. Ben-Ner and L. Putterman (eds.), *Economics, Values and Organization,* Cambridge: Cambridge Univ. Press, pp. 461-88.

Lanjouw, J. O., and Lanjouw, P. 1997. *Poverty Comparisons with Noncompatible Data*, The World Bank: Washington D.C.

Levitas, R. 2006. The concept and measurement of social exclusion. In *Poverty and Social Exclusion in Britain* (eds C. Pantazis, D. Gordon and R. Levitas). Policy Press.

Levitas, R., Pantazis, C., Fahmy, E., Gordon, D., Lloyd, E., and Patsios, D. 2007. *The Multi-Dimensional Analysis of Social Exclusion*, A Research Report for the Social Exclusion Task Force, viewed 30 June 2007.

Lewina, F. 1999. The Gender Bias and Development Theory, *Political and Economic Review*, issue-10, pp. 15-28. University of Limerick.

Lipsky, M. and Smith, S. R. 1989. Non-profit organizations, government, and the welfare state. *Political Science Quarterly,* 104(4): pp. 625–648.

Lipton, M. and Ravaillon, M. 1995. Poverty and Policy. Ch. 41 of J. Behrman and T.N. Srinivasan (Eds.) *Handbook of Development Economics.* Vol. IIIb. Amsterdam: Elsevier.

Lister, R. 2004. *Poverty,* Polity Press, Cambridge.

—. 2004. *Poverty*. Cambridge: Polity Press.

Littlefield, E., Murduch, J., and Hashemi, S. 2003. Is Microfinance an Effective Strategy to Reach the Millenium Development Goals?

Lokshin, M., Umapathi, N. and Paternostro, S. 2004. Robustness of Subjective Welfare Analysis in a Poor developing Country: Madagascar 2001, *World Bank Policy Research Working Paper*, Washington, D.C, World Bank.

Lorgelly, P., Lorimer, K., Fenwick, E., and Briggs, A. 2007. Using mixed methods to operationalize the capability approach: an application in public health. Paper presented in HDCA conference, 2007.

Mabughi, N. and Selim, T. 2006. Poverty as Social Deprivation: A Survey, *Review of Social Economy*, Vol. LXIV, No. 2, pp.181-204, June-2006.

MacCallum, R. C., Austin, J. T., 2000. Applications of Structural Equation Modelling In Psychological Research. *Psychological Research Journals*, 51, pp. 201-226.

MacCallum, R.C., Browne, M.W., and Sugawara, H., M. 1996. Power Analysis and Determination of Sample Size for Covariance Structure Modelling, *Psychological Methods*, 1 (2), pp. 130-49.

Macchiavello, R. 2008. Public sector motivation and development failures, Journal of Development Economics, 86, pp. 201-213.

Mack, J and Lansley, S. 1985. Poor Britain, George Allen and Unwin, London.

Mahbub, A., and Roy, R. D. 1997. Anaemic towards wellbeing. *Working Paper No. 20, BRAC-ICDDR,* B Joint Research Project, Dhaka.

Mahmud K. M., Ahmed, S. 2003. Relative efficiency of government and non-government organisations in implementing a nutrition intervention programme a case study from Bangladesh. *Public Health Nutrition*, 6 (1), pp. 19-24

Mahmud, W. 2008. Social Development in Bangladesh: Pathways, Surprises and Challenges. *Indian Journal of Human Development,* Vol-2, No. 1, pp. 79-91.

Majumdar, M. and Subramanian, S. 2001. Capability failure and group disparities: some evidence from India from the 1980s. *Journal of Development Studies*, 37(5), pp. 104-140.

Mansbridge J. 1998. On the contested nature of the public good. In Private Action and the Public Good, Powell WW, Clemens ES (eds). Yale University Press: New Haven, CT; 3–19.

Marsh, H. W., Balla, J. R., and McDonald, R. P. 1988. Goodness of fit indexes in confirmatory factor analysis: The effect of sample size. *Psychological Bulletin, 103*, pp. 391-410.

Max-Neef. 1993. *Real-Life Economics: Understanding Wealth Creation*, with Paul Ekins.

Mayoux, L. 1999. From Access to Empowerment: Gender Issues in Micro-finance. *CSD NGO Women's Caucus Position Paper for CSD-8,* 2000.

—. 2000. From Access to Empowerment: Gender Issues in Micro-finance. CSD NGO Women's Caucus Position Paper for CSD-8.

McGhee, T. 1999. Partnership and Disaster Response in Bangladesh. The Emergency Nutrition Network (ENN) Paper Series, Issue-6.

McGillivray, M and Noorbakhsh, F. 2007. Composite indexes of well-being: past, present and future, in McGillivray, Mark (eds), *Human well-being: concept and measurement,* pp. 113-134, Palgrave Macmillan, Basingstoke, England

McGranahan, D.V., et al. 1972. *Content and measurement of socioeconomic development,* United Nations Research Institute for Social Development and Praeger, New York) 39.

McGregor, J. A. 2007. Researching wellbeing: From concepts to methodology. In I. Gough and J. A. McGregor (eds.), Wellbeing in developing countries: From theory to research. Cambridge: Cambridge University Press.

McLeod D. 2007. Is poverty increasing in Bangladesh? Reconciling national and global monitoring estimates. Final Report to UNDP-BDP Poverty Group, New York

McNamara, C. 2010. Organizational Change and Development. Authenticity Consulting, USA.

Ministry of Finance (MOF), Government of Bangladesh. 2010. Economic Review.

—. 2008. *Economic Review-2008*. Chapter-13 and Page ixx.

—. 2004. A National Strategy for Economic Growth, Poverty Reduction and Social Development. BG Press, Dhaka.

—. 2005. Unlocking the Potential: National Strategy for Accelerated Poverty Reduction. BG Press, Dhaka.

—. 2010 and 2011. Economic Review.

Ministry of Food and Disaster Management (MFODM)-Government of Bangladesh, 2008. Cyclone SIDR Food and Non-Food Relief Operation. February 25, 2008.

Moore, K. 2001. Frameworks for understanding the intergenerational transmission of poverty and well-being in developing countries, CPRC Working Paper 8, 2001, Chronic Poverty Research Centre, ISBN Number: 1-904049-07-9

Moore, M., Choudhary, M., and Singh, N. 1998. How can we know what they want? Understanding local perceptions of poverty and ill-being in Asia'. *IDS Working Paper No. 80,* Institute of Development Studies, University of Sussex, Brighton.

Morduch, J. 2000. The Microfinance Schism. *World Development*, Vol. 28, No. 4, 617-629.

Morris, M.D. 1979. *Measuring the Condition of the World's Poor: The Physical Quality of Life Index*, New York: Pergamon.

Morshed, M. 2000. Micro credit programmes of NGOs: An Evaluation, paper presented at the Sixth Workshop of European Network of Bangladesh Studies, Oslo, 14 – 16 May.

Mubangizi, B. C. 2009. Poverty Alleviation and Service Delivery – Developing a Conceptual Framework for South Africa's Service Delivery System, *International NGO Journal*, Vol. 4 (10), pp. 446-455, October, 2009.

Mugavin, M. E. 2008. Multidimensional scaling: A brief overview. *Nursing Research*, 57(1), pp. 64-68.

Muhammad, A. 2006. Monga, Microcredit and the Nobel Prize in http://www.countercurrents.org/gl-muhammad041206.html

Mukherjee, D. 1997. Informal rents and property rights in land. In J. Roemer (Ed.), Property relations, incentives and welfare. Palgrave: Macmillan.

Mulaik, S. A.; James, L. R.; Vanaltine, J.; Bennett, N.; Lind, S.; Stilwell, C. D. 1989. Evaluation of goodness-of-fit indices for structural equation models. Psychol. Bull., 105 (3), pp. 430-445

Myers, D. G., and Diener, E. 1995. Who Is Happy? Summary in Ackerman et al. (eds.) pp. 174-7.

Nabi, R., Datta, D., Chakraborty, S., Belgum, M. and Chadhury, N. J. 1999. *Participatory poverty assessment in Bangladesh*, Washington: PREM, World Bank.

Narayan, A., Yoshida N., Zaman H. 2007. Trends and Patterns of Poverty in Bangladesh in Recent Years. A Background paper for Bangladesh Poverty Assessment 2007. South Asia Region, World Bank.

Narayan, D. 1999. Bonds and Bridges: Social Capital and Poverty. *PRE Working Paper No. 2167.* Washington D.C: The World Bank.

Narayan, D., Chambers, R., Shah, M. K. and Petesch, P. 2000. *Voices of the Poor: Crying Out for Change*, Oxford University Press for the World Bank, New York.

Narayan, D., *et al*, 2000. Voices of the Poor-can anyone hear us, Vol-I. *The World Bank Publication-2000*. ISBN-13: 9780195216011

Narayan, D., Patel, R., Schafft, K., Rachemacher, A., and Koch-Schulte, S. 1999. Voices of the poor: Can anyone hear us?, Washington DC: World Bank.

Narayan, D., Walton, M. and Chambers, R. 2000. *Voices of the poor: Crying out for change,* USA: Oxford University Press

NASA, 2008. Track of Cyclone Reshmi in Bangladesh.

Neely, C., Sutherland, K., and Johnson, J. 2004. Do Sustainable Livelihoods Approaches Have a Positive Impact on the Rural Poor? A Look at Twelve Case Studies. Livelihood Support Programme of FAO.

Nelson, R., and Krashinsky, M. 1973.Two major issues of public policy: Public policy and organization of supply. In D. Young (Ed.), *Public subsidy for day care of young children*. Lexington, MA: D. C. Heath and Co.

Newton, J. 1980. Child care decision making surveyPreliminary report. Yale University, Program on Non-profit Organizations.

NGO Affairs Bureau (NGOAB), Bangladesh. 2010. See, http://www.ngoab.gov.bd/Files/statistics.pdf

NGOAB (Non-Government Organizations Affair Bureau of Bangladesh), Annual Report, 2009-10.

—. See for instance, http://www.ngoab.gov.bd/

North, D. C. 1991. Institutions. *Journal of Economic Perspectives* 5(4):97-112.

Nunnenkamp, P. 2008. The Myth of NGO Superiority. Development Research Paper Pedia

Nussbaum, M. 1993. Non-relative Virtues: An Aristotelian Approach, *The Quality of Life*, Edited by Martha C. Nussbaum and Amartya Sen, Oxford University Press, pp.242-269.

Nussbaum, M. C. 2005a. Well-Being, Contracts and Capabilities in Lenore Manderson (ed.), *Rethinking Well-Being*, Perth: API Network, pp.27-44.

Nussbaum, Martha. 1995. Human Capabilities, Female Human beings. In Martha Nussbaum and Jonathan Glover (eds.) Women, Culture and Development, pp. 61-104.

—. 2000. Women and Human Development. The Capabilities Approach. Cambridge: Cambridge University Press.

—. 2003. Capabilities as Fundamental Entitlements: Sen and Social Justice. Feminist Economics.

Osmani, S. R. 1990. Notes on some recent estimates of poverty in Bangladesh. The Bangladesh Development Studies, 18 (3), pp. 60-72.

—. ed. 1992. *Nutrition and poverty*, Oxford Clarendon Press.

Paitoonpong, S. 1999. *Consultations with the poor. National synthesis report: Thailand* (preliminary draft), Thailand Development Research Institute Foundation/The World Bank.

Parasuraman, A, Valarie, A, Zeithaml, A, Leonard, L., and Berry, L. (1985). A conceptual model of service quality and its implications for future research. *Journal of Marketing*, 49, pp. 41-50.

Parasuraman, A., Zeithaml, V., and Berry, L. 1988. SERVQUAL: a multi-item scale for measuring consumer perceptions of SQ. *Journal of Retailing,* 64 (1), pp. 12-40.

Paul, S and Israel, A. 1991. *Non-governmental Organizations and The World Bank: Cooperation for Development*, Washington DC.

Permut, S. 1981. *Consumer perceptions of non-profit enterprise: A comment on Hansmann*, Yale University, Program on Non-profit Organizations.

Piketty, T. 1999. Theories of Persistent Inequality and Intergenerational Mobility, in A. Atkinson and F. Bourguignon (eds), Handbook of Income Distribution, Elsevier.

Pitt, M. M. and Khandker, S. R, Cartwright, J. 2006. 'Empowering Women with Micro Finance: Evidence from Bangladesh' *Economic Development and Cultural Change*, Vol. 54, pp. 791–831. Available at SSRN: http://ssrn.com/abstract=636360

Pitt, M. M. and Khandker, S. R. 1998. The Impact of Group-Based Credit Programs on Poor Households in Bangladesh: Does the Gender of Participants Matter? *Journal of Political Economy, 106 (October)*: 958-96.

Poggi A. 2007a. Does persistence of social exclusion exist in Spain? *Journal of Economic Inequality*, 5(1): pp. 53-72.

—. 2007b. Social exclusion mobility in Spain, 1994-2001, *Research on Economic Inequality*, Vol. 15 (1), pp. 53-72.

Pradhan, M., and Ravallion, M. 2000. Measuring poverty using qualitative perceptions of consumption adequacy. *Review of Economics and Statistics* 82, pp. 462–71.

Prahalad, C.K., and Ramaswamy, V. 2000. Co-opting customer competencies. *Harvard Business Review*, pp. 79-87.

Qizilbash, M. 2005. Capabilities, Happiness and Adaptation in Sen and J. S. Mill., *Utilitas*.

Raftopoulos, B. 2001. The state and poverty reduction in Zimbabwe, 1980–1997, in F. Wilson, N. Kanji and E. Braathen, eds, Poverty Reduction: What Role for the State in Today's Globalized Economy? Comparative Research on Poverty (CROP) Program/Zed Books, London, pp. 196–217.

Rahman M. H. 2000. Fighting Poverty: Government and NGO perceptions and interventions in Bangladesh. Paper presented at the Development Studies Network Conference on Poverty, Prosperity and Progress Victoria University of Wellington, Wellington

Rahman, H. Z and Hossain, M. 1991. *The Anatomy of Mora Kartik: An Enquiry into the Economic Health of the Countryside*, Dhaka, BIDS.

Rahman, H. Z. et. al. 2005. Monga Forecast 2005 Field Assessment and Action Plan, PPRC.

Rahmato, D. and Kidanu, A. 1999. Consultations with the poor: A study to inform the world development report 2000/2001 on poverty and development (National Report, Ethiopia.

Ramsay, M. 1992. *Human Needs and the Market* (Aldershot: Avebury).

Ramsey, G. 1992. Adult education and school programs: The two co-funded ABC Educational TV Services. *Australian Journal of Educational Technology,* 1992, 8(1), pp. 35-50.

Ravallion, M. 1994. Poverty Comparisons, Fundamentals of Pure and Applied Economics Volume 56, Chur, Switzerland: Harwood Academic Publishers.

Ravallion, M., Shah, S., and Wodon, Q. 1999. Bangladesh: From Counting the Poor to Making the Poor Count, A World Bank Country Study, The World Bank, Washington.

Razafindrakoto M., Roubaud F. 2000. The multiples facets of poverty in a developing country: The case of Madagascar capital city, actes du séminaire International Comparison of poverty, Bratislava, SUSR/INSEE/EUROSTAT, pp. 339-371.

Razafindrakoto M., Roubaud F. 2005b. Les multiples facettes de la pauvreté dans un pays en développement Le cas de la capitale malgache », *Economie et Statistique*, no383-384-385, pp. 131-155.

Roach, J. L., and Roach, J. K. 1972. Introduction. In Poverty, edited by Jack L Roach, and Janet K Roach. Harmondsworth: Penguin.

Robeyns, I. 2002. Sen's Capability Approach and Gender Inequality, *Conference Proceeding-Promoting Woman's Capabilities: Examining Nussbaum's Capabilities Approach*, 9-10 September-2002, St Edmund's College Cambridge.

—. 2003. Sen.s Capability Approach and Gender Inequality: Selecting Relevant Capabilities., *Feminist Economics*, 9(2-3), pp. 61-92.

Rodgers, G., Gore, C., and Figueiredo J. B. 1995. *Social Exclusion: Rhetoric, Reality, Responses*, International Labor Organization, Geneva.

Roemer, John. 1996. *Theories of Distributive Justice*. Cambridge: Harvard University Press.

Rojas, M. 2007. The complexity of wellbeing: A life satisfaction conception and a domains-of-life approach in Gough, I. and McGregor, J.A. (Eds) *Wellbeing in Developing Countries: From Theory to Research*. Cambridge: Cambridge University Press.

Rose, K. 1992. *Where women are leaders. The SEWA movement in India.* London: Zed Press.

Rowntree, B. S. 1901. *Poverty: A Study of Town Life*. London: Macmillan.

Ruggeri Laderchi, C. 2001. Participatory Methods in the Analysis of Poverty: A Critical Review. *QEH Working Paper 62*. Queen Elisabeth House, Oxford.

Ruggeri Laderchi, C., Saith, R., et al. 2003. Does it matter that we do not Agree on the definition of poverty? a comparison of four approaches. *Oxford Development Studies*, 31(3), pp. 243–274.

Ruggeri-Laderchi, C. 1997. Poverty and its Many Dimensions: The Role of Income as an Indicator., *Oxford Development Studies*, 25(3), pp. 345-60.

—. 2008. Do concepts matter? An empirical investigation of the differences between a capability and a monetary assessment of poverty, in COMIM, Qizilbash and S. Alkire (eds), *The Capability Approach: Concepts, Measures and Application*, CUP, 2008.

Runciman, W. 1966. *Relative Deprivation and Social Justice,* Routledge, London.

Ryan, R. M., and Deci, E. L. 2001. On Happiness and Human Potentials: A Review of Research on Hedonic and Eudaimonic Well-Being. *Annu. Rev. Psychol.*, 52, pp. 141-66.

Saith, R. 2001. Social Exclusion: The Concept and Application to Developing Countries. *QEH Working Paper 72*. Queen Elisabeth House, Oxford.

Salamon, L. M. 1987. Partners in Public Service: The Scope and Theory of Government-Non profit Relations, in Powel (ed), pp. 99-117.

Sanyal, P. 2007. Credit Versus Coalition: Exploring The Influence Of Microfinance Programs On Women's Agency. Paper presented at the *annual meeting of the American Sociological Association.*

Saul, J. 2004. Benchmarking for Non-profits: How to Measure, Manage and Improve Performance. Wilder Publishing Centre, Wilder Foundation.

Scheaffer, R. L., Mendenhall, W., and Ott, R. L. 1996. *Elementary Survey Sampling*, New York: Duxbury Printers.

Schischka, J., Dalziel, P. and Saunders, C. 2008. *Applying Sen's Capabilities Approach to Poverty Alleviation Programs.* Journal of Human Development Vol. 9, pp. 229-246.

Schokkaert, E. and Van Ootegem, L. 1990. Sen.s Concept of the Living Standard Applied to the Belgian Unemployed., *Reserches Economiques de Louvain*, 56(3-4), pp. 429-450.

Schwartz, S.H. 1994. Are there universal aspects in the structure and conduct of human values? *Journal of Social Issues*, 50, no. 4, pp. 19-45.

Scoones, I. 1997. Sustainable Rural Livelihoods – A Framework for Analysis. IDS Working Paper-72

Sen, A. K. 1992. Inequality Reexamined. Oxford: Oxford University Press. 54

—. 1997. Maximization and the Act of Choice. *Econometrica* 65(4): pp. 745-79.

—. 1998. Mortality as an Indicator of Economic Success and Failure. *The Economic Journal* 108: pp. 1-25.

—. 1999. *Development as Freedom.* New York: Random House.

—. 1973. *On Economic Inequality.* Reprinted in 1997 by Clarendon Press.

—. 1977. Rational Fools: A Critique of the Behavioural Foundations of Economic Theory, reprinted in Sen, A.K. 1982.

—. 1979b. *Equality of What?* Tanner Lecture on Human Values, Stanford University. *www.tannerlectures.utah.edu*

—. 1980. Equality of What, in Sterling M. McMurrin (ed.), *The Tanner Lectures on Human Value*, Salt Lake City: University of Utah Press, pp. 195.220.

—. 1981a. *Poverty and Famines: An Essay on Entitlement and Deprivation.* Oxford: Clarendon Press.

—. 1982. *Choice, Welfare and Measurement.* Oxford: Basil Blackwell.

—. 1983. Poor, Relatively Speaking. *Oxford Economic Papers* 35, pp. 153-169

—. 1983a. Development: Which Way Now?, *Economic Journal*, 93, pp. 745. 62.

—. 1984. *Resources, Values and Development*, Oxford: Basil Blackwell.

—. 1985. *Commodities and Capabilities*. Oxford: Elsevier Science Publishers

—. 1987. The Standard of Living. Cambridge: Cambridge University Press.

—. 1993. Capability and Wellbeing, *The Quality of Life*, Martha C. Nussbaum and Amartya Sen (eds.), Oxford University Press, pp. 30-53.

—. 2000. Social Exclusion: Concept, Application and Scrutiny. *Social Development Paper No. 1.* Asian Development Bank. Manila.

—. 2001. Many Faces of Gender Inequality. *Frontline,* 19 November-18: pp. 4-14.

—. 2005. The Argumentative Indian, Allen Lane.

Sen, B. 1995. Rural Poverty trends: 1963-64 to 1983-90. In Z. R. Hossain and M. Hossain, eds., Rethinking Rural Poverty: Bangladesh as a case study. Sage Publication, New York.

—. 2003. Drivers of Escape and Decent: Changing Household Fortunes in Rural Bangladesh. Bangladesh Institute of Development Studies, Dhaka.

Sen, B. and Hulme, D. 2004. Chronic poverty in Bangladesh: tales of ascent, descent, marginality and persistence, Bangladesh Institute of Development Studies, Dhaka.

Serrat, O. 2008. *The Sustainable Livelihoods Approach,* Asian Development Bank.

Shaffer, P. 2008. New Thinking on Poverty: Implications for Globalization and Poverty Reduction Strategy, RER, Issue-47, pp. 192-231.

Shimp, T. A., Sharma, S., 1987. Consumer Ethnocentrism: Construction and Validation of the CETSCALE. *Journal of Marketing Research,* Vol. XXIV, pp. 280-9.

Siddique, M. A. B. 1998. Gender Issues In Poverty Alleviation: A Case Study Of Bangladesh. *International Journal of Social Economics,* 25 (6/7/8), pp. 1095-1111.

Siddiqui, K. 1982. Political Economy of Rural Poverty in Bangladesh. Dhaka: NILG

Sidorenko, A. 2006. Empowerment and Participation in Policy Action on Ageing, International Design for All Conference, 2006, Finland.

Silver, H. 2007. The process of social exclusion: the dynamics of an evolving concept. CPRC Working Paper-95.

Sobhan, R. 1998. How Bad Governance Impedes Poverty Alleviation in Bangladesh, OECD Development Centre, Working Paper No. 143.

Srinivasan, T. N. 1994. Human Development: A New Paradigm or Reinvention of the Wheel? *Human Development.* 84. 2, pp. 238-243.

Stewart, F. 2001. Women and Human Development: The Capabilities Approach by Martha C. Nussbaum., *Journal of International Development*, 13(8), pp. 1191-2.

Stiglitz, J. 1996. Some Lessons from the East Asian Miracle, The World Bank Research Observer, Vol. 11, No. 2, pp. 151-177.

Streeten, P. 1984. Basic Needs: Some Unsettled Questions. *World Development*. Vol. 12, No. 9, pp. 973-978.

—. 1998. Beyond the Six Veils: Conceptualizing and Measuring Poverty. *Journal of International Affairs.* Vol. 52. No.1, pp. 1-21.

Streeten, P., Burki, J. S., Haq, M. U., Hicks, N. and Stewart, F., 1981. First Things First: Meeting Basic Human Needs in Developing Countries. New York: Oxford University Press.

Sugden, R. 1993. Welfare, resources and capabilities: a review of Inequality re-examined by Amartya Sen. *Journal of Economic Literature*, vol 31, no. 4, pp. 1947-62.

Suh, E., Diener, E., Oishi, S. and Triandis, H. C. 1998. The shifting basis of life satisfaction judgements across cultures: emotions versus norms, *Journal of Personality and Social Psychology* 74: pp. 482-493

Sukhatme, P. V. 1978. Assessment of Adequacy of Diets at Different Income Levels, *Economic and Political Weekly*, Special Number, pp. 1373-1384.

—. 1977. Measurement of Poverty Based on Nutritional Needs, *Bulletin of the International Statistical Institute*, Vol XLVIIBook 4, Contributed Papers, pp 553-556.

Sundaram, I. S. 1986. Voluntary Agencies and Rural Development, B. H. Publishing Corporation, New Delhi.

SUPRO. 2007. Increasing poverty and MDGs achievement: Is poverty-free Bangladesh possible? Supro Position Paper 15. Available at:

http://www.supro.org/pdf&doc_files/MGD%20English-1.pdf Accessed 15 July 2011.

Teas, R. K. 1993. Consumer expectations and the measurement of perceived service quality. *Journal of Professional Services Marketing*, 8(2), pp. 33-54.

Tilly, C. 2006. The Politics of Exclusion. Paper produced for the World Bank 'Moving out of Poverty' project.

Tiwari, M. 2008. Poverty and Wellbeing at the Grassroots-How Much is Visible to Researchers? *Social Indicators Research*, Vol. 90, No. 1, pp. 127-140.

Townsend, P. 1979. Poverty in the United Kingdom. London: Allen Lane.

—. 1985. A Sociological Approach to the Measurement of Poverty: A Rejoinder to Professor Amartya Sen. *Oxford Economic Papers*. No. 37.

—. 1987. Deprivation, *Journal of Social Policy*, 16(2), pp. 125-146.

Transparency International Bangladesh (TIB), Annual Report-2007

Tsakloglou, P. and Papadopoulos, F. 2002b. Poverty, material deprivation and multi-dimensional disadvantage during four life stage: Evidence from ECHP, in C. Heady (eds) *Poverty and social exclusion in Europe*, Cheltenham ; Northampton, MA : E. Elgar.

Tucker, L. R., and Lewis, C. 1973. A Reliability coefficient for maximum likelihood factor analysis. *Psychometrica*, 38, pp. 1-10.

Twigg, J. 2009. Tools for Mainstreaming Disaster Risk Reduction. 14 guidance notes were produced by the ProVention Consortium. Switzerland.

UN Humanitarian Affairs, Different years.

Un Nabi, R. 1999. Consultation with the Poor. Participatory Poverty Assessment in Bangladesh, NGO Working Group on the World Bank, Bangladesh.

UNDP Annual Report, 1995

—. 1996. Human Development Report 1996. Oxford: Oxford University Press.

—. 1997. Human Development Report 1997. Oxford: Oxford University Press.

—. 2000. Human Development Report 2000. Oxford: Oxford University Press.

—. 2003. Poverty Reduction and Human Rights: A Practice Note, UNDP Publication, pp. 1-15.

—. 2005. Human Development Report-2005: International cooperation at a crossroads, aid, trade and security in an unequal world. New York.

—. Human Development Report – 2003, 2010.

—. 2006. World Development Report.

—. UNDP. 2010. Human Development Report. Oxford: Oxford University Press.

UNICEF, 2007. UNICEF Situation Report Bangladesh Floods-External. September.

USAID, 2008. Bangladesh Cyclone Fact Sheet-11. March 31, 2008.

Veenhoven, R. 1991. Is Happiness Relative? *Social Indicators Research* 24, no.1: pp.1–34.

Vinson, T. 2007. *Dropping off the edge: the distribution of disadvantage in Australia*, Jesuit Social Services, Melbourne.

Wade, R. 1990. *Governing the Market: Economic Theory and the Role of Government in East Asian Industrialization*, Princeton University Press.

WeD, 2004–2007. Wellbeing in developing countries program, University of Bath.

Weisbrod, B. 1974. Toward a theory of the voluntary non-profit sector in a three-sector economy. In Phelps, E. (Ed.), *Altruism, morality, and economic theory, economic theory.* New York: Russell Sage.

Weisbrod, B.A. 1975. Toward a theory of the voluntary nonprofit sector in a three-sector economy, in E.S. Phelps (ed.) *Altruism, Morality, and Economic Theory,* Russell Sage Foundation, New York. Reprinted in S. Rose-Ackerman (ed.) (1986) The *Economics of Nonprofit Organizations: Studies in Structure and Policy,* Oxford University Press, New York. Also reprinted in D.L. Gies, J.S. Oft and J.M. Shafritz (eds) (1990) The *Nonprofit Organization: Essential Readings,* Brooks/Cole Publishing, Pacific Grove, California.

—. 1977. The *Voluntary Nonprofit Sector,* Lexington Books, Lexington, Massachusetts.

Whelan, C.T., Layte, R. and Maitre, B. 2002. Persistent deprivation in the European Union, *Journal of Applied Social Science Studies*, 12 (2), pp. 91-105.

White, S., and Petit, J. 2004. Participatory approaches and the measurement of human well-being, WeD Working Paper 8. Bath Wellbeing in Developing Countries (WeD) Research Group.

Wood, G. 1997. States without Citizens: the problem of the Franchise State in M.Edwards and D.Hulme (Eds) Too Close for Comfort: NGOs and the State, MacMillan.

World Bank Annual Reports of 1991, 1995, 2000, 2005, 2007

World Bank, 1990. *World Development Report 1990: The 2.5 point Strategy*, Washington D.C: The World Bank.

—. 1996. *World Bank Annual Report*, Washington DC.

—. 2000. *World Development Report 2000*. Oxford: Oxford University Press.

—. 2000. *World Development Report 2000: Opportunity, Empowerment and Security*. Washington D.C: The World Bank.

—. 2001. Social Protection Sector Strategy. Washington D.C: The World Bank.

—. 2005. Poverty Manual.

World Food Program, 2009. Khulna District-Tropical Cyclones AILA Areas Affected with Surface Water. Rapid Disaster Impact Map. June 3, 2009.

—. 2009. Potuakhali District-Tropical Cyclones AILA Areas Affected with Surface Water. Rapid Disaster Impact Map. June 3, 2009.

—. 2009. Satkhira District-Tropical Cyclones AILA Areas Affected with Surface Water. Rapid Disaster Impact Map. June 3, 2009.

Yolande, M., Michel W., Joy W., July 2002. Evolving Partnerships: The Role of NGOs in Basic Education in Africa. USAID, Bureau of Africa, Office of Sustainable Development

Young, D. R. 1983. *If Not For Profit, For What?*, DC Heath, Lexington, Massachusetts.

Yunus, M. 2008. *Creating a World without Poverty*. PublicAffairs, New York. ISBN-13: 978-1-58648-493-4.

Zaidi, S. A., 2000. *NGOs and Local Government in Pakistan*. Rupa & Co., Dakshin.

Zaman, H. 2004. Microfinance in Bangladesh: Growth, Achievements, and Lessons, Paper presented in Scaling Up Poverty Reduction: A Global Learning Process and Conference Shanghai, May 25–27, 2004.

Zohir, S. 2007. NGO Sector in Bangladesh: An overview. Online Publications.

Zug, S. 2006a. Monga Seasonal Food Insecurity in Bangladesh Bringing the Information Together, in *The Journal of Social Studies*, No. 111, pp. 1-14, Centre for Social Studies, Dhaka. The paper can be found at: http://www.bangladesch.org/pics/download/S_Zug_Article_Monga.pdf

Zug, S. 2006b. Monga: Seasonal Food Insecurity in Bangladesh: Understanding the Problem and Strategies to Combat it. Paper prepared on behalf of NETZ.

INDEX